After
The
Midst

They said they found me floundering inside a carrousel, tied to a plastic horse, bent for a ride (obviously with mayonnaise and ketchup all around), playing with genitals, oozing demonic sounds and nimble melodies, and an old Christmas tree dangling behind, asking for more.

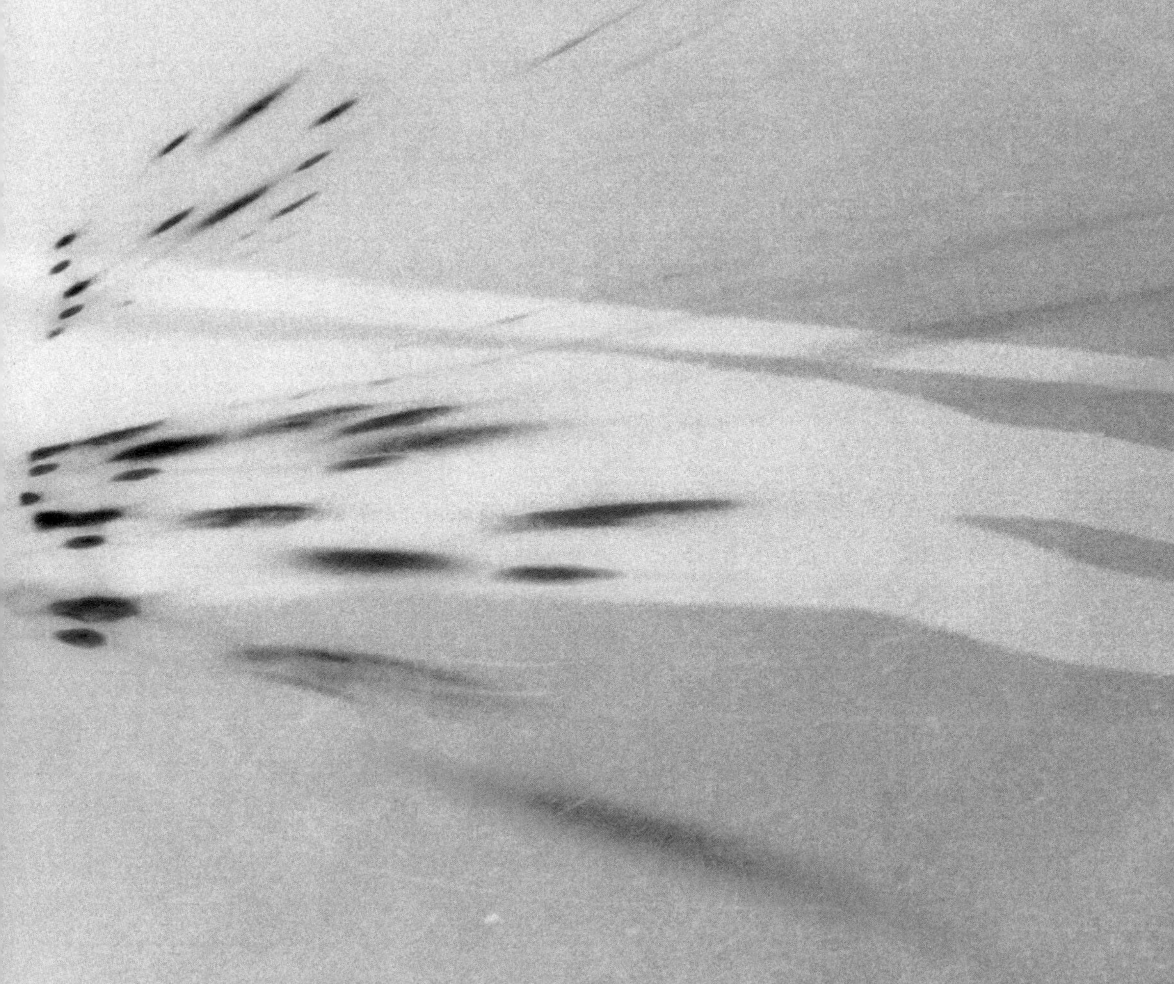

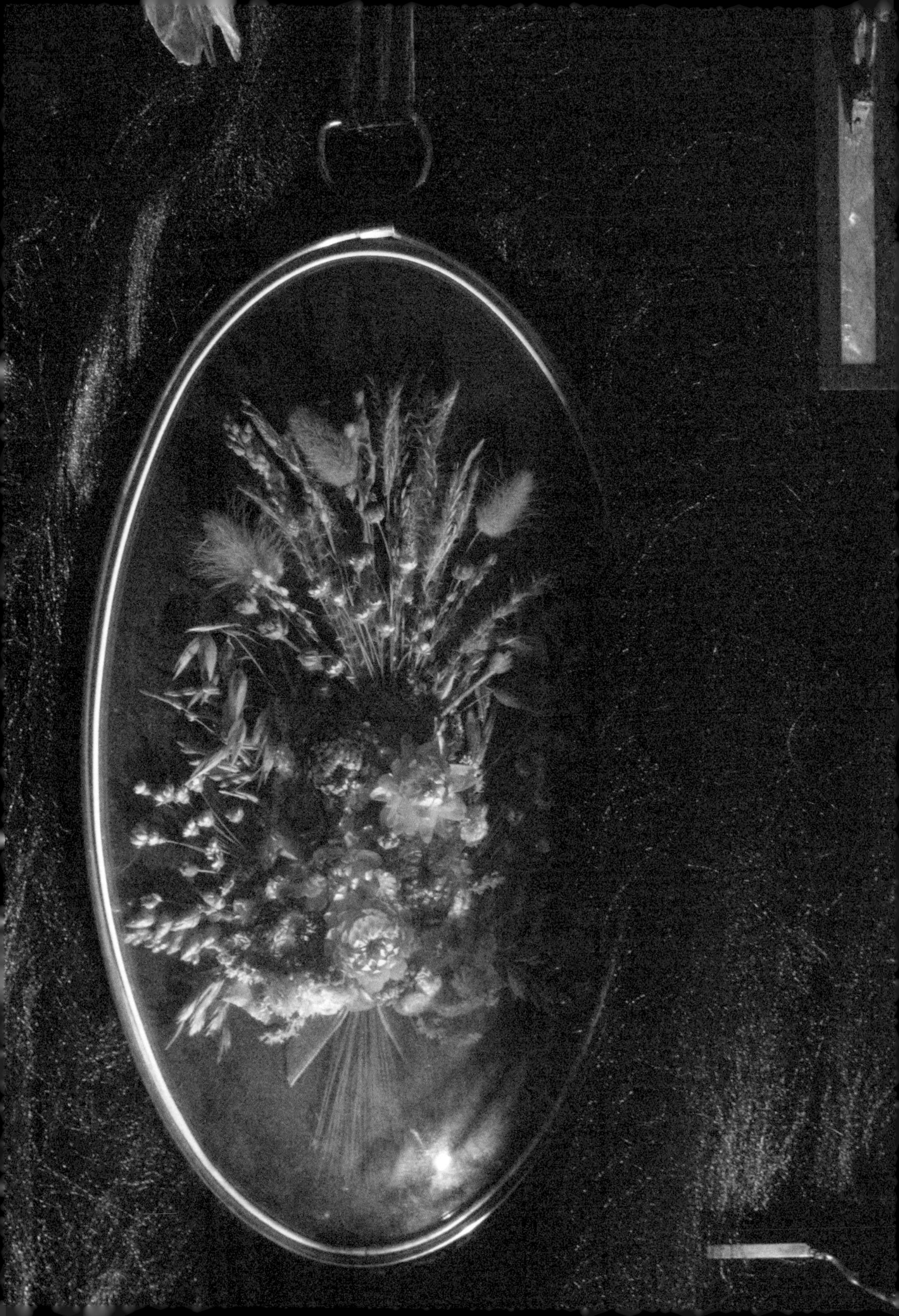

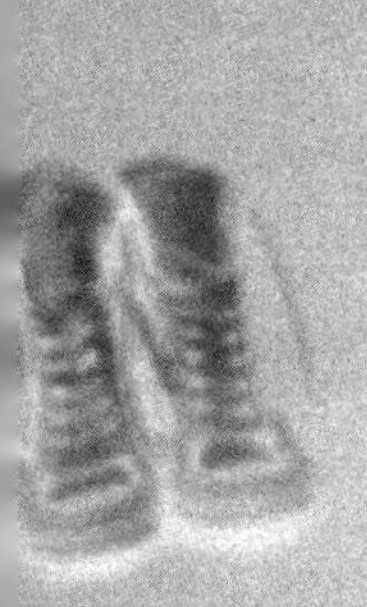

They said they found me in a carrousel, under a plastic chair, stuck between the four legs, sucking my thumb (obviously with mayonnaise and ketchup all around), oozing and bubbling unceremoniously, yes, bubbling like the infamous tea, and an old Christmas tree dangling behind, asking for more.

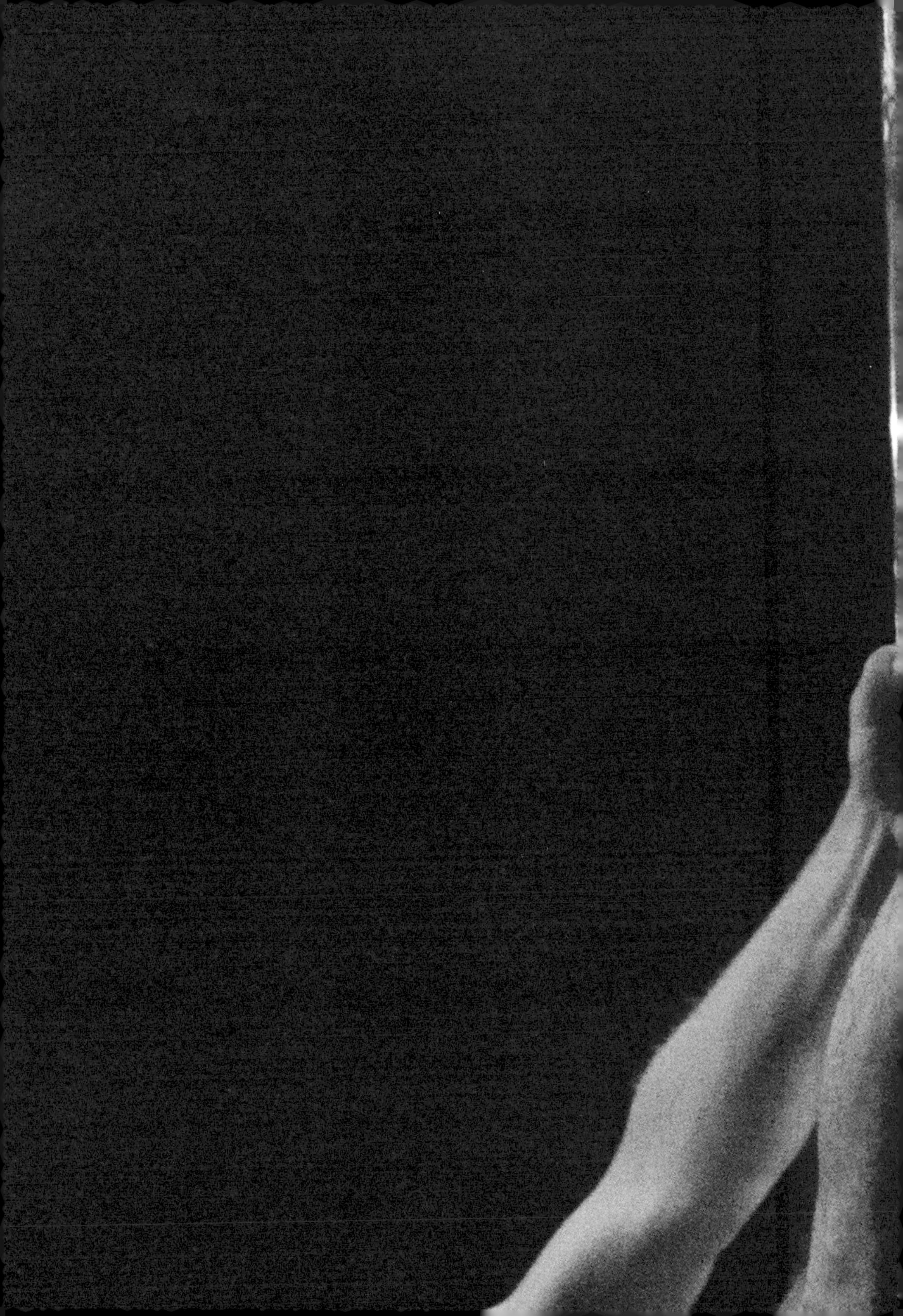

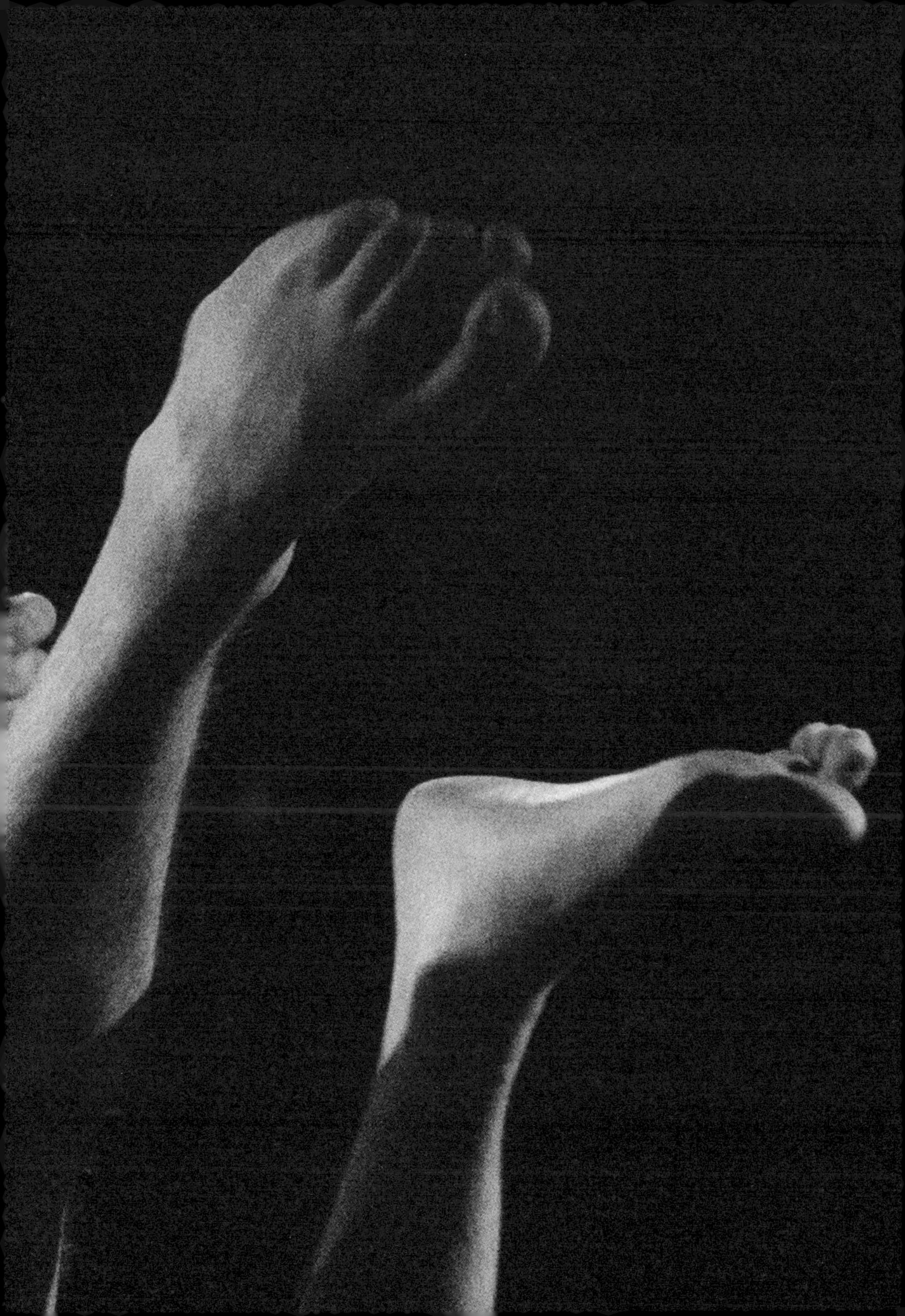

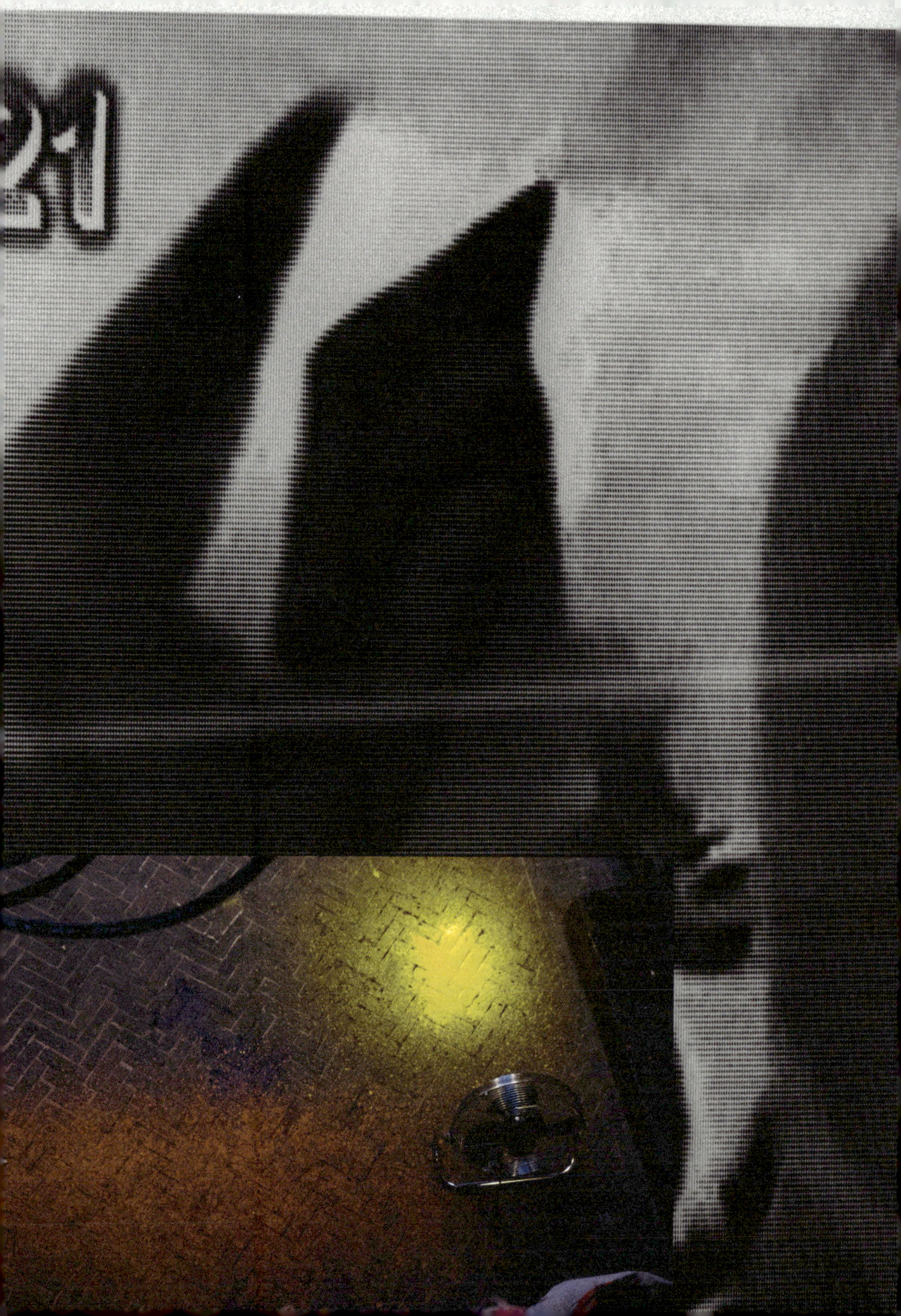

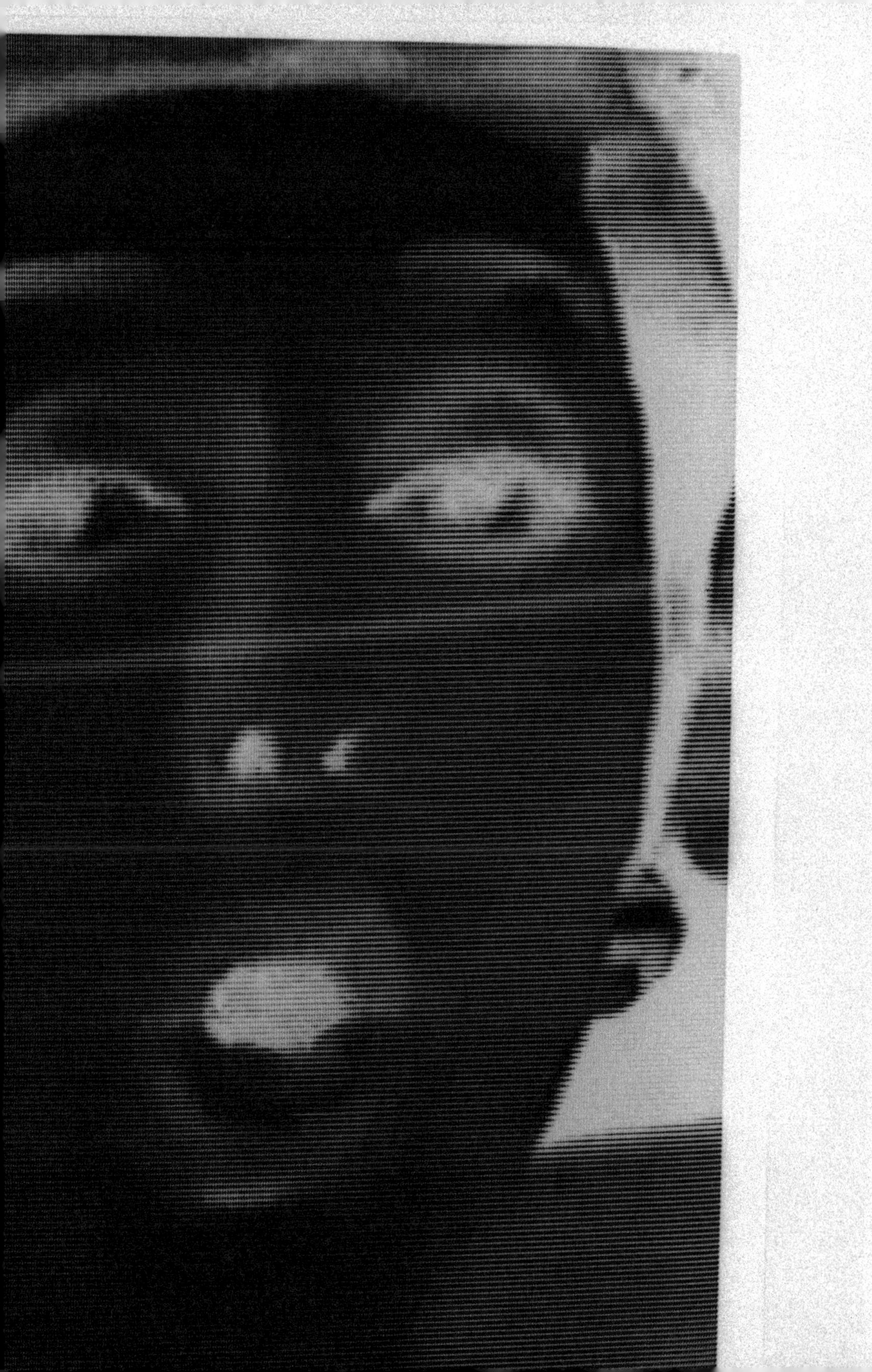

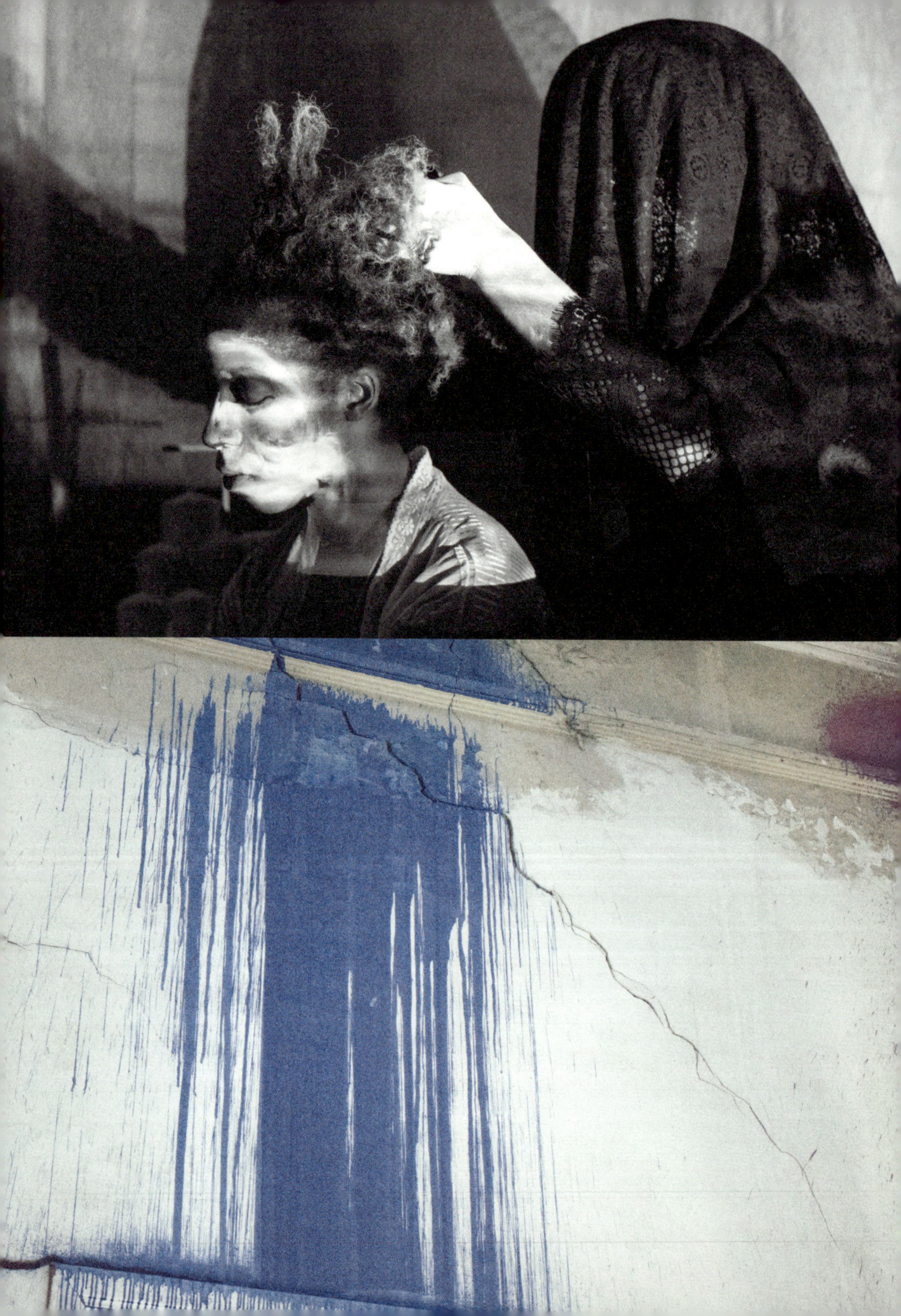

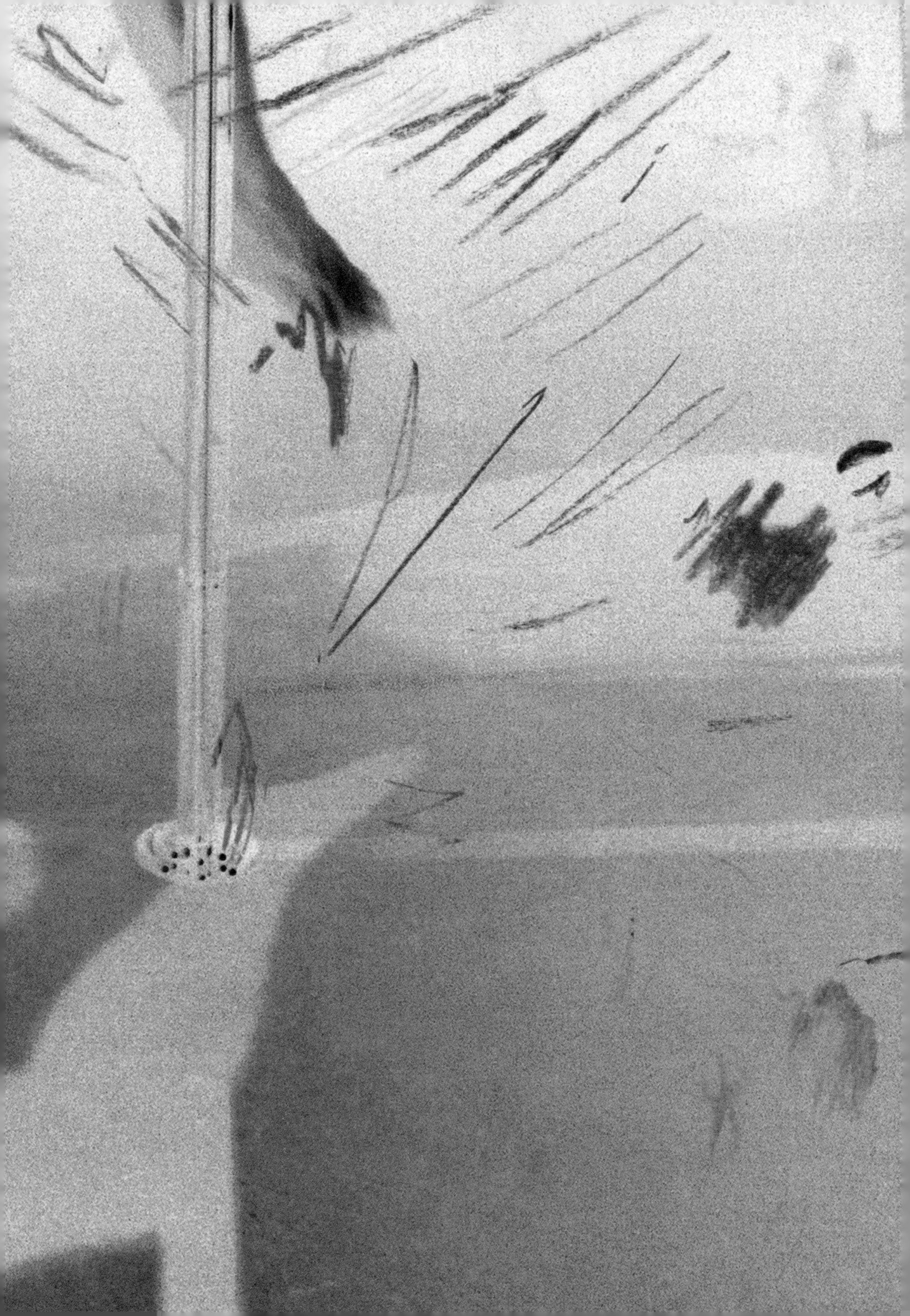

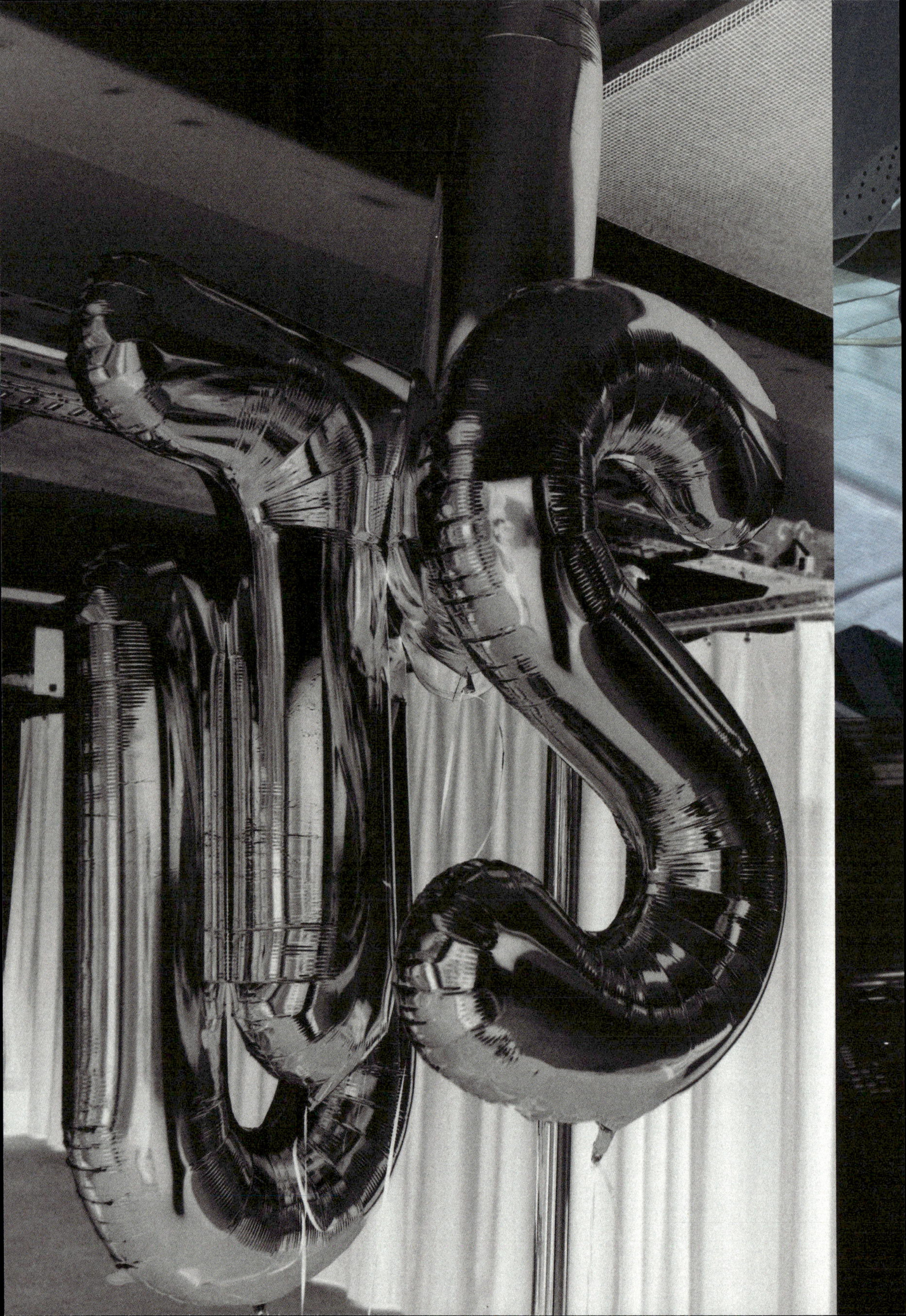

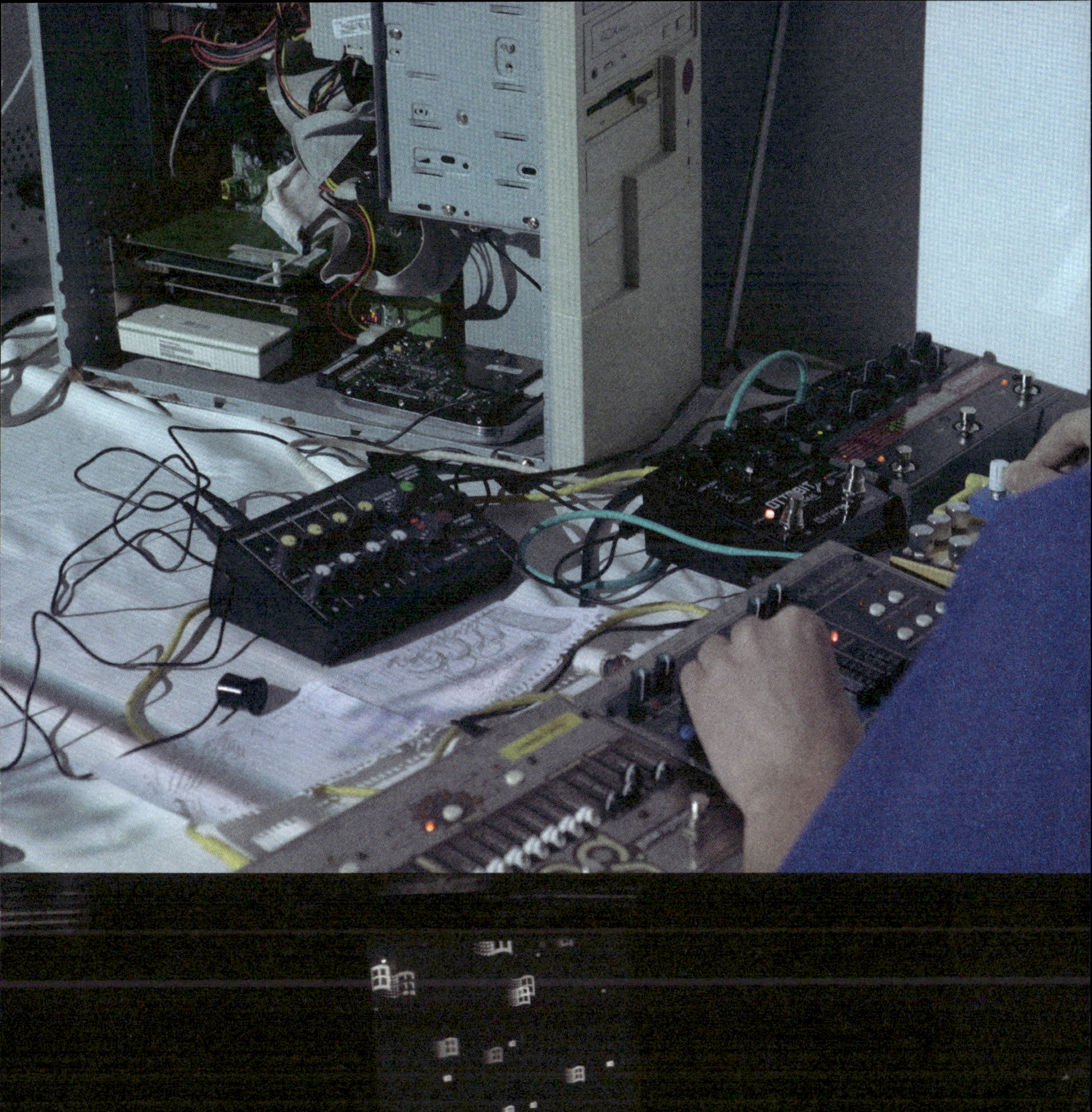

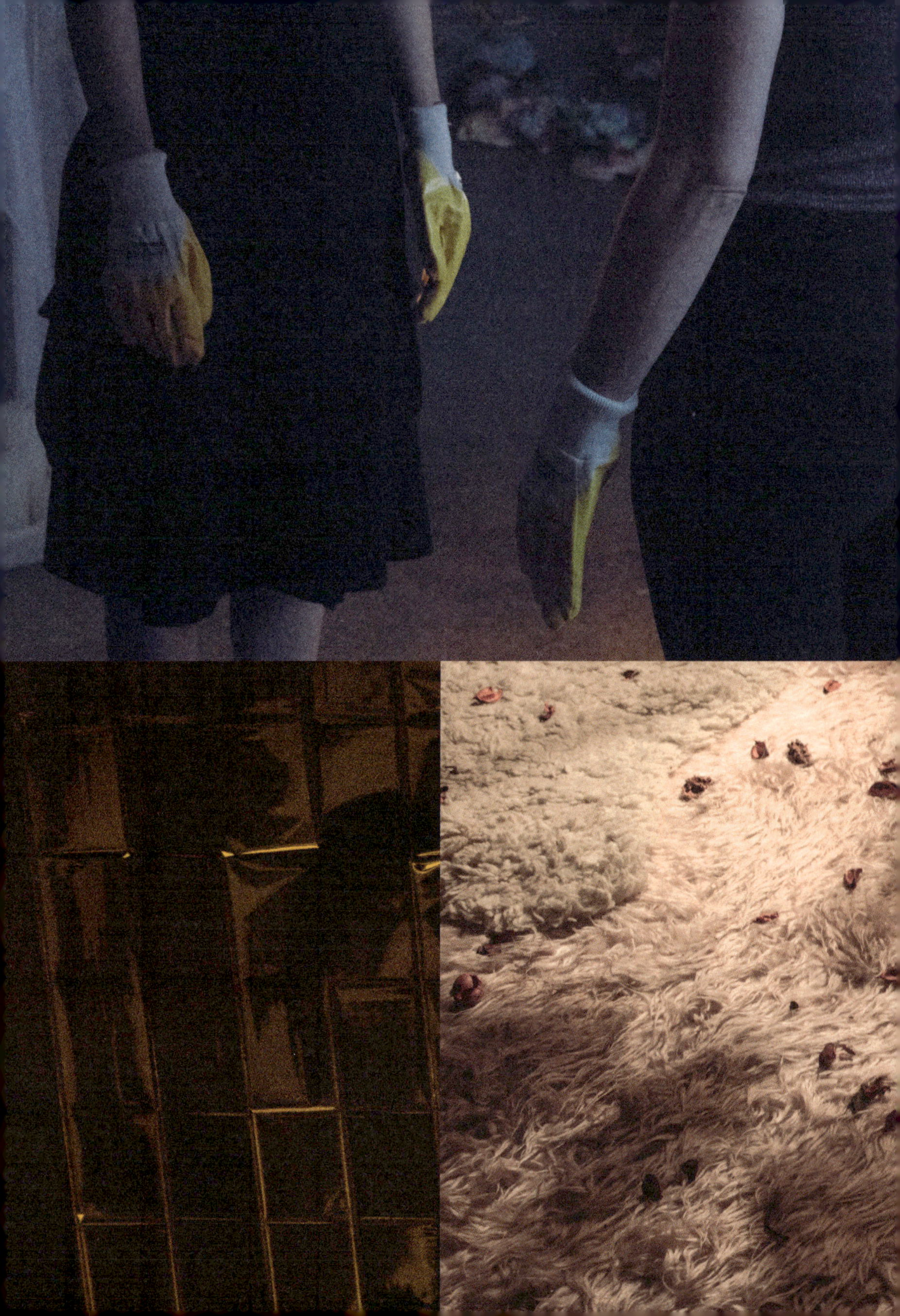

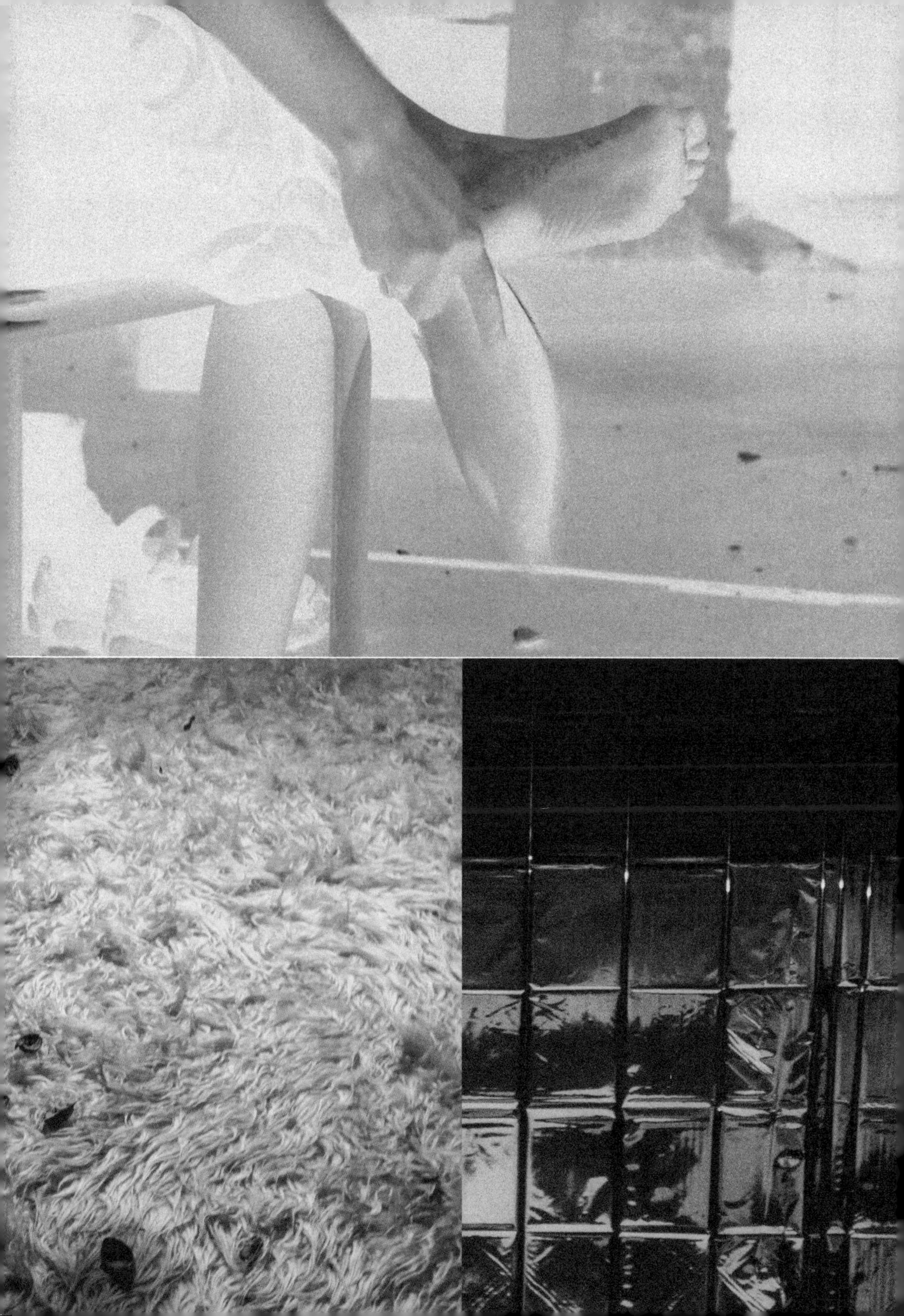

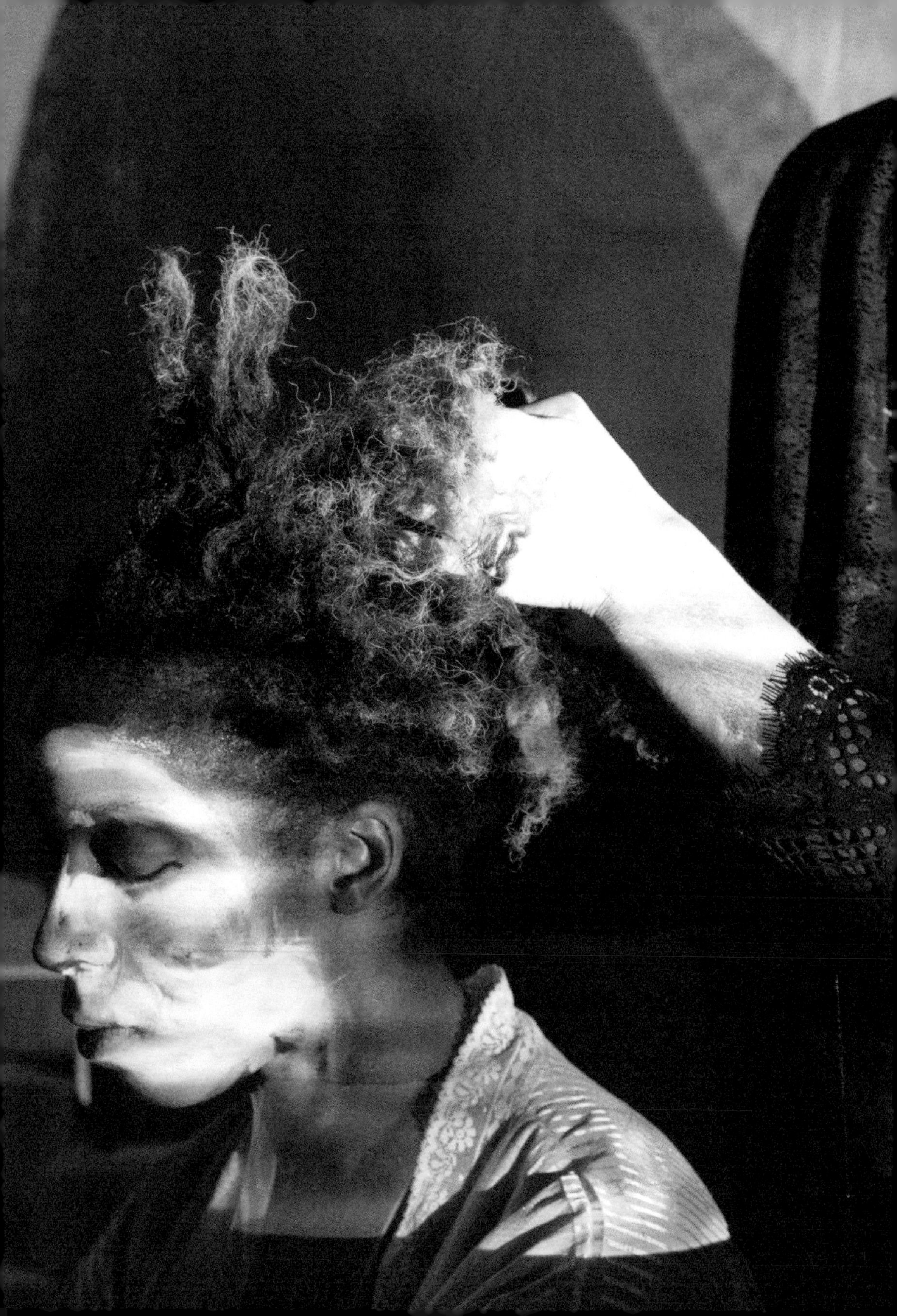

They said they found me in a car, under a plastic chair, stuck between Tuna and Margarita, in whatever order they ordered it (obviously with mayonnaise and ketchup all around), oozing pure nonsense without apology, and an old Christmas tree dangling behind, asking for more.

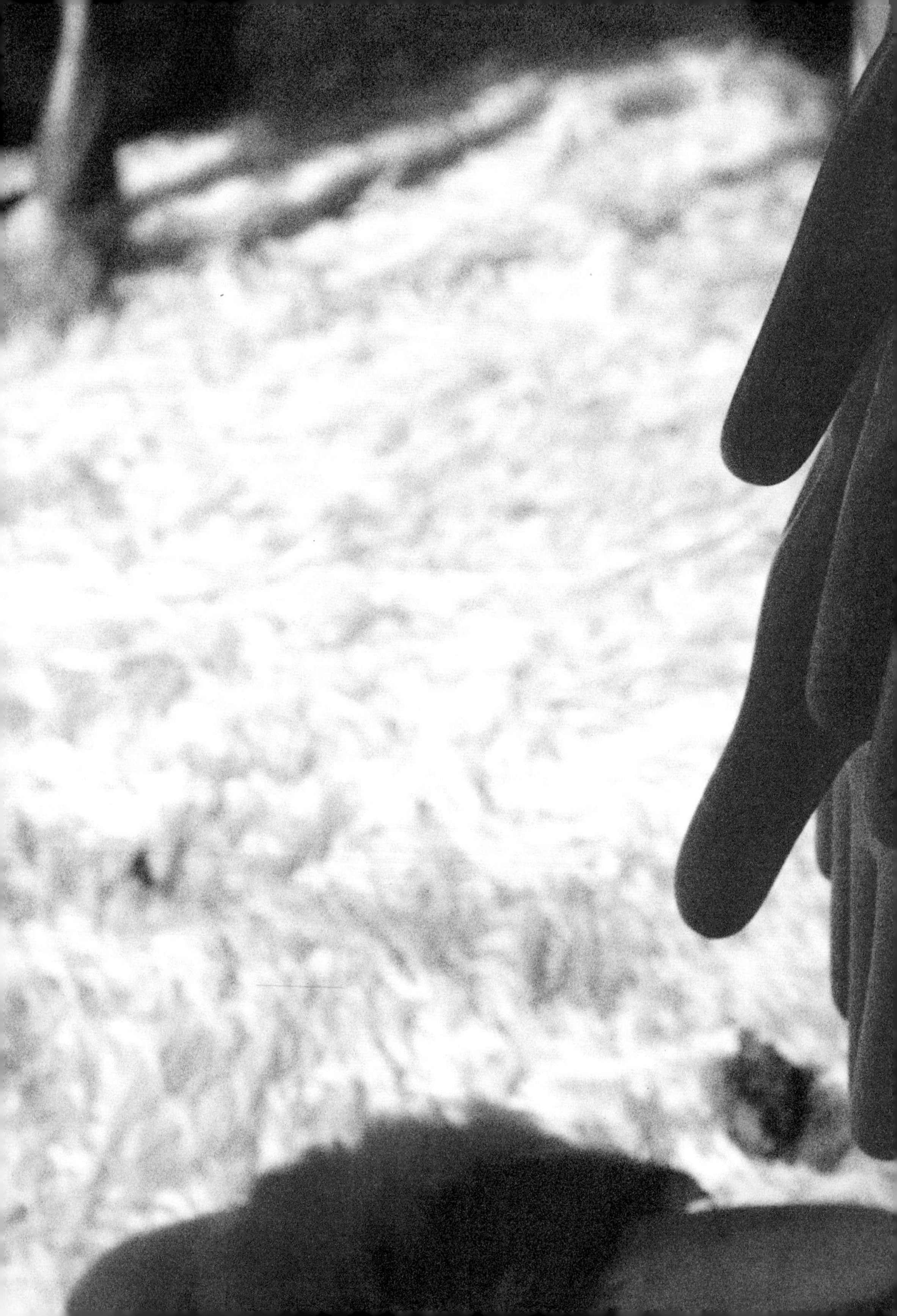

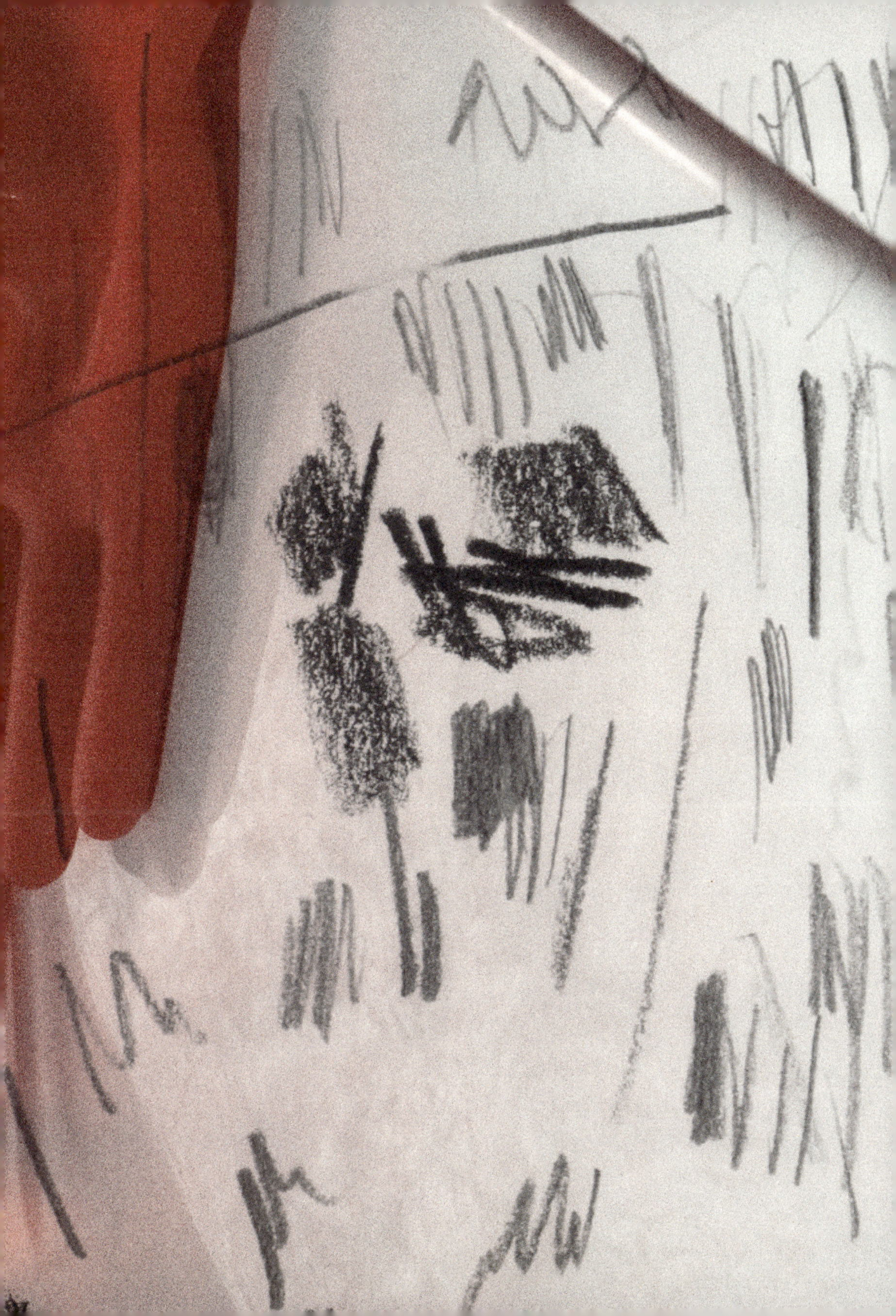

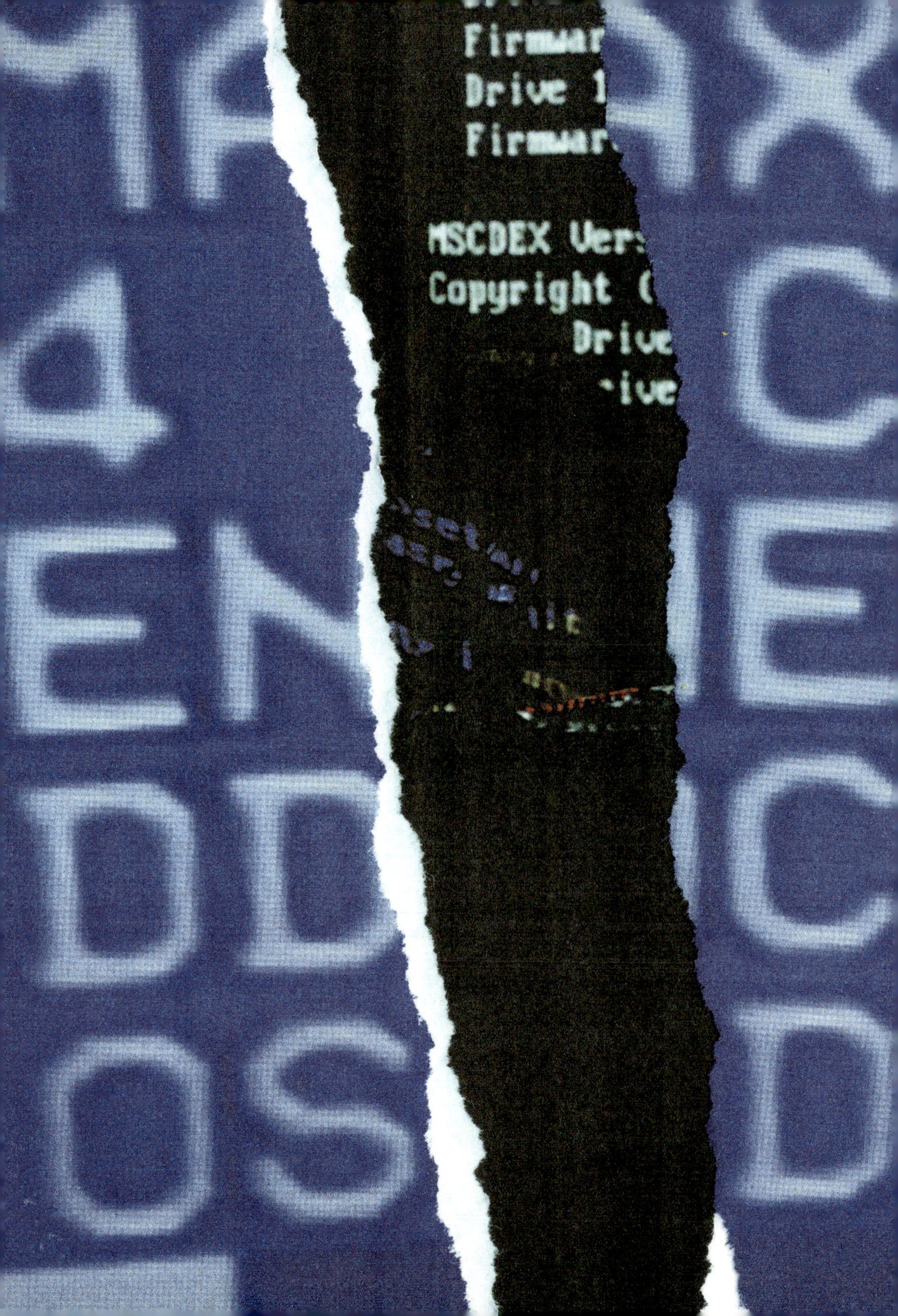

Firmwar
Drive 1
Firmwar

MSCDEX Vers
Copyright (
Drive
ive

condary Chan

1E

Corp. 1986-1

r BANANA unit

r BANANA unit

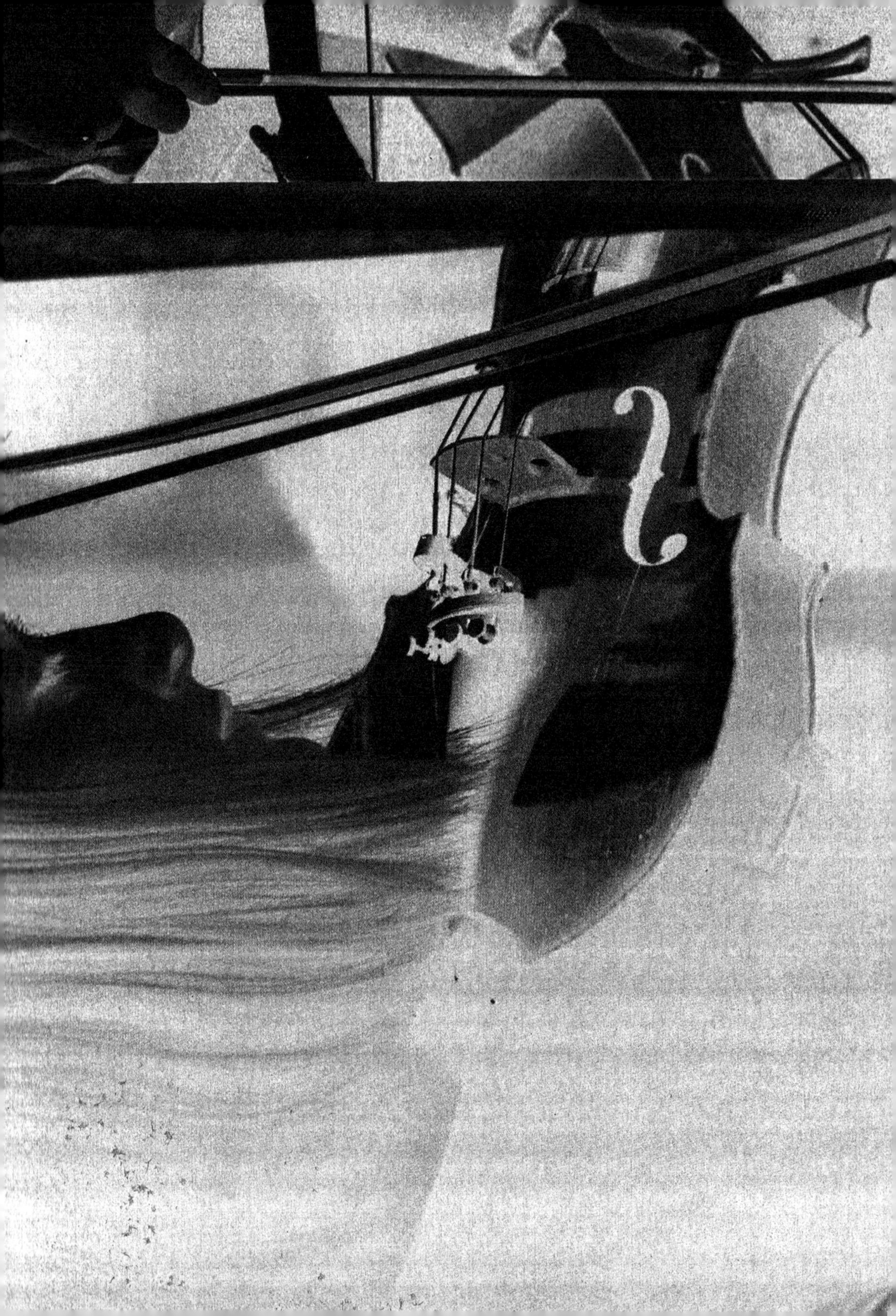

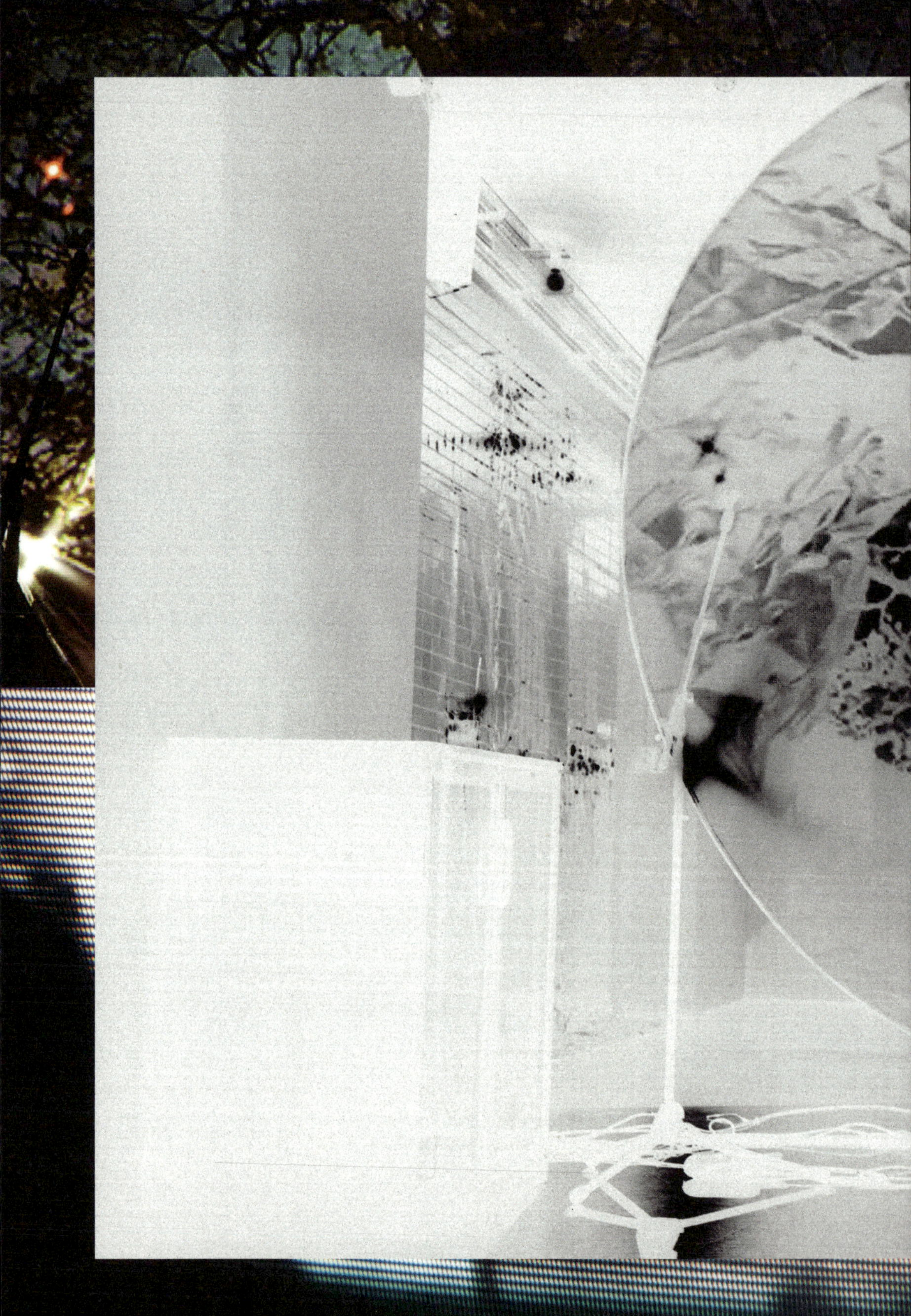

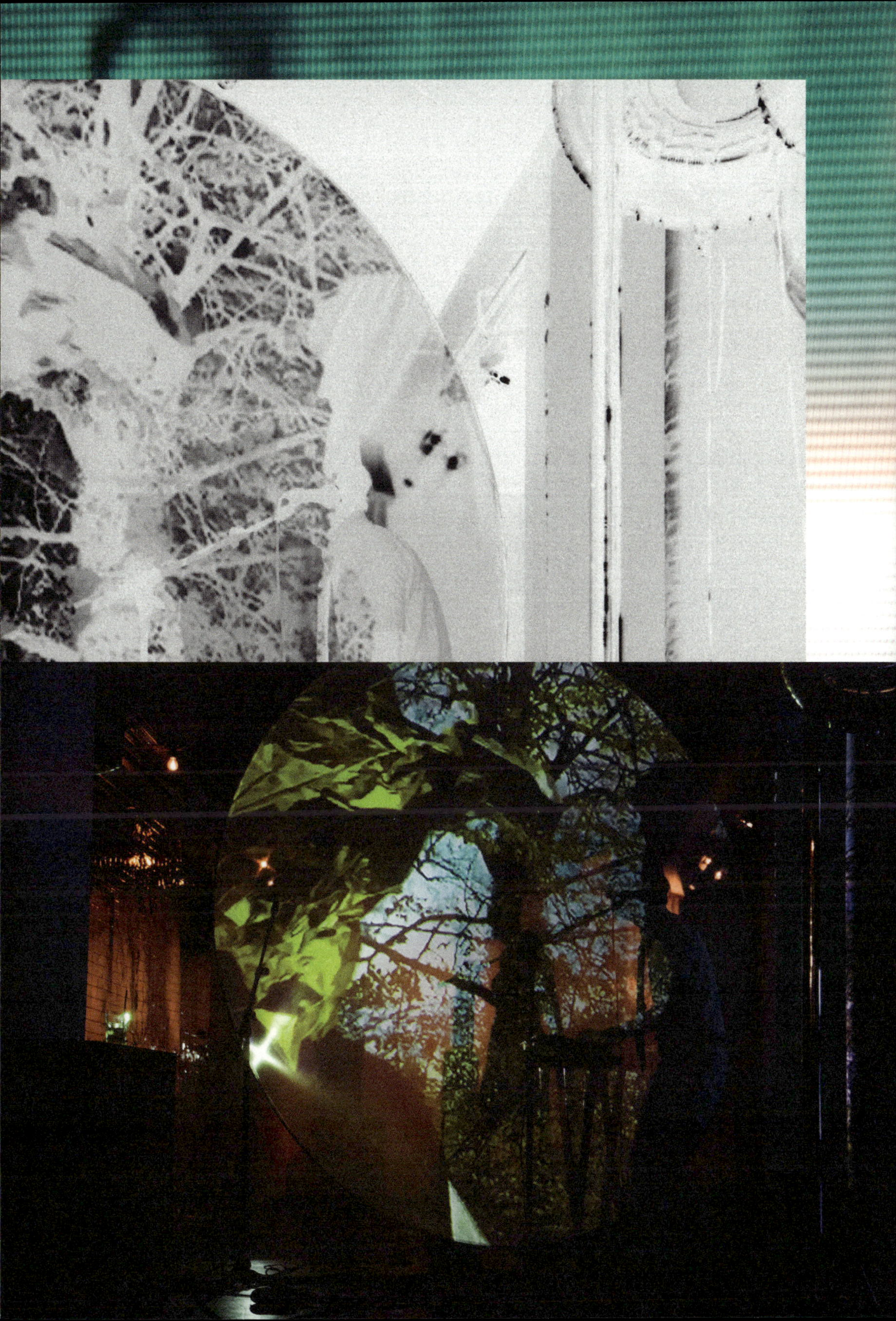

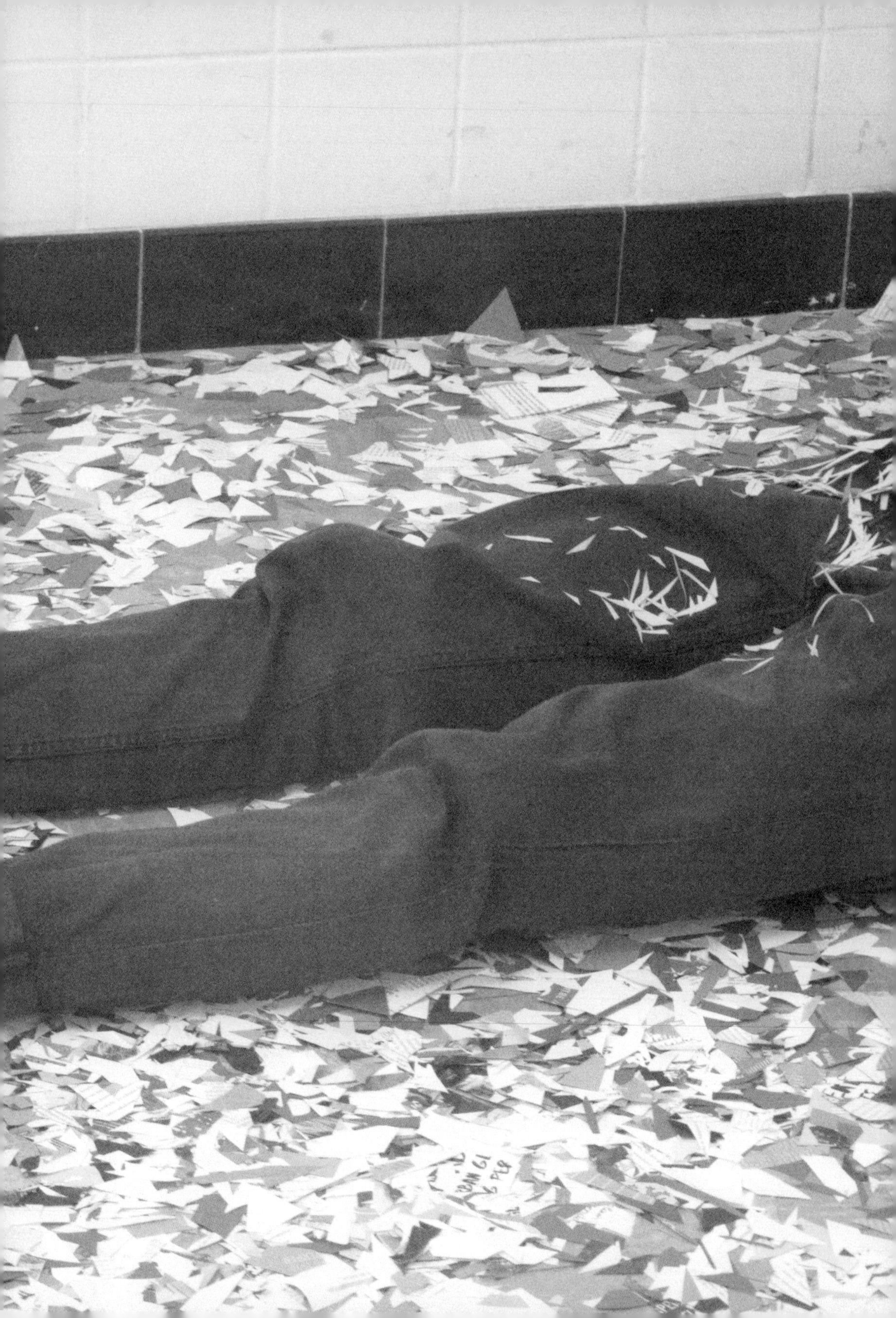

They said that they found me inside a piñata, XL size, near a carpark, dressed as wafel and falafel, dressed as Liza and Matilda, dressed as Lindsay and Malcolm, with a hell moving out of my stomach, now on my face (a heavy load to carry especially for future achievements, none of us know how it goes, obviously with mayonnaise and ketchup all around), and still that old Christmas tree dangling behind, asking for more.

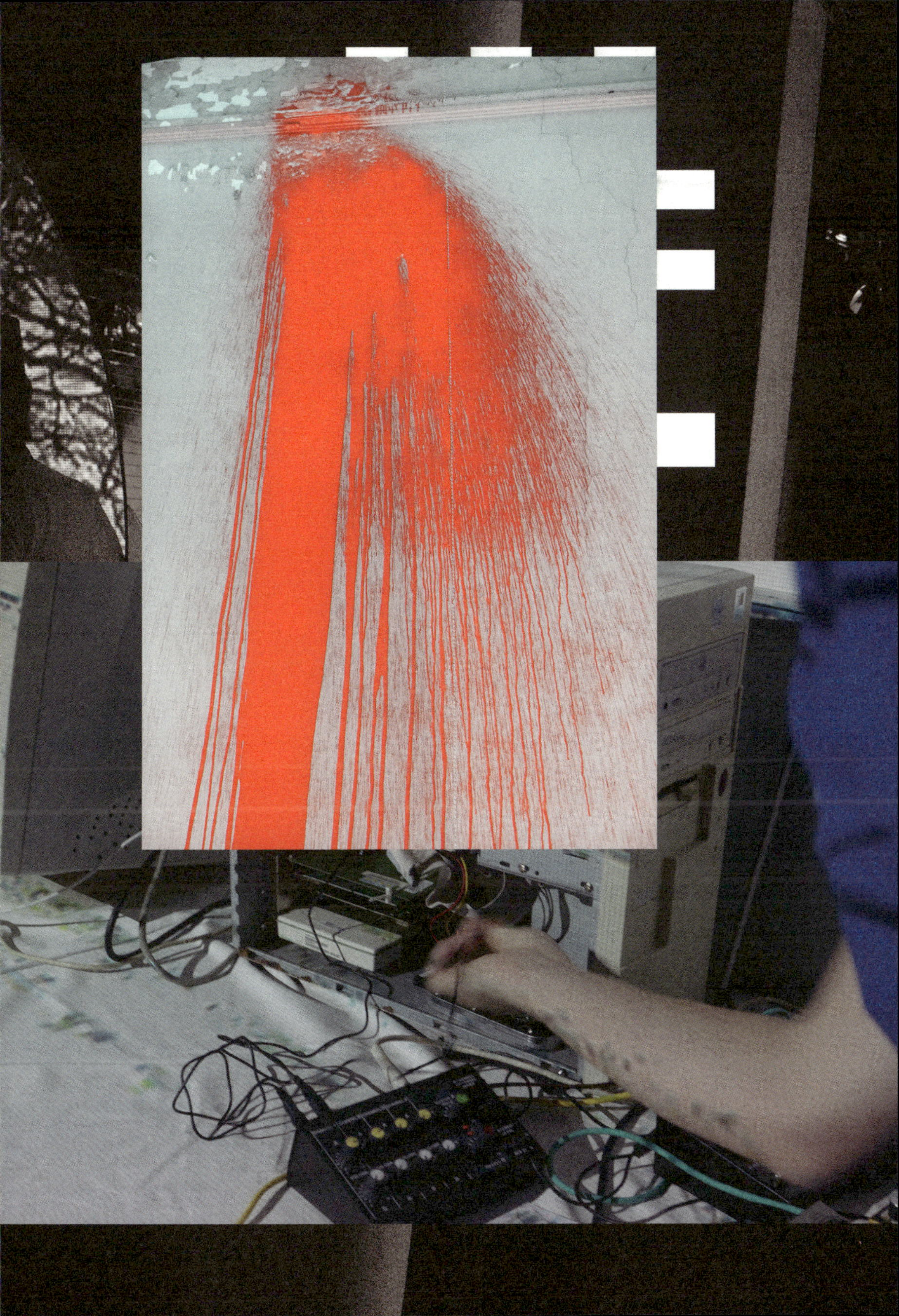

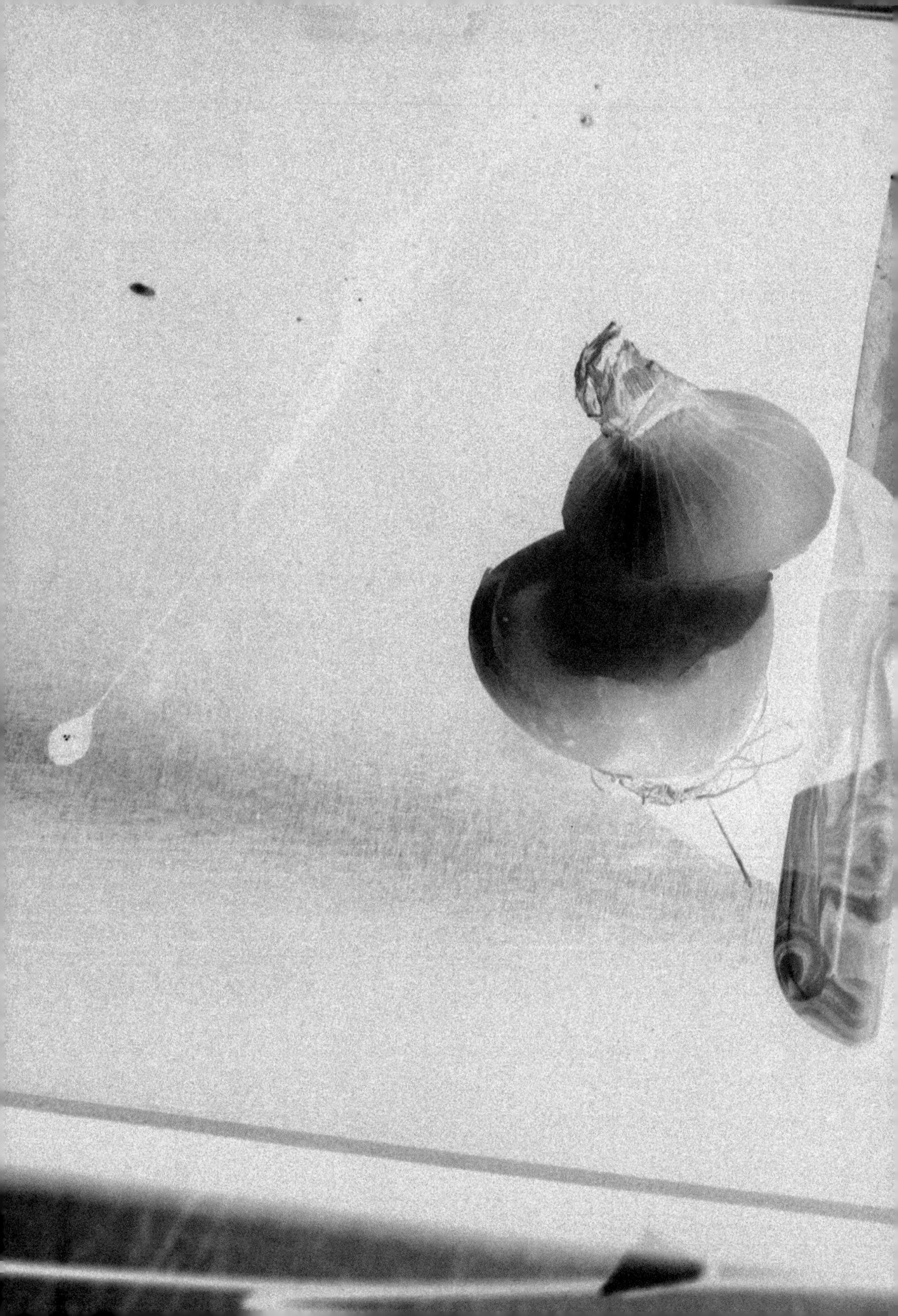

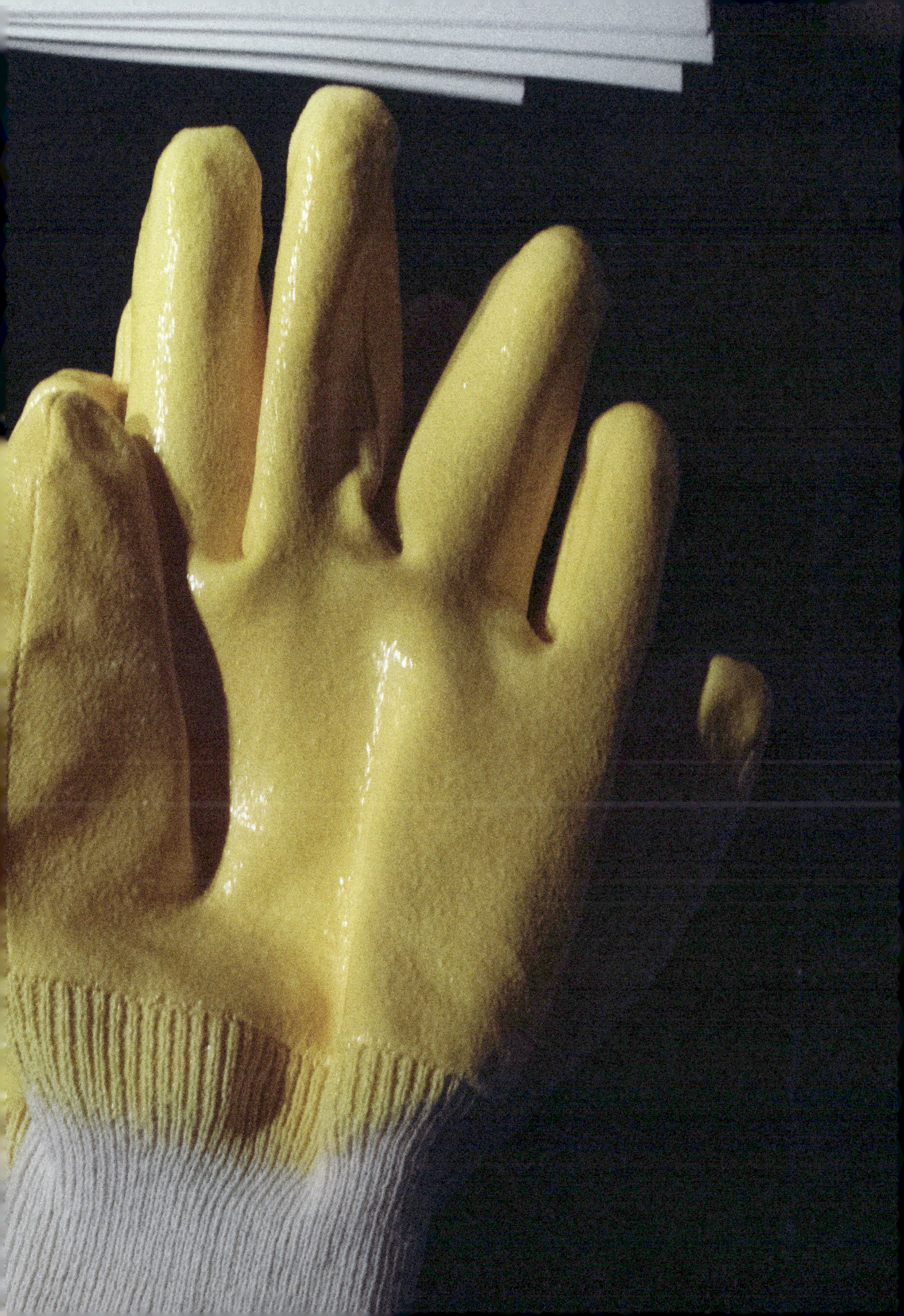

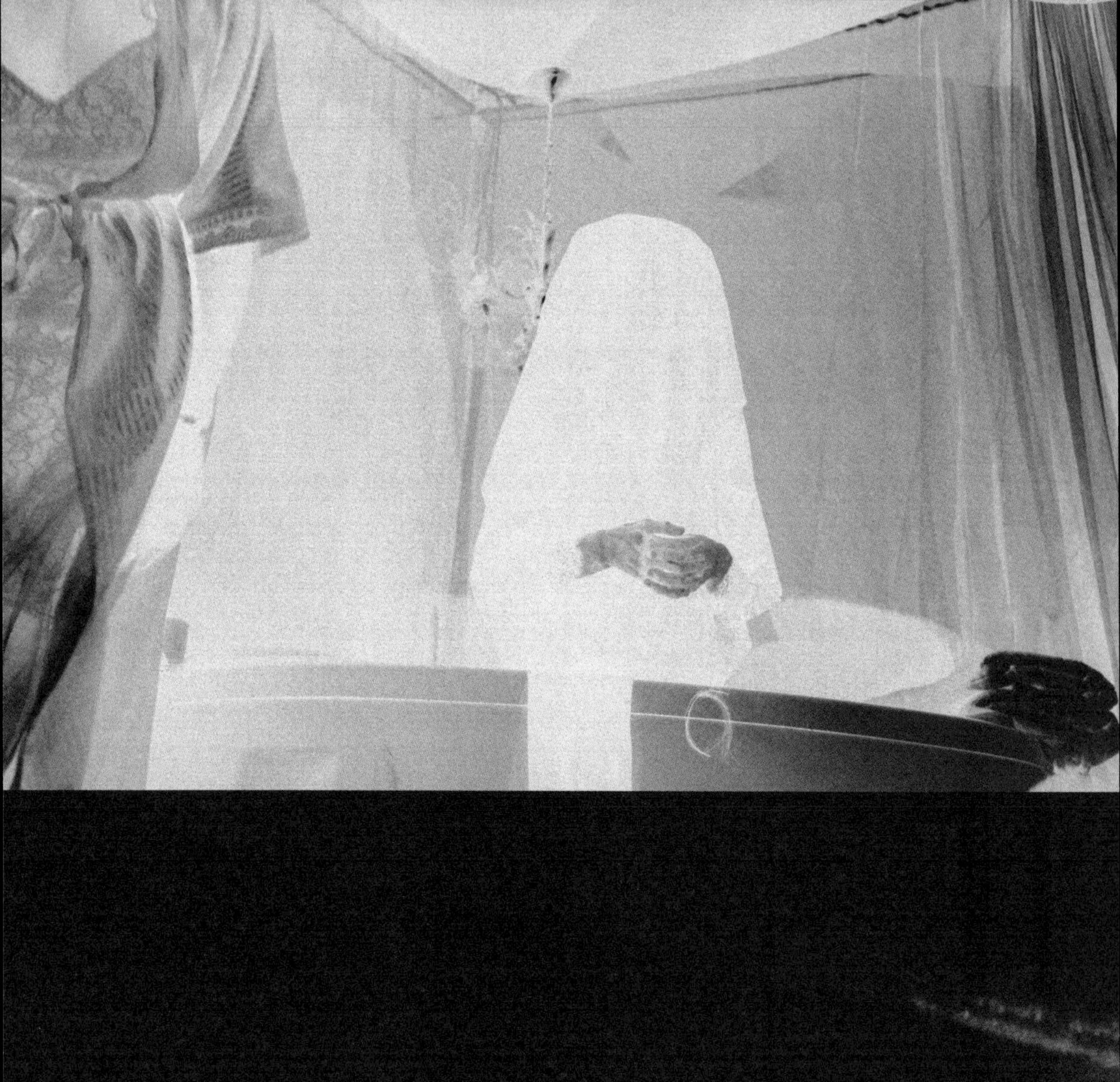

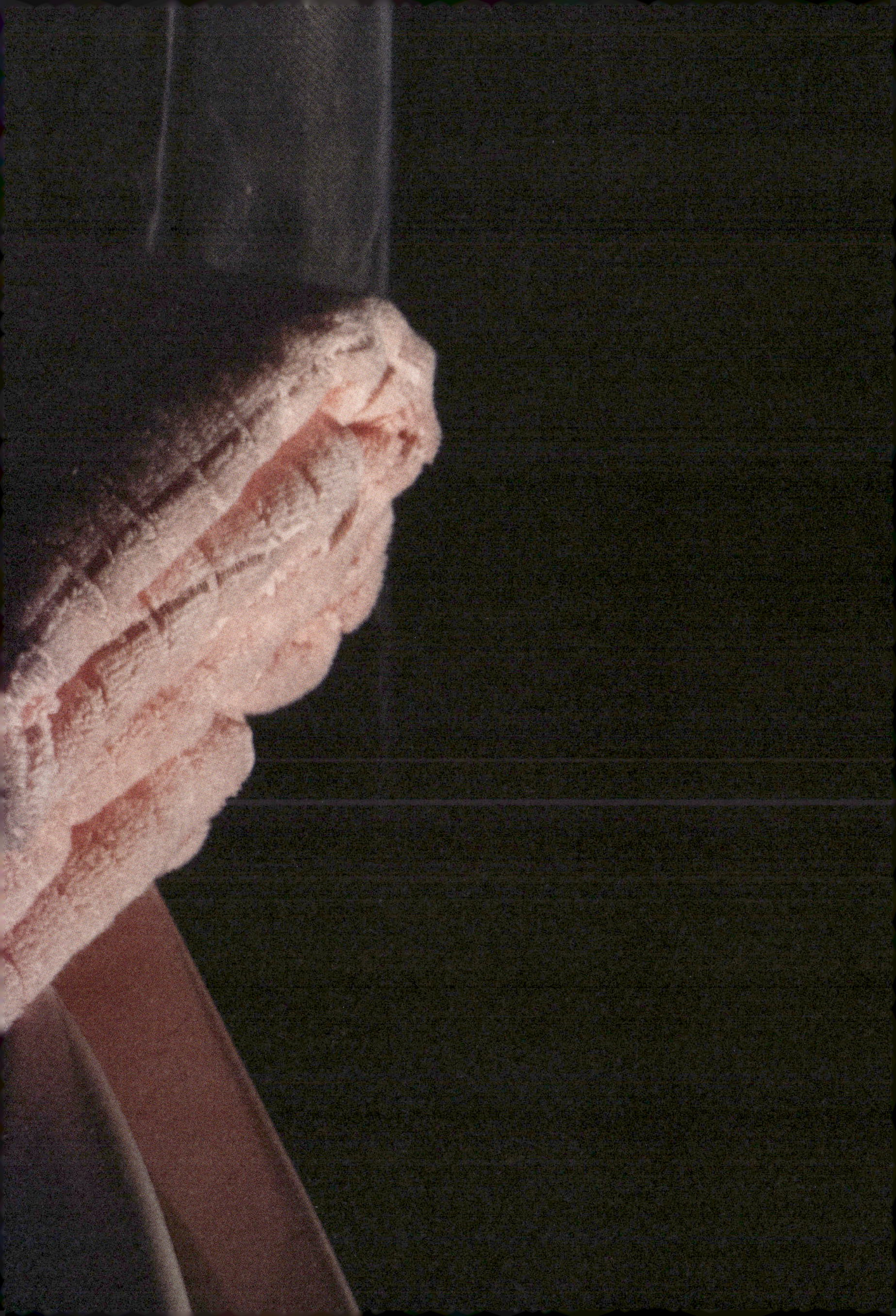

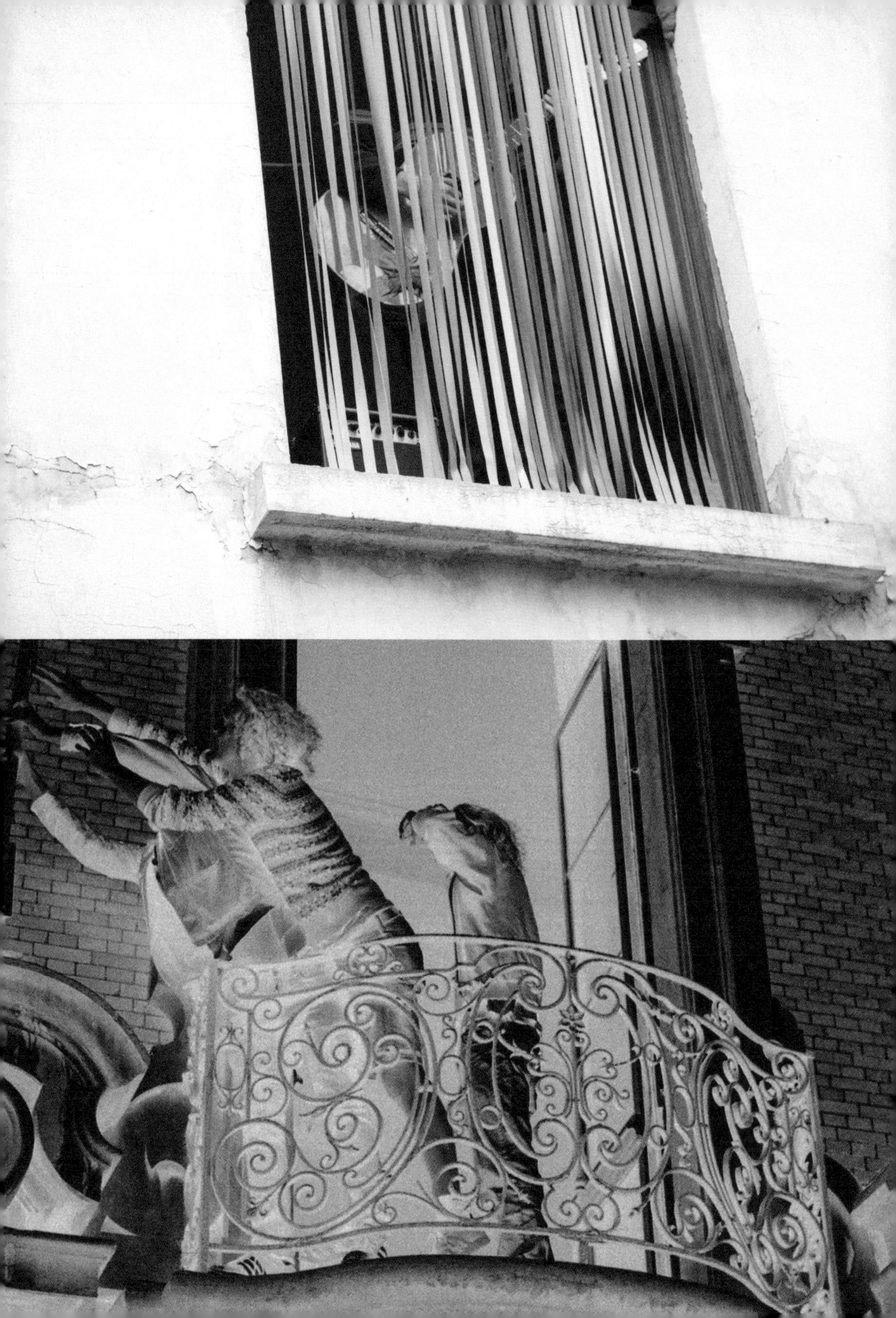

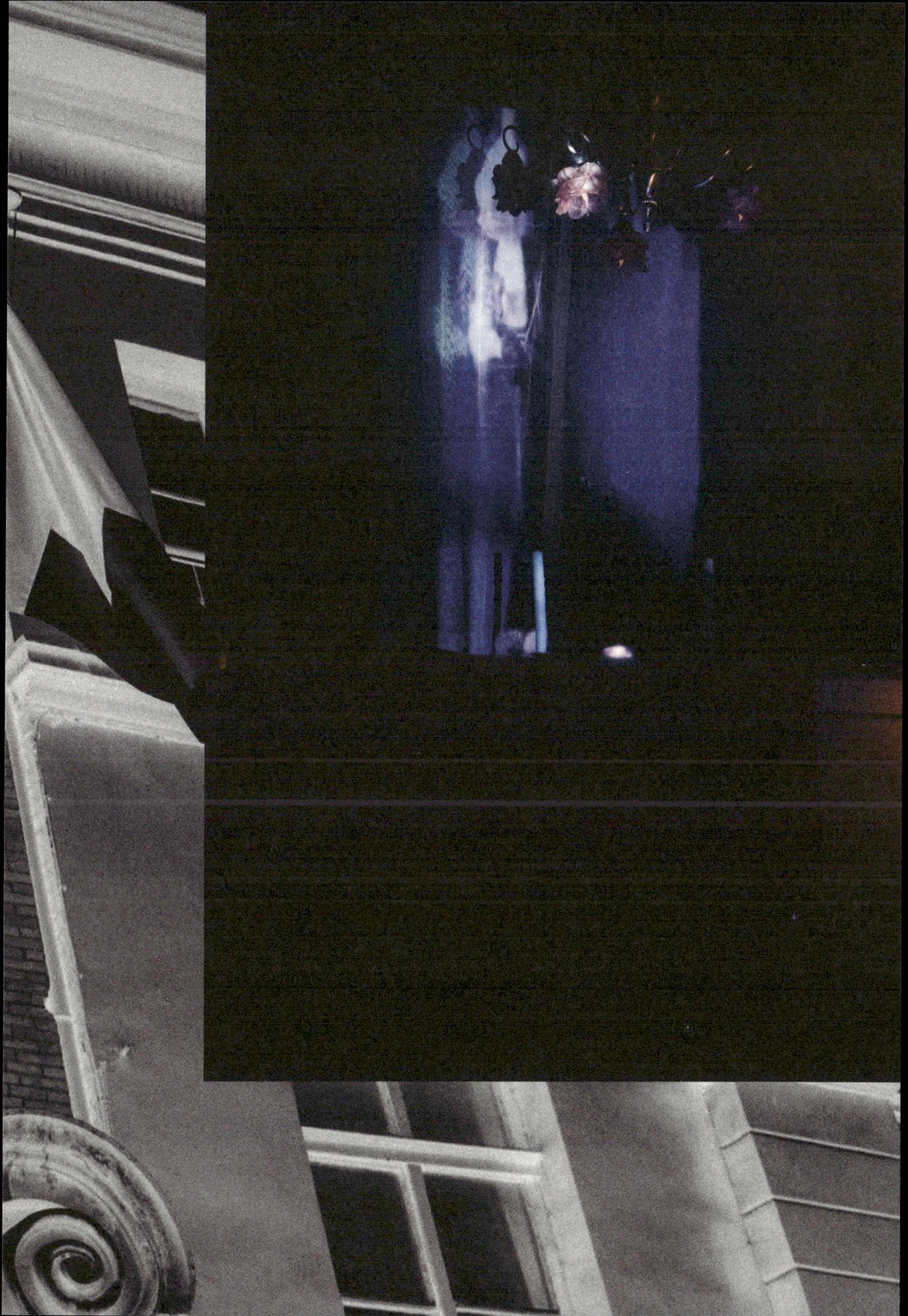

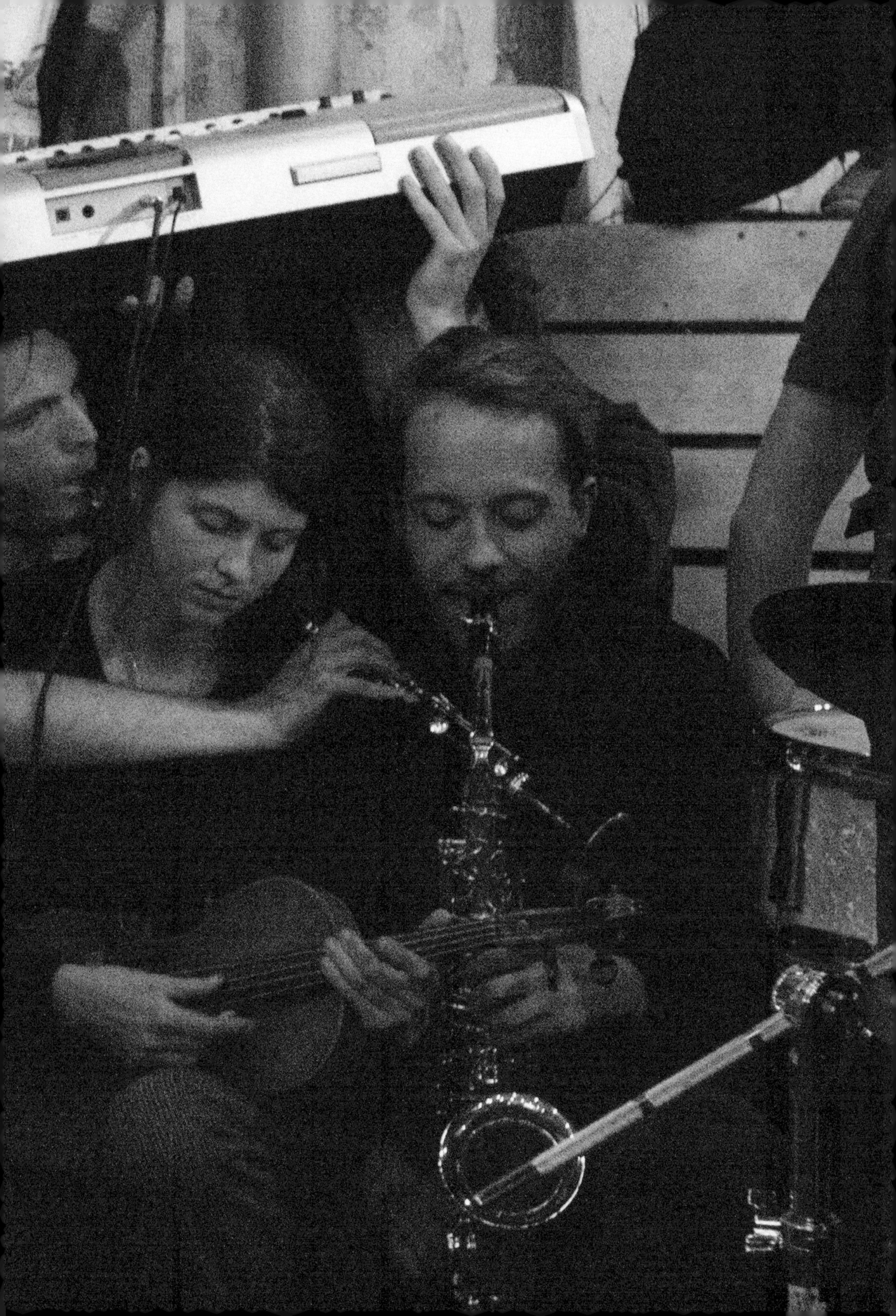

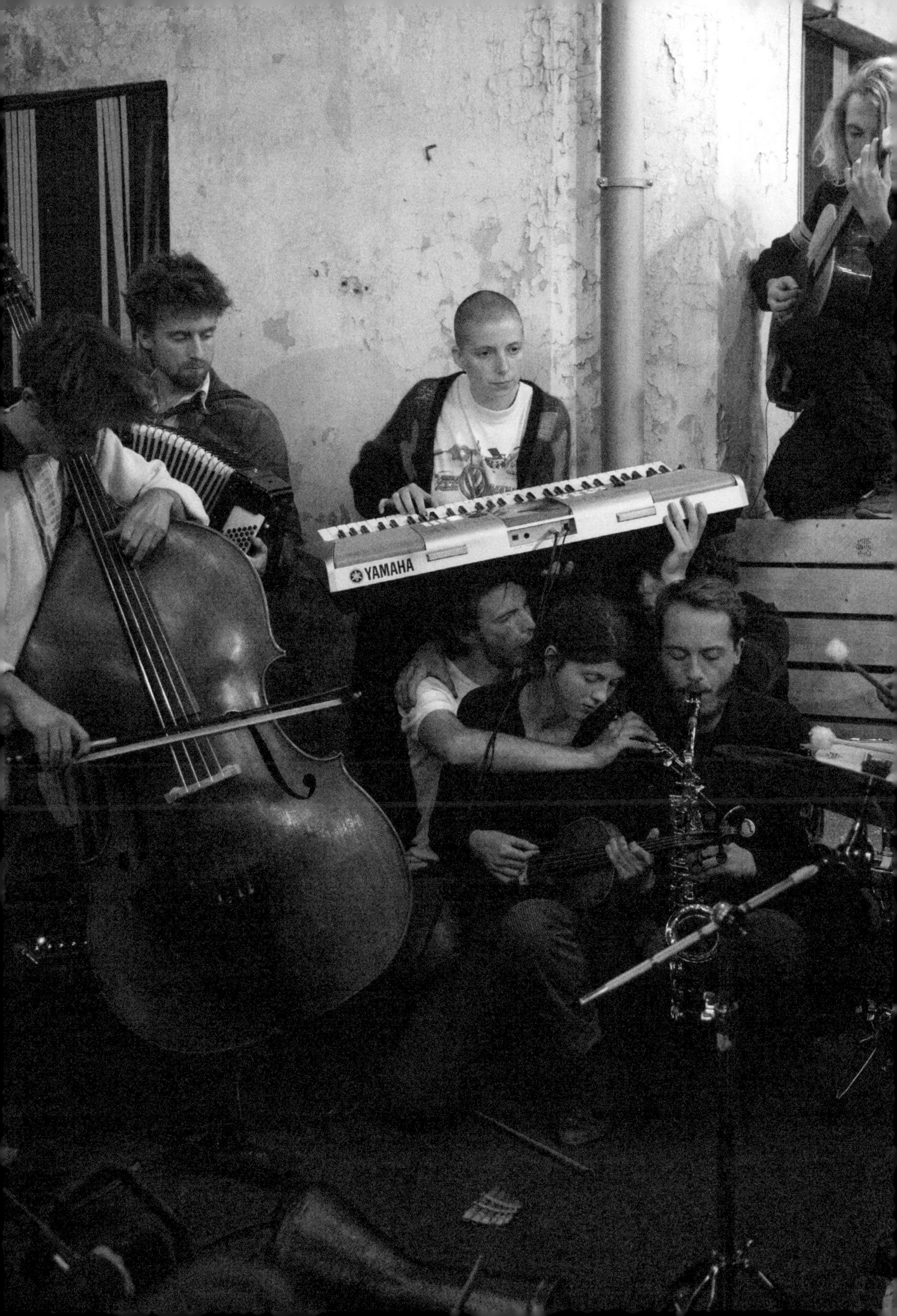
YAMAHA

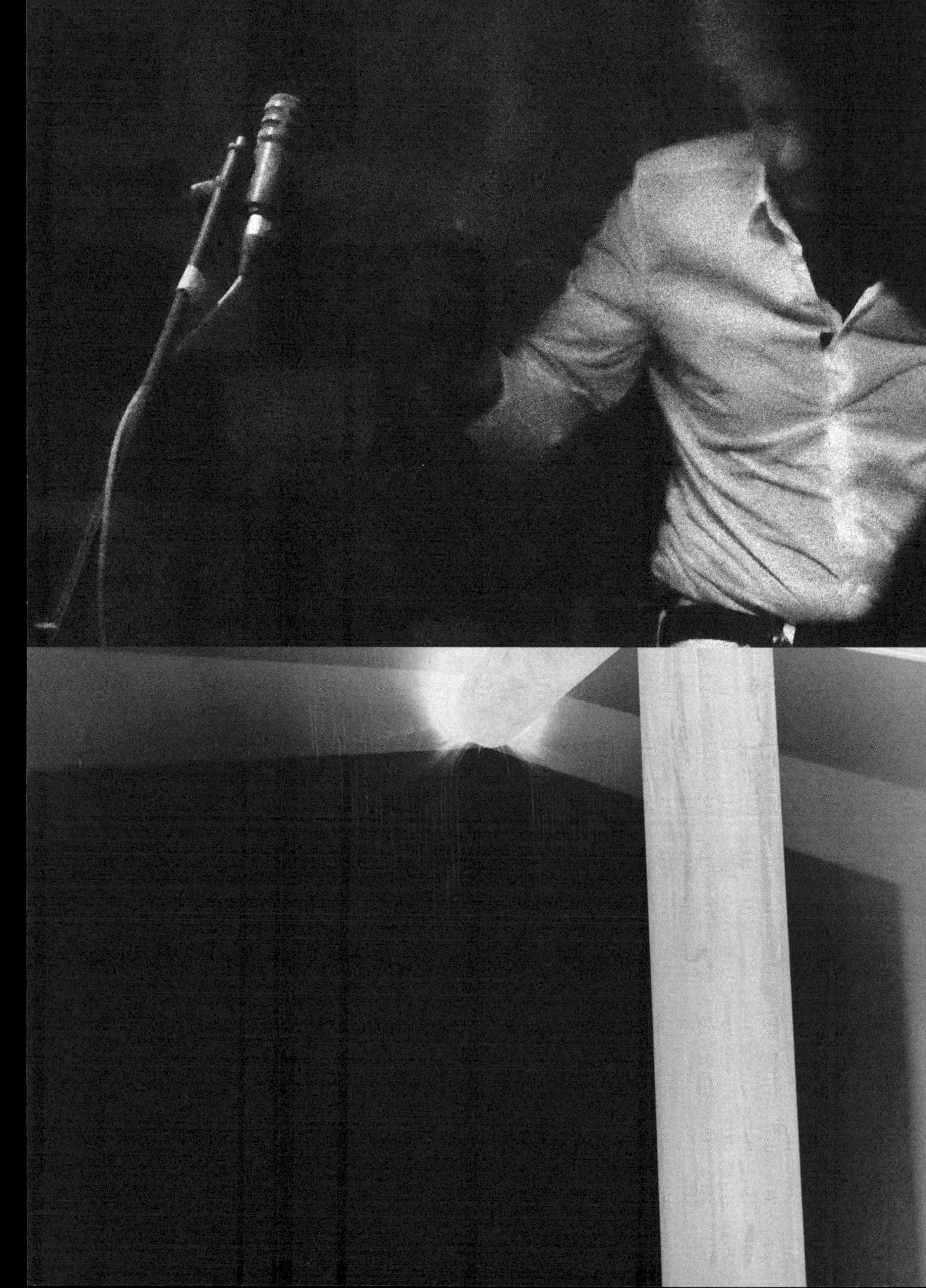

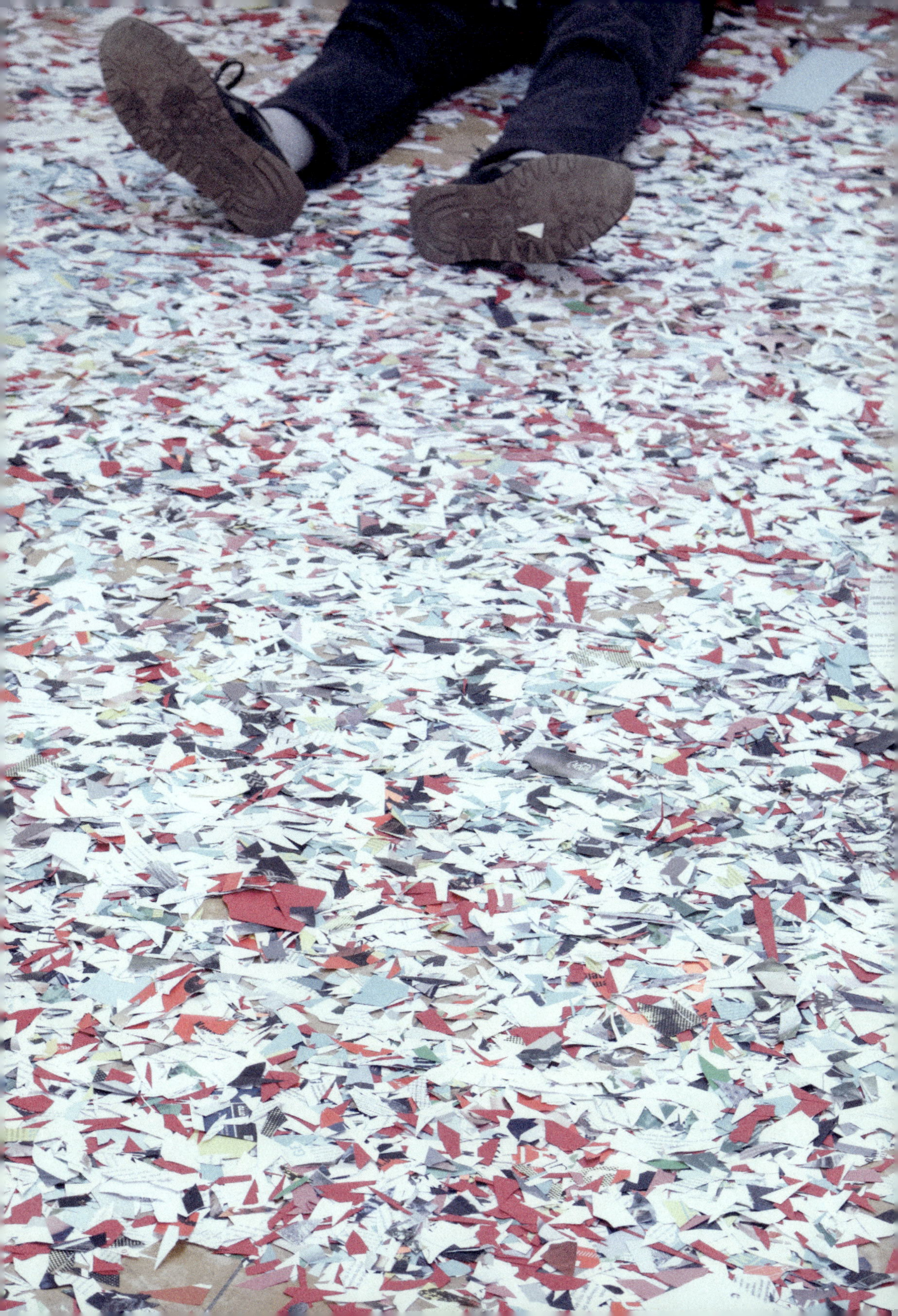

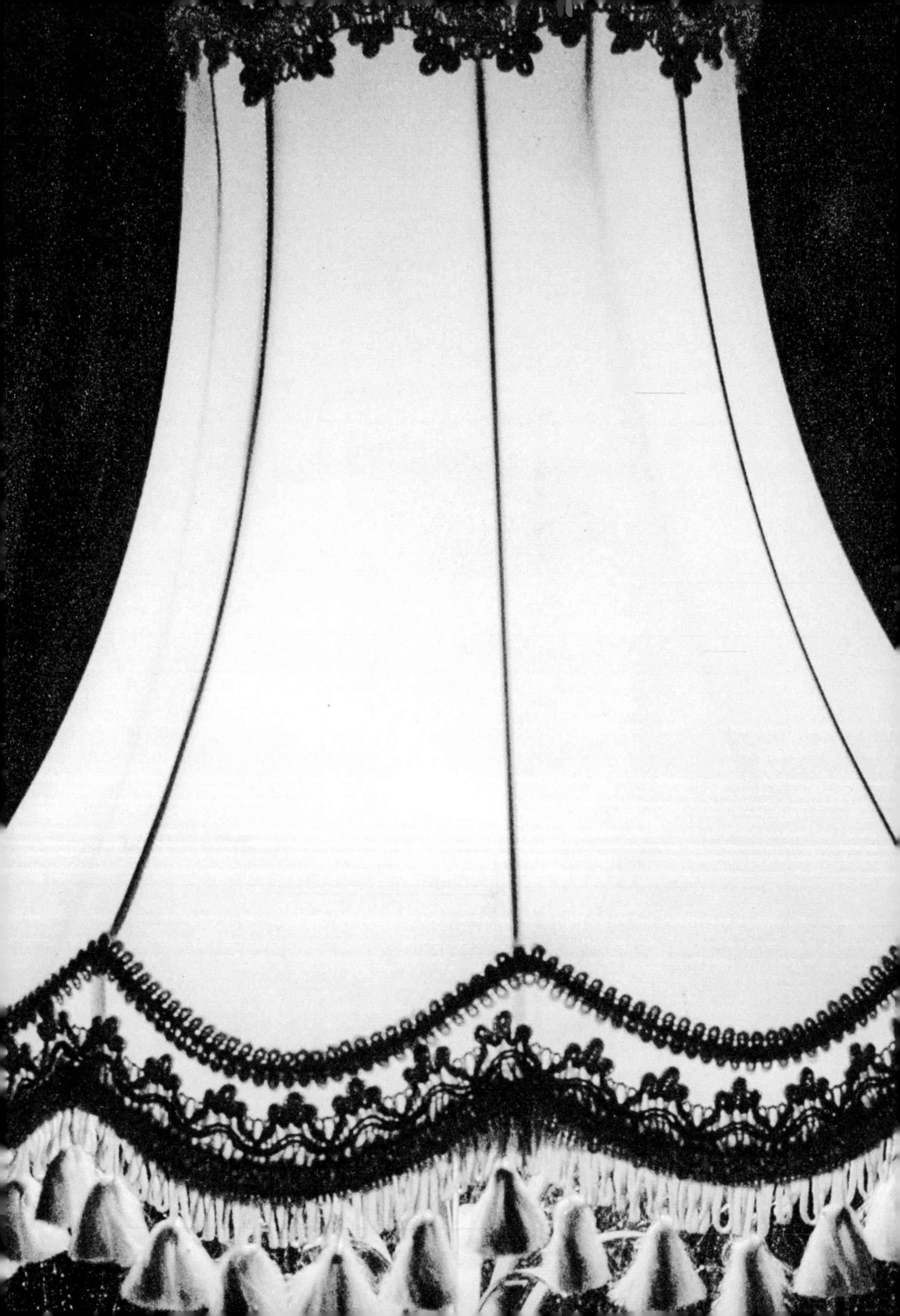

They said they found me inside a car dressed as a bag of frietjes, XL size, soaked in enough fat to keep my aura burning forever. Stringent in gestures, I was unable to speak, obviously, with mayonnaise and ketchup all around, some curry on the bottom, and an old Christmas tree dangling behind, asking for more.

More of what? I wondered. The image is grotesque, even if the mood is slightly familiar. *Is there something I am not aware of that I should know?*

Supposedly I smelled of Irish coffee and escargots (not dozens, but hundreds). Was I downing them as a chaser? They are too sluggish to chase anything.

Look, I drink Irish coffee all night long to keep myself fuzzy-faced and awake. Not to please anyone. A combination of whiskey, sugar, and coffee works. Loopy conversations and dreamy drifts are my forte. I crawl from one stage of music to another in a spirit of discovery while everything around me (the crowd, the color of the trash bins, that old WWII veteran holding a dog to his chest) suggests that I've stumbled upon the same AC/DC tribute band. In fact, it could be a different one—edgier, rougher and more distant from the original, which is precious.

I will come back tomorrow night, and the next. My fans know it.

A stamp on my right hand indicated that I had visited the EO Club prior to that. I couldn't explain my appearance near the carpark in the first place, so the question of how one would arrive there in a bumper car didn't seem crucial. But the EO club? The one that closed many years ago?

Are you sure it was a club door stamp? Not, say, a tattoo or a bruise? I ask.

I've never been to EO, even in its heyday. Only heard about all those 90s 'as if there is no tomorrow' techno raves. Of course, not many records of that period remain—decadence asks no witness. Years later, the club became a restaurant where Soromimi would cook elaborate meals for a dedicated crowd of gourmands, improvising on the character of various ethnic cuisines: fresh ingredients, a hearty approach, family-like management. Words flow so easily that I close my eyes to inhale the smell from the kitchen. But something else, rather post-ethnic, pops up right after a hint of grey shrimp soup.

Candles and flutes, the smell of burning sage. Echoes and loopholes. Everything softly embraces vulnerability, even the fire traps and safety hazards, visible only from my perspective. There is a woman wearing a swaddle and a headpiece, all in white with gold leaves shimmering behind her. Snare, undulating rhythm, humming and nodding, circular movement. The sounds of tranquility heading somewhere.

Heading to the next stage? I ask

It could be a more recent memory though. I open my eyes. The smell of burning sage lingers like a feeling that I've woken up not just from one dream, but from at least two. One took place many years ago and the other is one breath away. But they could be the same: like a shell inside a shell or one breath inside another. The same, as well as two or three. But never one. Oneness is disgusting. Oneness is an attempt to put all the ingredients into one cocktail and call it Universal Screwdriver X. The burning sage crawls around and smoke weaves the sound of a flute into a misty desert, or a river, depending on where you are. It could be a balcony too. I cannot contain this image, nor comprehend it. It does not contain itself, nor is it contained by anything else. I can only experience it, be captured by it, and soaked with it. This is what happens now.

You are witnessing it, too. You are witnessing the dawn of the image as you breathe slowly and your attention is moving in open circles. An image opens up like someone's shirt button. *Ping.* It could be your phone too. *Pong.* Everything matters. Nothing stays closed. Smoke tickles your nose and something is hurting—perhaps it is your limb, or maybe someone else's. Someone in the same room, or somewhere else sitting in a slightly uncomfortable position. But it is also softly numbing. You are accustomed to feeling the pain of others, or at least acknowledging it. This comes with numbing.

How can I re-sense myself in this state?

This room is organized like a multi-practice lounge for music, ideas, and social performance. A space of aimless drift and engaged attention, social rest and productivity. Maybe even re-drawing some axis of life. There are several here, ranging from tri-colored coasters to a constellation of rotating stages. One of them is a pole to dance on. I first smell it, then touch it. The sense of warm metal brings back a quick sensation: how fluently I spun on it yesterday! How could I have forgotten it? Spinning up and down, naked, kinky, and loose. My beard swaying around like the shamelessness after a good comb. A glamorous and self-centered introspective, according to someone (could have been me). But have you ever seen a pole-dance that was not self-centered? Introspection might work differently, though.

Did I wear cowboy boots?
Yes, maybe. I don't remember.
Did I look at the flourishing fanfares?

I did, and they did too. Looking for me in every corner of the building, in every blow of air that went through brass that night.

They found me singing in Farsi, my ancient language, and my favorite leather skirt, in matching lunatic beats, on the highest heels and in the lowest pitch. They also found me talking to strangers: something about the I Ching, mathematics, and quails. Then smashing plates on the floor, stealing a cylinder of paint, and asking for more. Who knows what. The room was packed with incense smoke.

The next thing I remember is playing Gamelan tapes. Entrenched in piles of cassettes and retro-gear, entranced by my own voice and guitar riffs. Blessed by a yearning for the spiritual. *Let's go deeper into trance*, I whisper to my partner. *To be here and there, and many other dimensions. To be true and fake, real and mad, cool and spiritual, conflicted and peaceful, sexy and shy, sometimes transcendental, all at once, more than once.* I hear our voices climbing the intensity ladder, drone by drone. Now I can see those cowboy boots climbing too. More than two. Enough for an entire boy band to march around in. But I have no doubt they will arrive in Nikes and Adidas.

Am I stepping in someone else's shoes? I wonder, looking around.

Everybody is in someone else's shoes, or socks at least. Intimately friendly, we are well trained in appropriation and a sense of fairness.
We must be at a pyjama party, I say, expecting someone on the carpet (yes, I remember there was a carpet!) to crack a joke back. A good joke to remember afterwards or before (there is no sequence). Maybe even a bad joke, like this guy wearing a bandana could probably drop. But nothing cracks, not even an innocent quip. The guy with bandana is out of his shit. We are in viscous elasticity, wearing each other's sensibilities. All those things we've brought from home and travels: goods, recipes, skills. You can bend them incessantly or tie them around your head and nothing will crack unless I touch the hair of a black woman who told me not to last time. Confronted with the controversy, I cried about my lack of sensitivity then promised to be

respectful to all the things I don't understand. But I did it last time too, way before the EO Club opened. Probably not even in this country, not in this century, or even the last one. So, what changes? Learning is also elastic, as I've already said (forgive me if I repeat myself about elasticity. Some people are just arriving, and I have to inform them of what's going on here, while sitting only in my socks.).

Maybe this is what brought me from the EO Club to the future? Those socks! I suddenly realize.

I am so content that in this environment I am being appreciated for what I am—my creative/ destructive persona—and the resources of attention I bring. I know the next thing I will do is spit all the alcohol I've drank tonight: cava,iko e, rijstmelk, fanta, drankjesj whisk,y, watea, fruitsep, cola, lrtte, p ntje. Halfway through that I will be cutting paper to infinity, filling up the floor. Soromimi will find it most beautiful, and when she is grown up I will not be able explain to her why. I can't explain it now.

In juxtaposition, these two actions may seem like a cause and effect, or an abuse and a punishment. But trust me, I'm not here to bring some pedagogical narrative. I am not here to talk about waking or sobering up.

You set your alarm clocks yourself, people. I still have to install Windows 96 on a computer instead. It won't just crack, it'll blow your ears away.

Although … if you really want to know … maybe I am here to bring some teaching, a voice of self-inflicted authority. To tell you the truth, I am dying to tell you how to live. I am dying to show you that by installing old operational software I can create so much noise that this brain can't even operate anymore. But at the moment I am denying that voice, afraid of appearing authoritarian and old. Do you really want to hear my voice when I am in this mood? Take any tram in this town and I am announcing the stations. Live. And that's only where my trip starts.

Another Dirty Soromimi please!

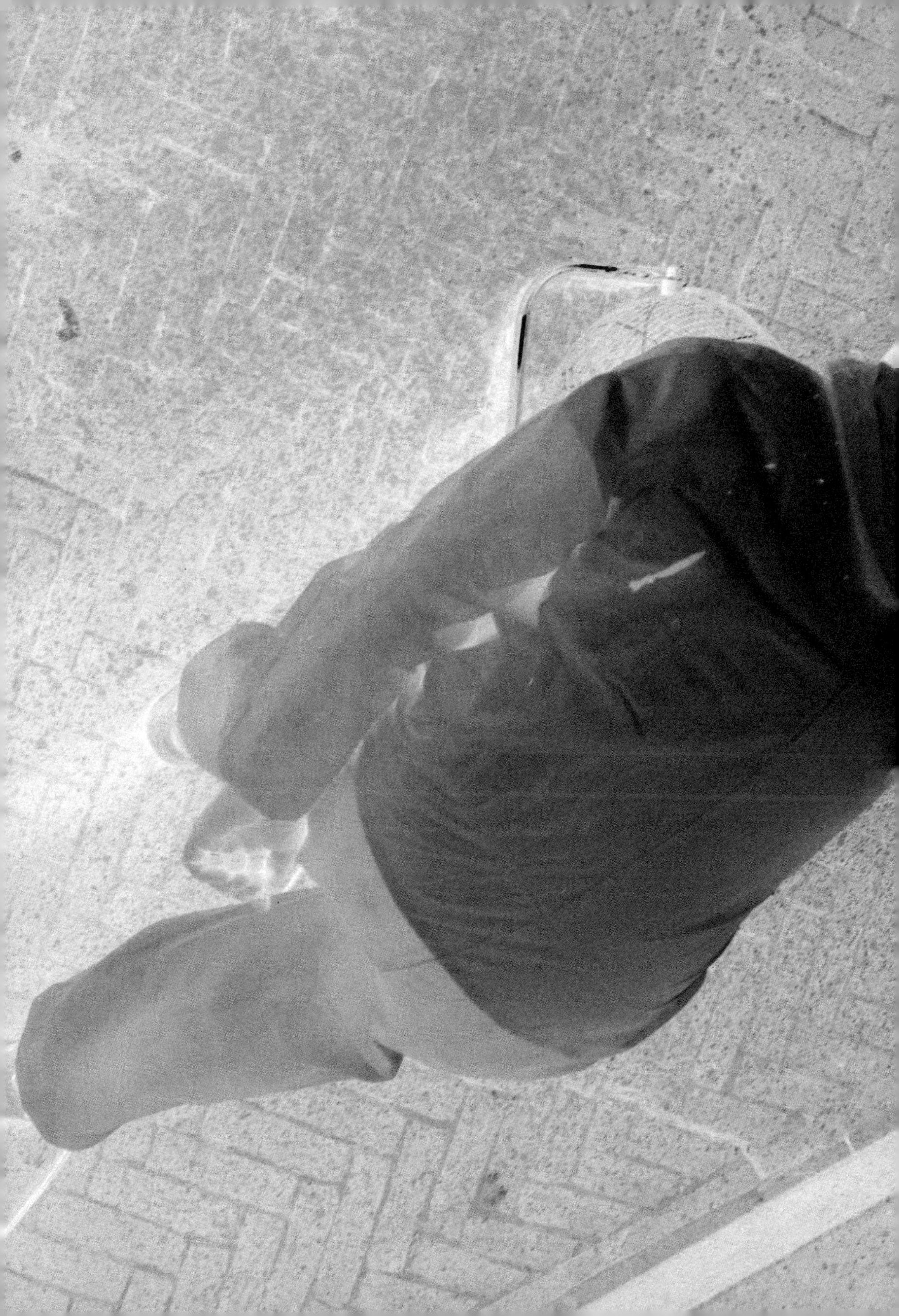

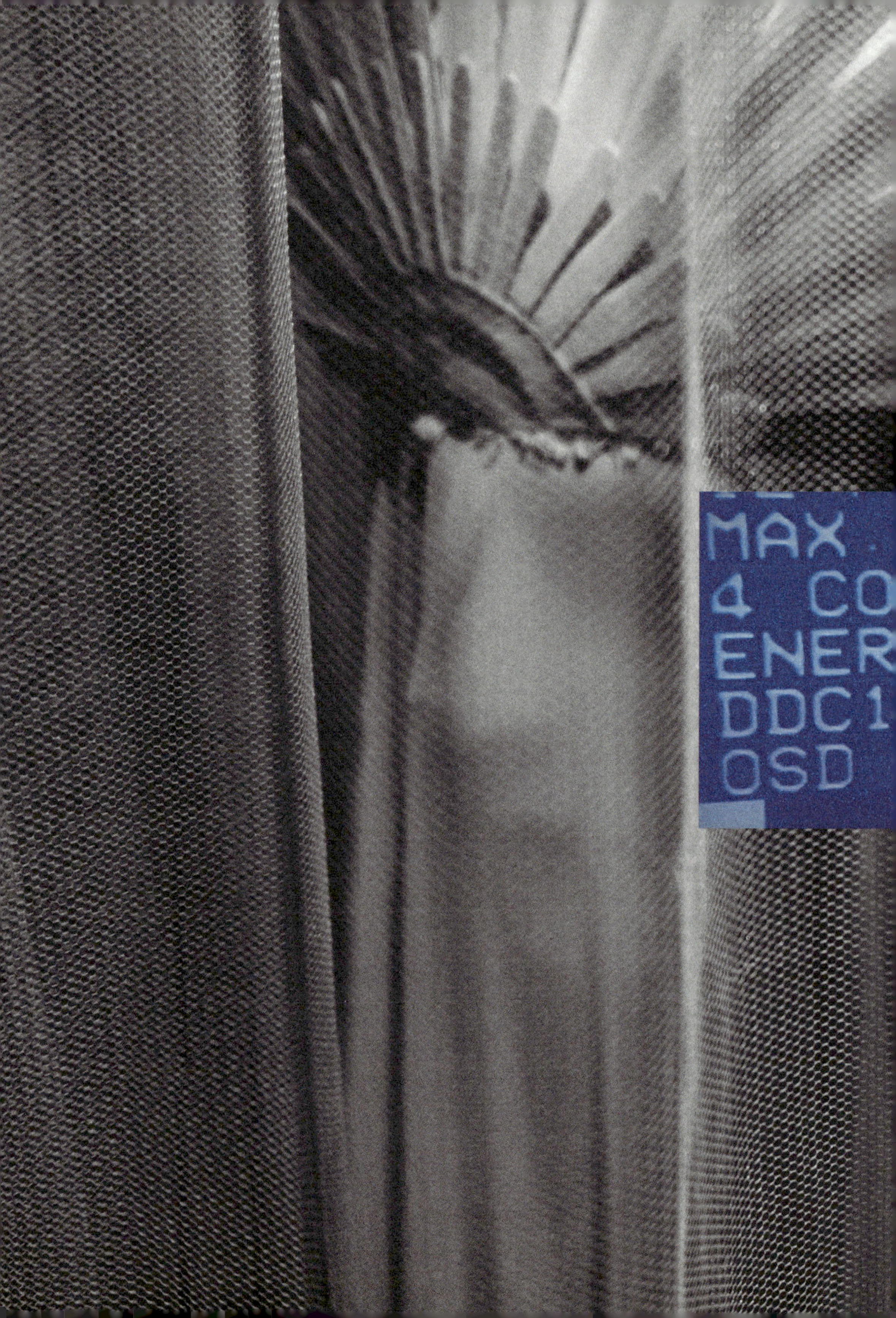
MAX
4 CO
ENER
DDC1
OSD

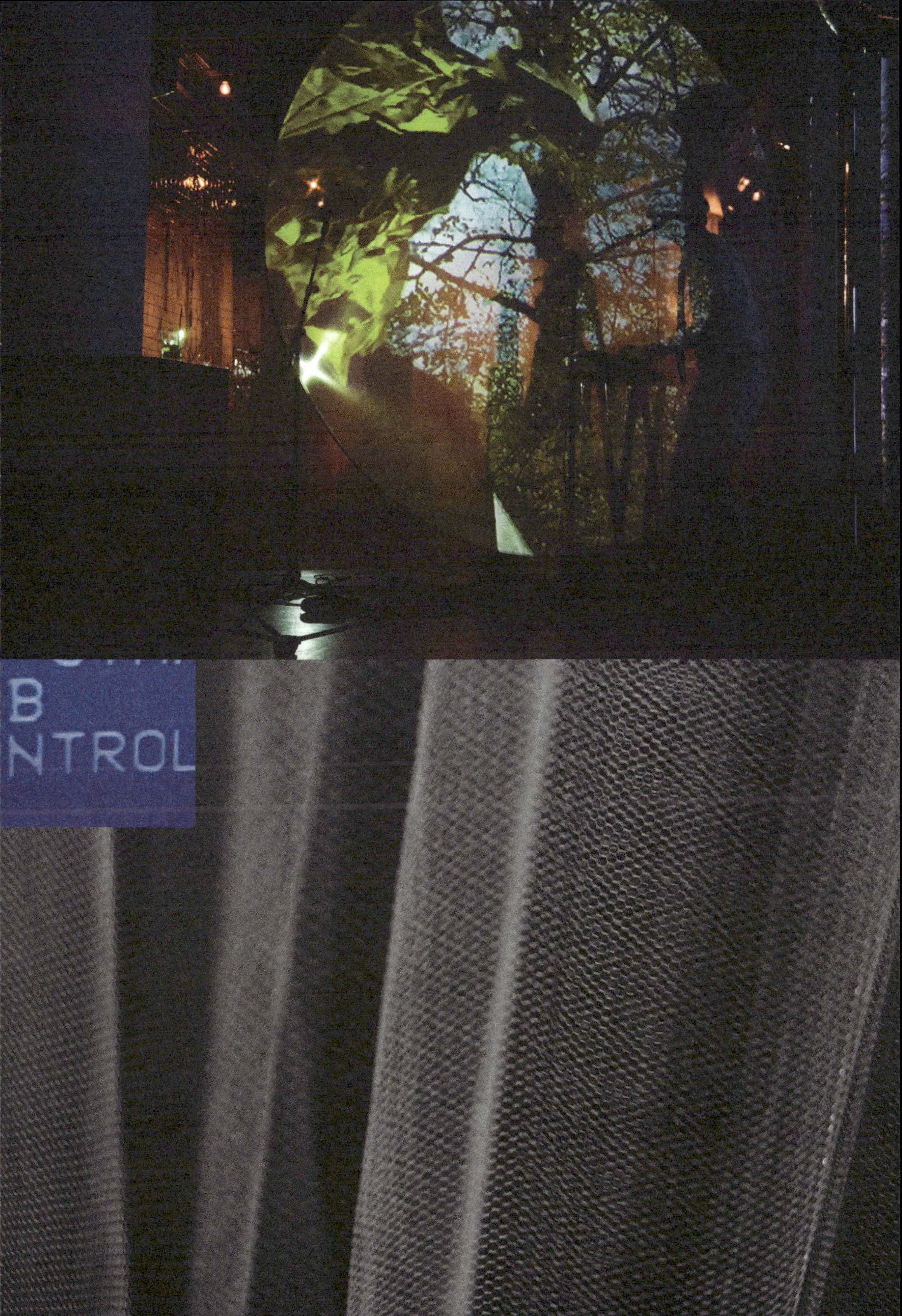
B
NTROL

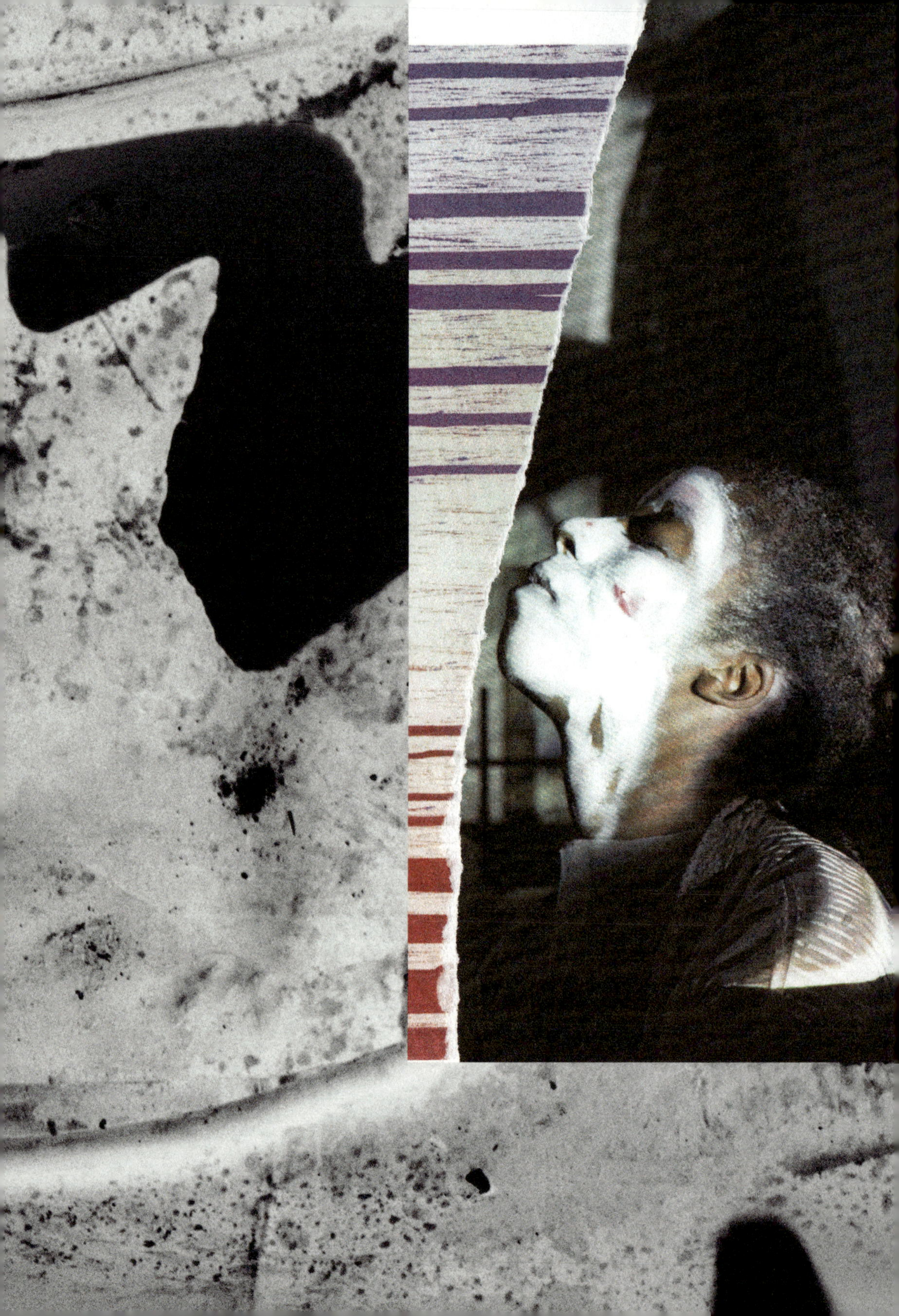

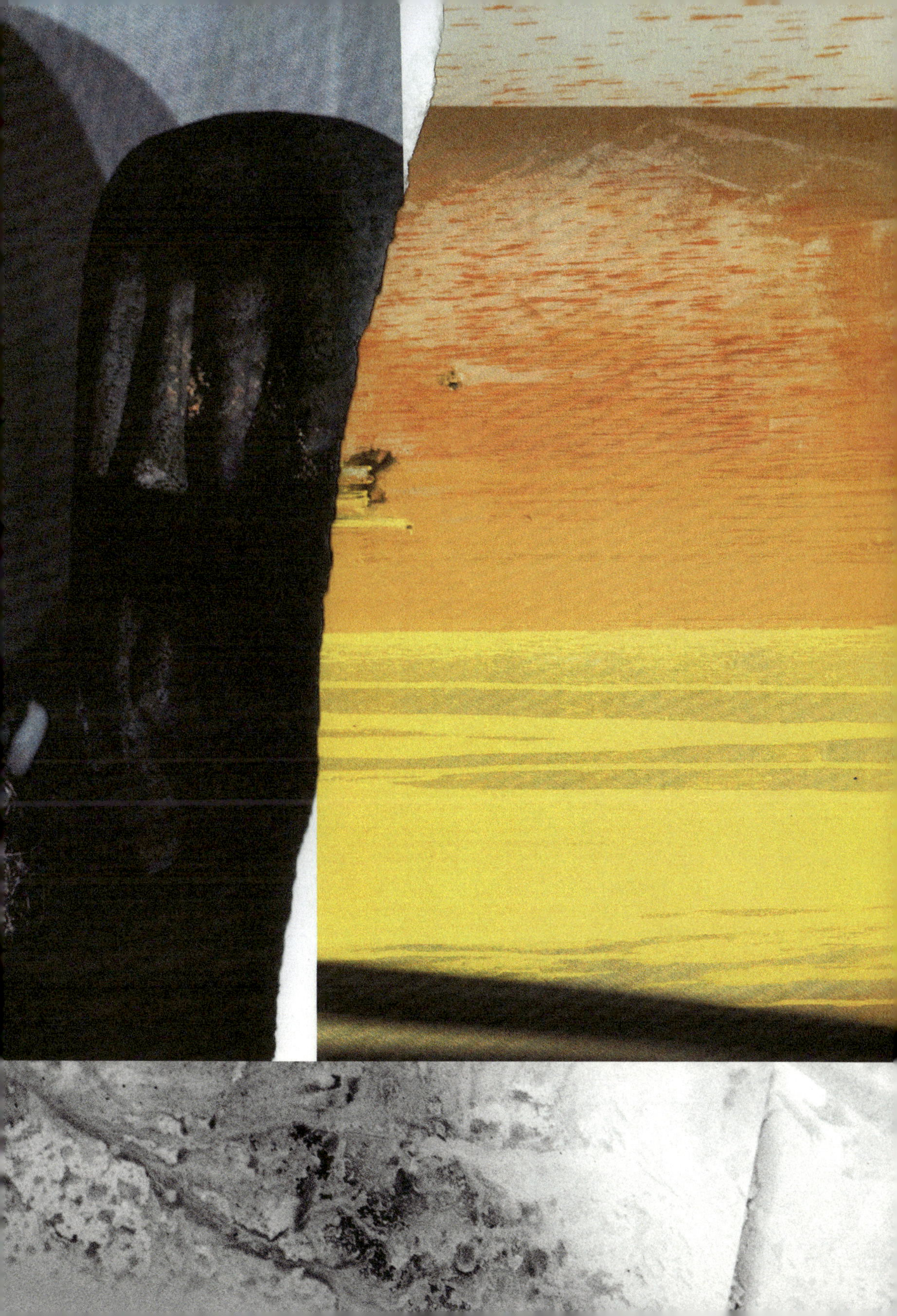

AsiaMusic.Com

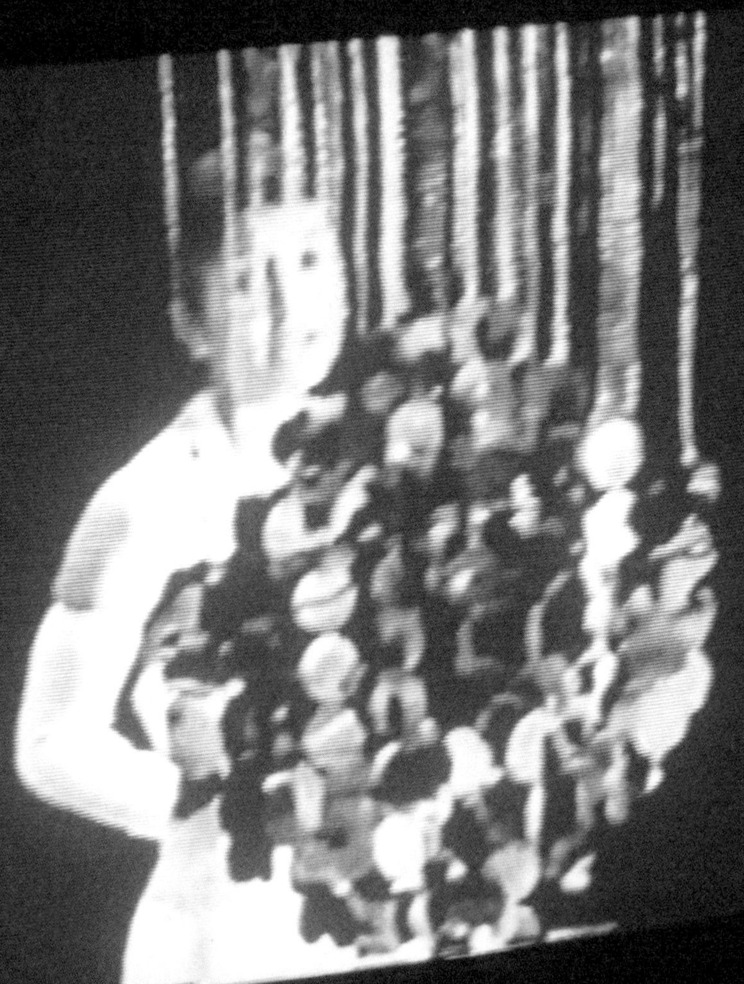

My body is saturated with tattoos. Saturn and a teddy bear on one leg. Scissors and a city skyline merge on biceps. The scissors are slightly open and city is falling off. A red carnation flower on a neck. A paper plane neatly folded on a shoulder. It is almost impossible to read what the paper says. By the time it reaches another hand the letters will be entirely gone. Naturally, as they say. Today they are still legible, dying from longing for a voice to say: I love your hands.

Are you sure it was a club door stamp? I ask again. *Not, say, a tattoo or a bruise?*

Soromimi is making a cocktail at the bar. A fly on the wall is staring at the cocktail. What does a fly see? A porthole made of droplets, neatly woven by the crystalline structure of the fly's eye. When one looks really deep into a porthole, a wave of something as large as an ocean appears. *The South China Sea, probably. Or another apparition without scale*, thinks the fly, right in front of me, crushed on ice.

I have to admit that coining names for bodies of water and dropping coins into water, usually fountains, has been one of my favorite activities since I can remember anything. Not only coins. I remember we dropped a dead mammal into a fountain, but that was a long time ago. Why was it so funny then? Good question. I still don't know the answer, but it's not funny anymore.

The way one would name a lake was to stare long enough at the body of water, hanging in space like a cloud or a piñata. Then someone would say a word or a phrase and if the piñata broke open and spilled out all its contents, the person had guessed the name right. Same with a lake in the sky: you either guess it right and it lands, or you keep guessing until something else snatches your attention. While I am looking at the piñata hanging above the bar, I am swooning inside a ship inside the glass that Soromimi is holding, reflecting the colors of the mystic care room. Soromimi is holding a spotlight. The porousness of matter binds these distant bodies of water—one far away and the other inside a straw. There is no separation between the two. That's probably how I woke up from two dreams at once. Or I am still dreaming? Somewhere at a distance, or at several distances, another ship appears. It is elegant, retro-fit, and dimly lit from the inside with what could be a gang of lighters. They are everywhere. Not only lighters, but also curls of clipped hair. I zoom slowly into one of the portholes, as much as a drinking glass can gather, and swallow myself into a room. A human-scale room.

Can one say 'swallow into'?
Yes, Soromimi, you can swallow into anything.

It is like sensing something and then putting yourself into the position of what could possibly be there, without even knowing what it is. Some shit will happen. You can swallow yourself into the cocktail you are making. You may think that there is no living being in it at that moment. But if you stare at it long enough, something may happen. If two of us are staring, it is even more likely.

I've come to this stage where I can stare long enough without trying to guess anything. At the same time, I am very hungry for the next performance. I am literally craving the next character to arrive on stage. Pauses can be too petite and polite, too ambient-like, too relaxing.

Where is the stage?
Everywhere.
OK.

I want a character that would open a bar door and sit down not far from me, the distance of a word or a phrase, and then order a body of liquid. A character whose purpose in life is to open this door at this specific moment and change the course of the situation. Or to change nothing at all. Perhaps this character is not familiar with their purpose, and not familiar with me either. But he or she is definitely familiar with the idea of the purpose of life.

You may accept what is given by god, state, or family, and repeat a particular routine every day, like cutting magazine pages with scissors, or simmering the best escargot in town. Or you may keep wondering about your individual purpose in life and frequent bars to discuss it with like-minded friends. Or you may abolish the whole idea of it because the purpose of life also requires a commitment.

At this moment in my life I am waiting for a character that would open the door and in a few hours become my best childhood friend embodied in one person, in two people, or more. Perhaps we would wake up the next morning together and I would die of pleasure saying *I love you! I always loved you! I love you so much and what you called yesterday is no more than—*

With the utterance of   suddenly a piano enters the room. There is a bird cage on top of it and a wedding cake. No, it is someone's head. What could be a piano player turns out to be Soromimi, putting photographs together. In one of them I see you sitting in a limousine, heading somewhere. *Heading to the next stage?* I check. Although the piano is still there and the bird cage open, Soromimi starts pouring some soy sauce into it.

Really??

Now the ocean disappears. Probably forever. I feel the misery and horror of the shrinking openness, similar to the moment of sobering up. The glass you found this publication in is gone, too. But if you zoom into another porthole of the ship you will still find Soromimi there. They are like a disco track: you feel the groove is ending, but again the main theme picks up and continues, taking you to a different level of excitement. From there you go somewhere else exciting and different, with no happy-end. Infinite outro. That's why disco is so good.

So, what is this cocktail called? I ask.

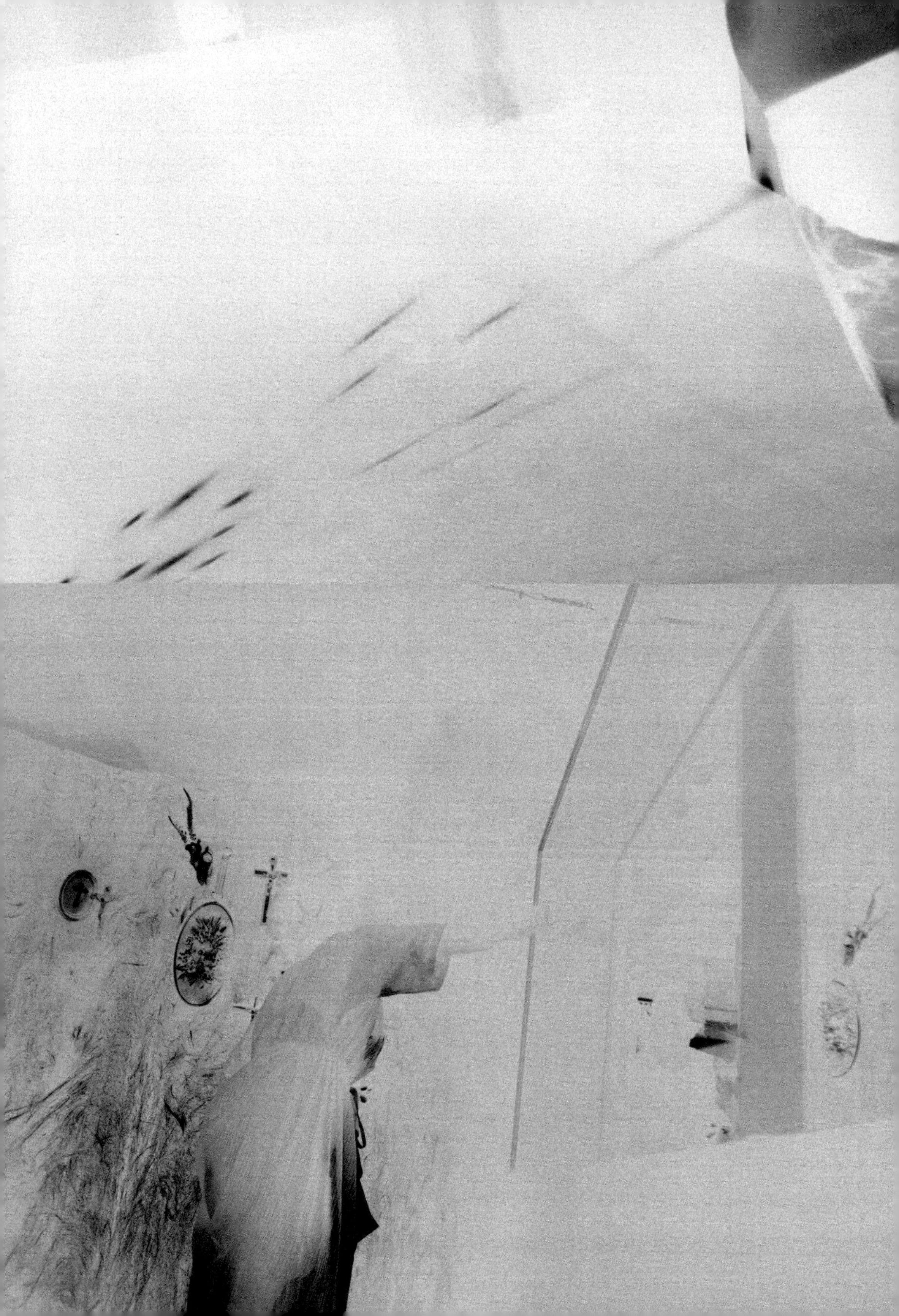

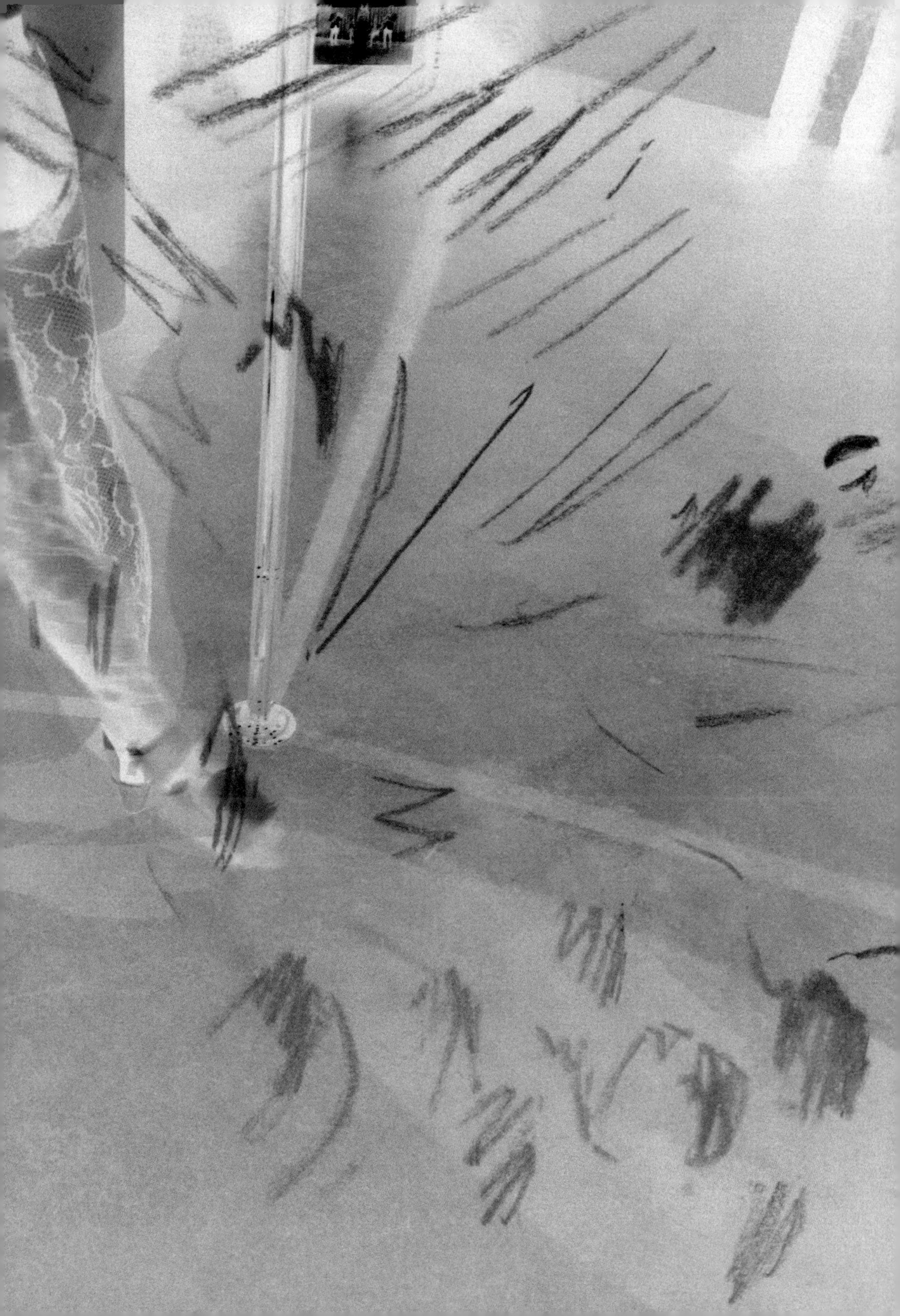

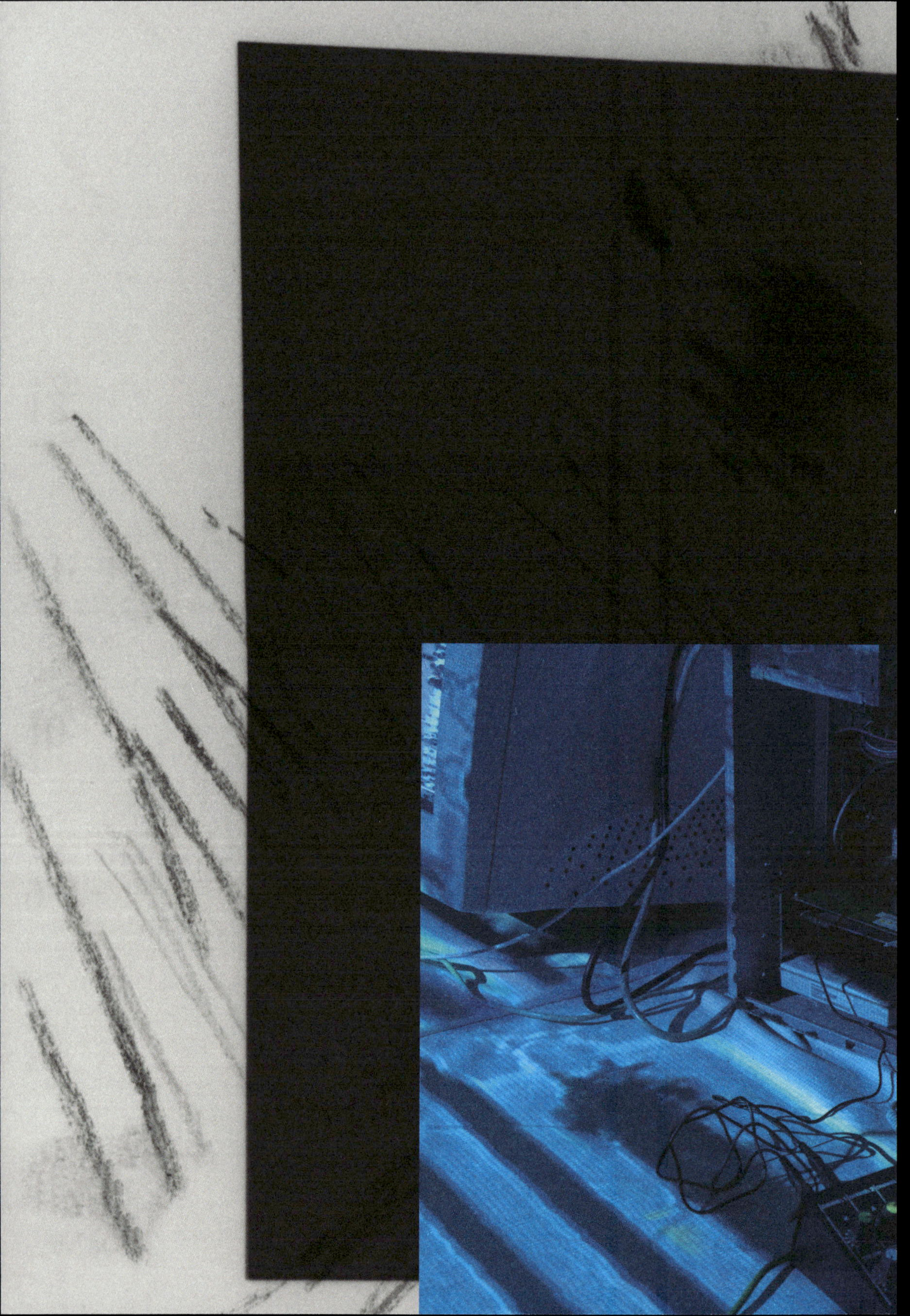

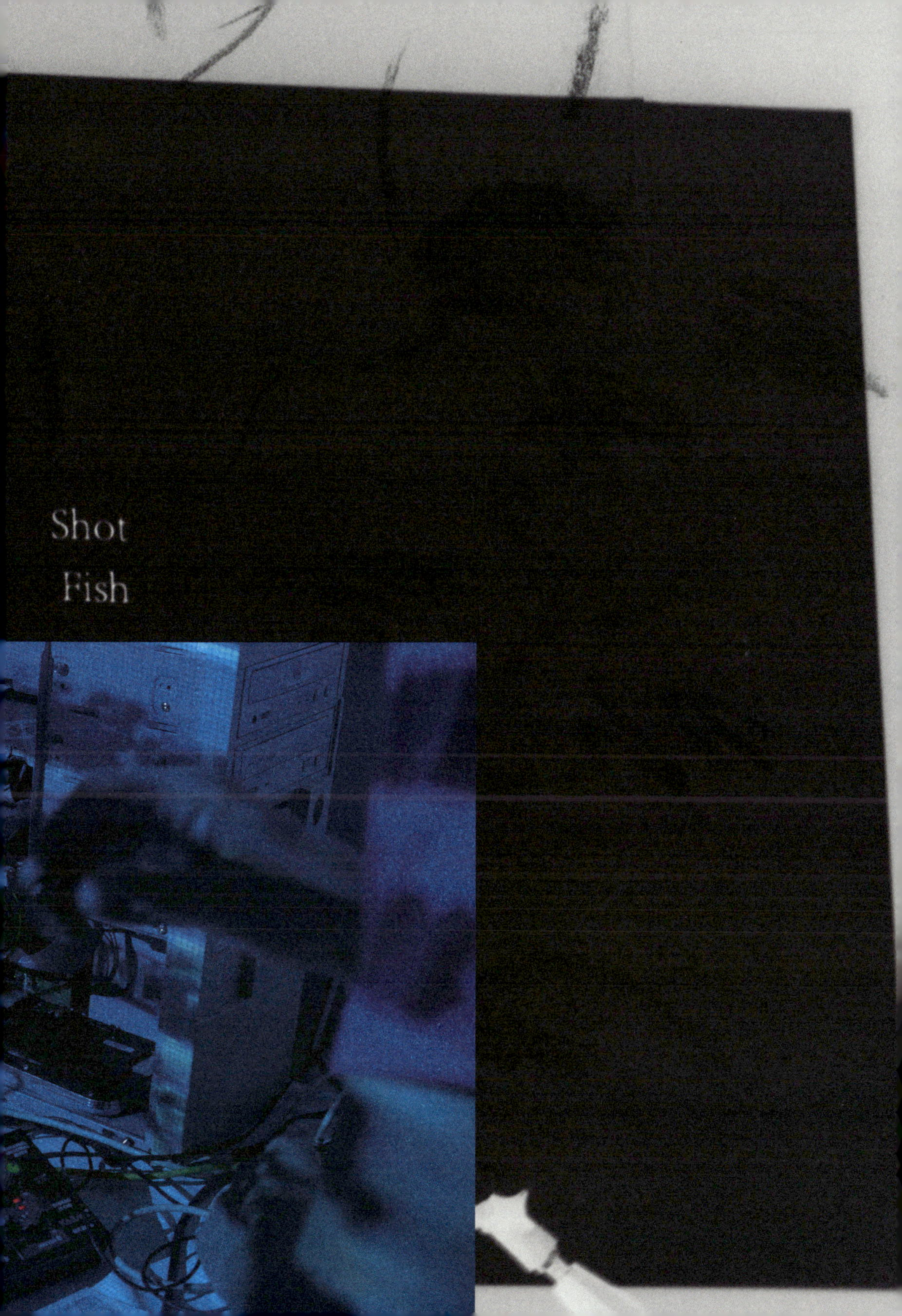
Shot
Fish

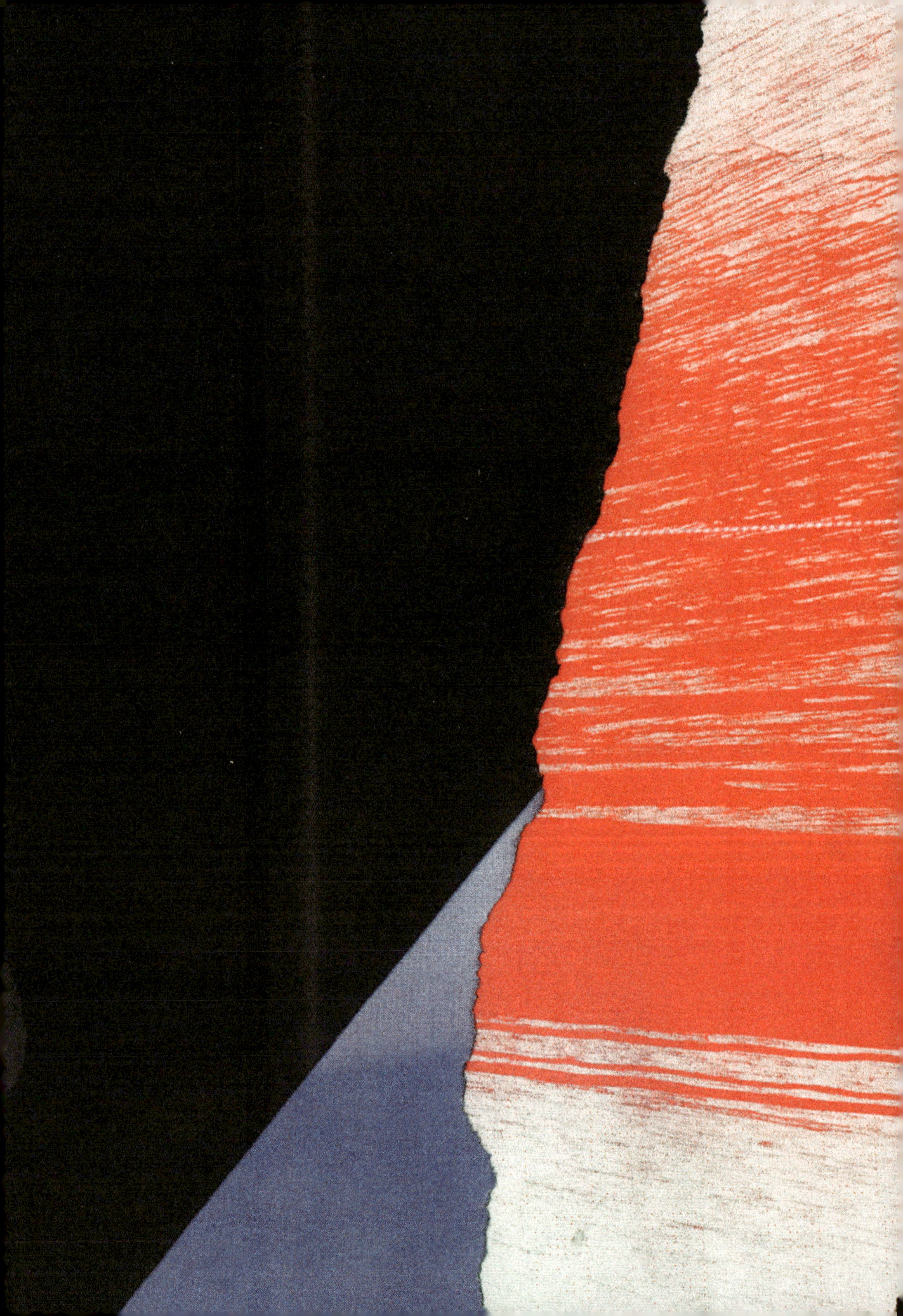

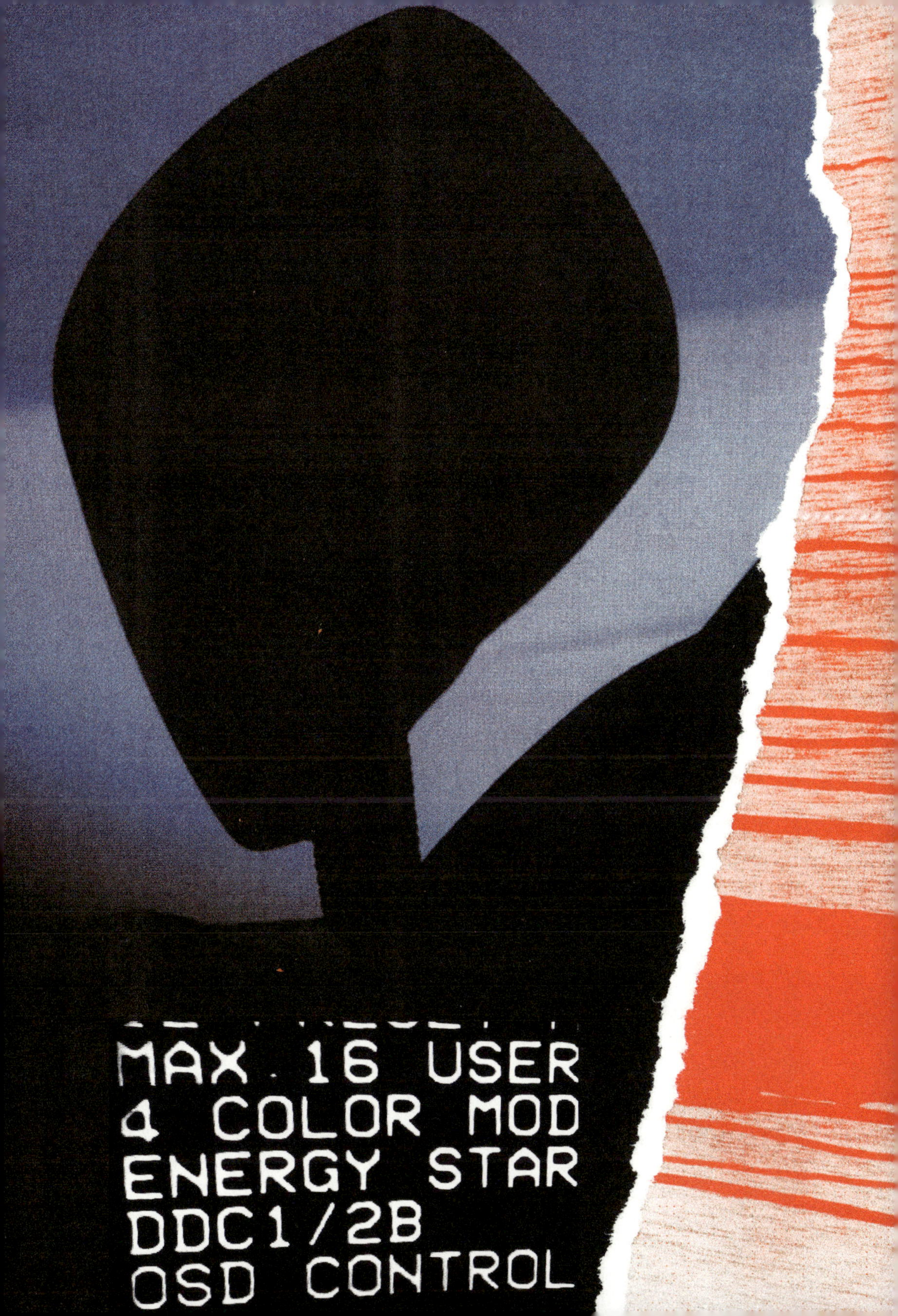
MAX 16 USER
4 COLOR MOD
ENERGY STAR
DDC1/2B
OSD CONTROL

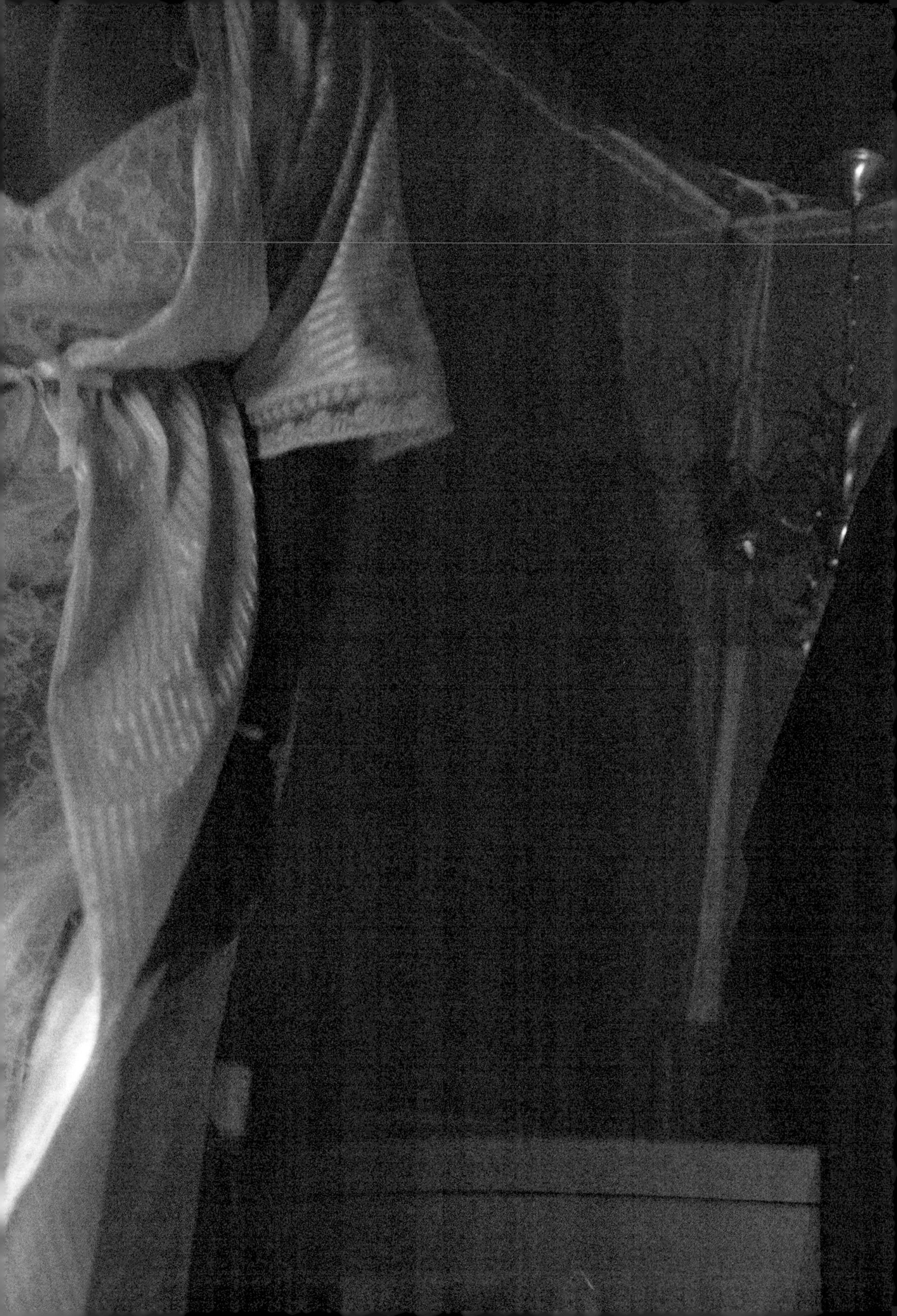

Every night starts with squirting.
Every day has a different color.

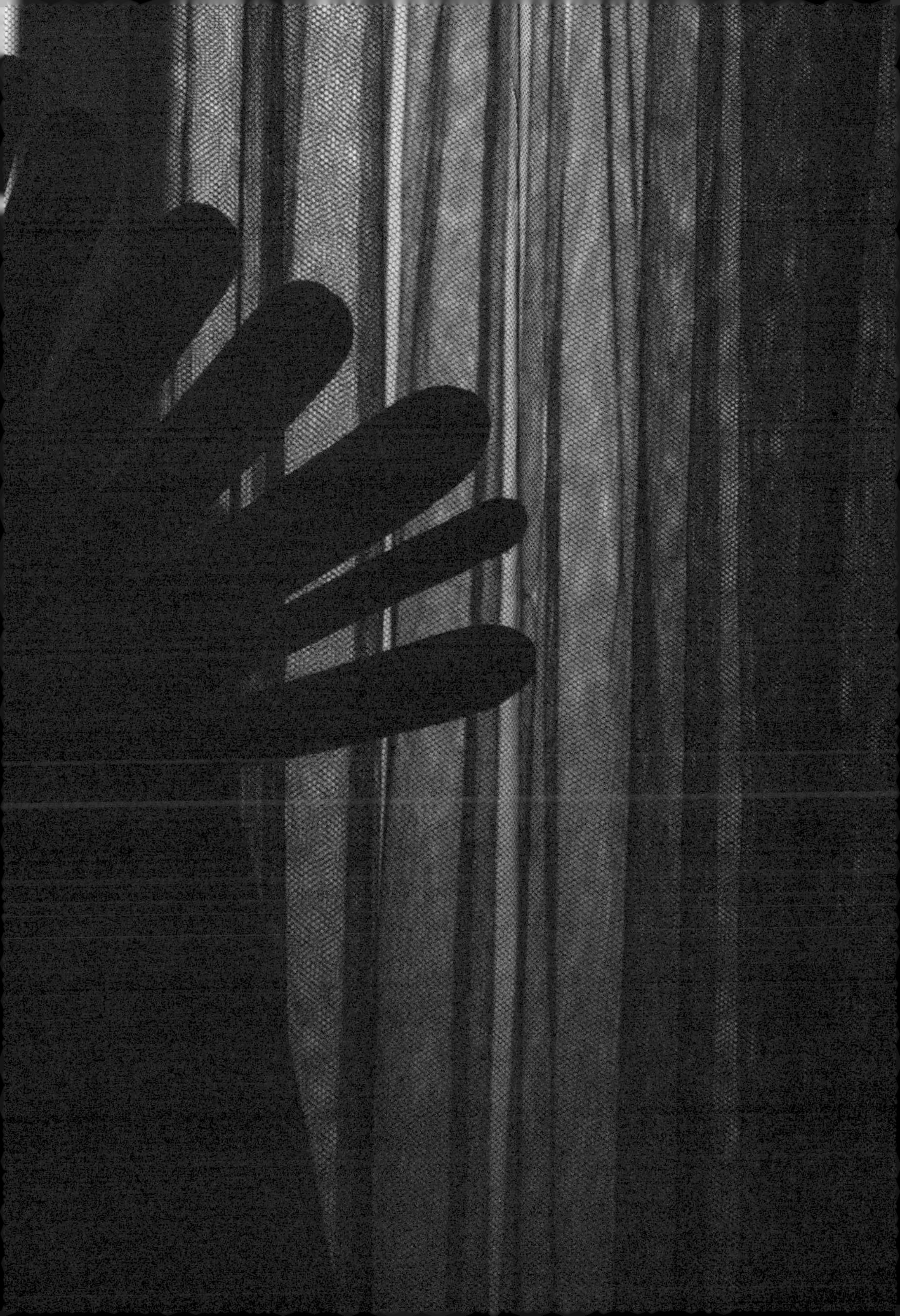

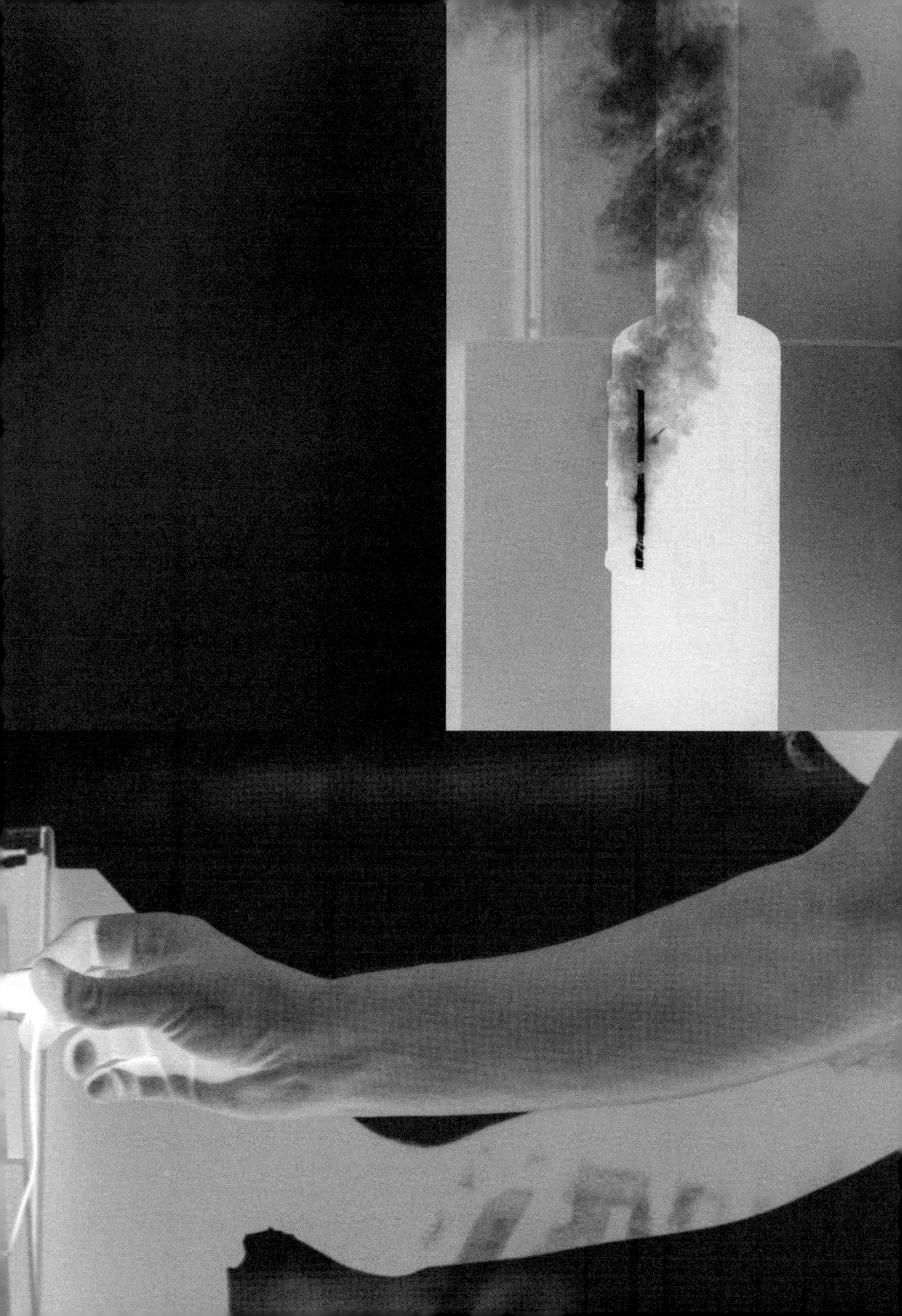

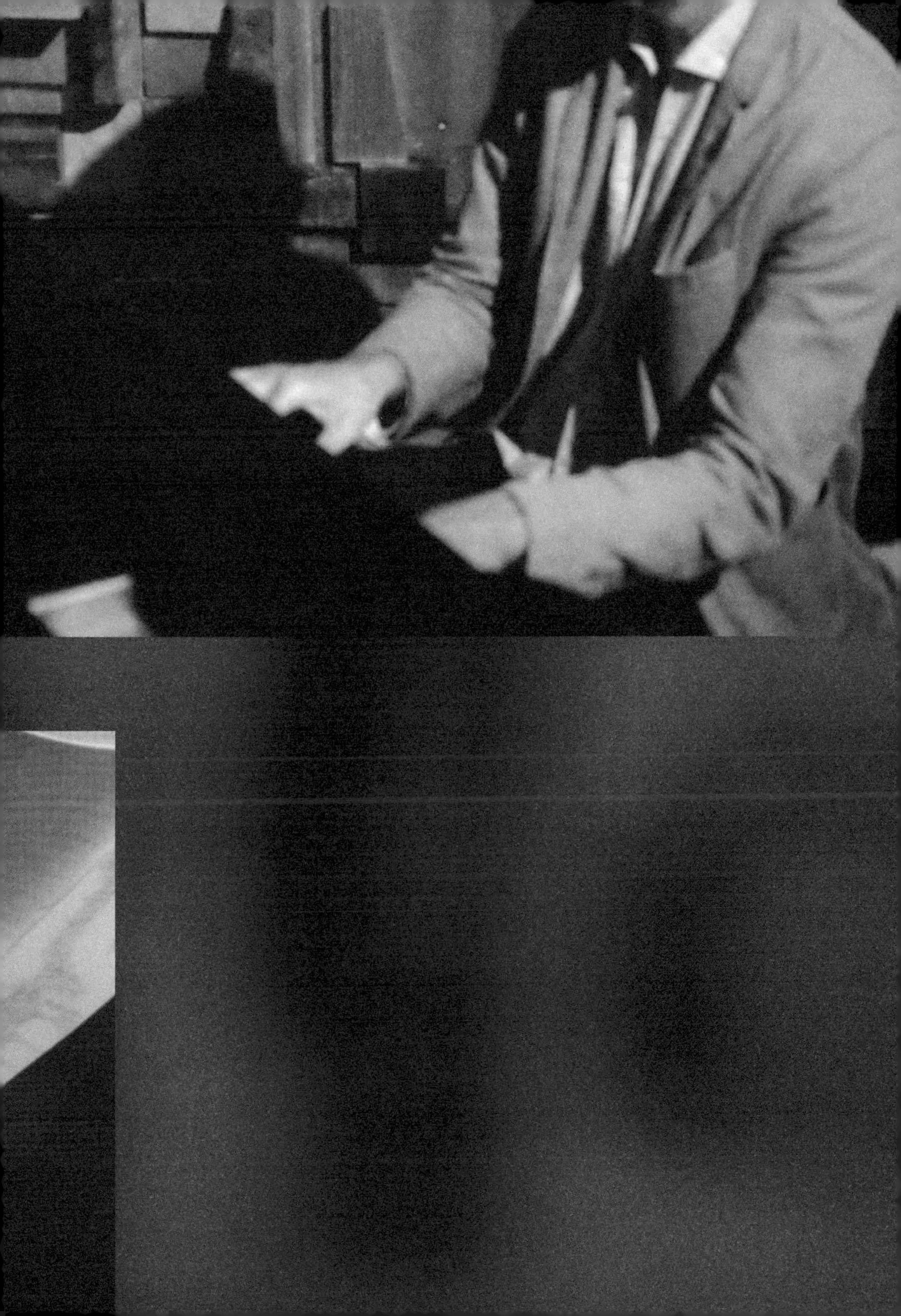

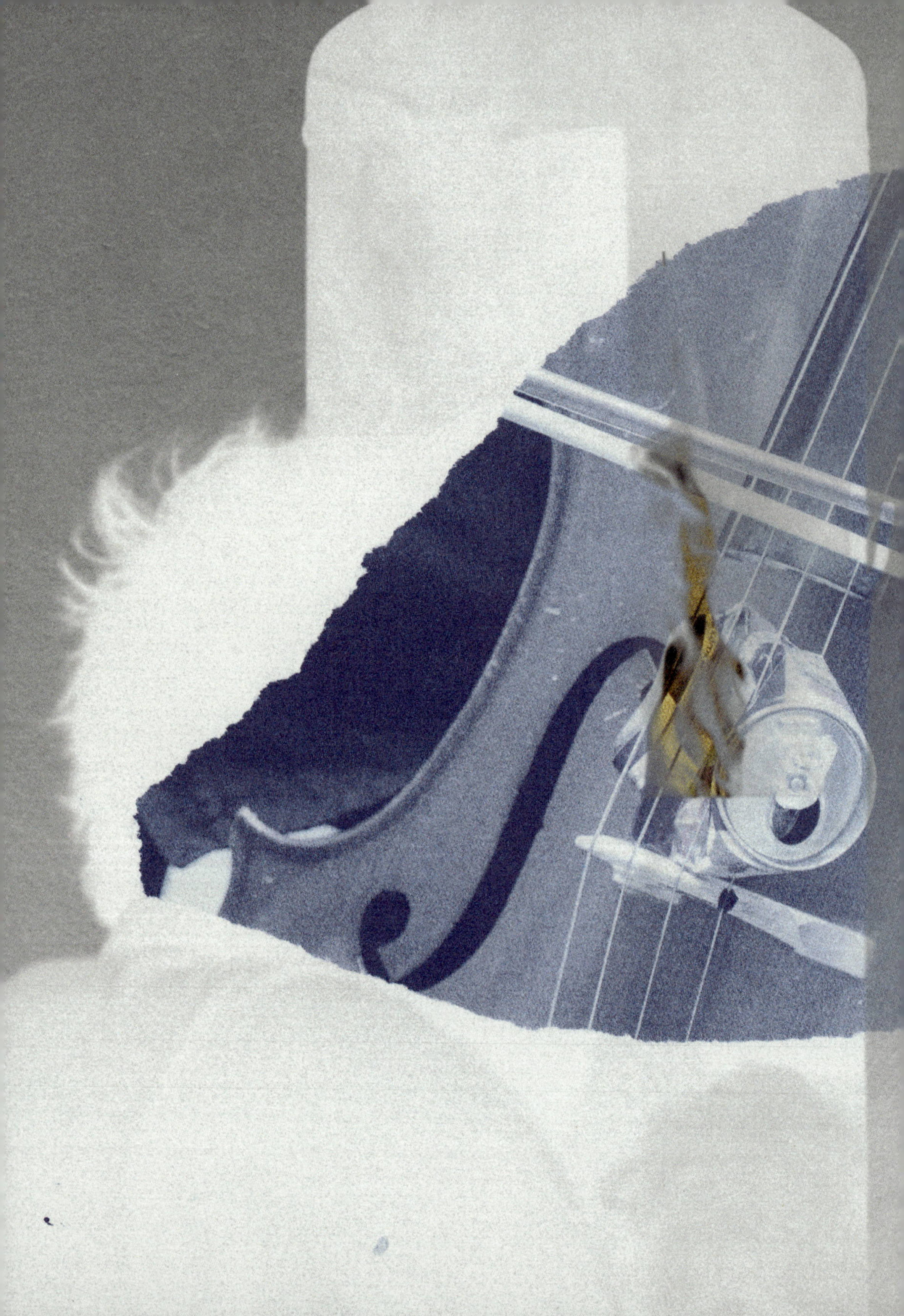

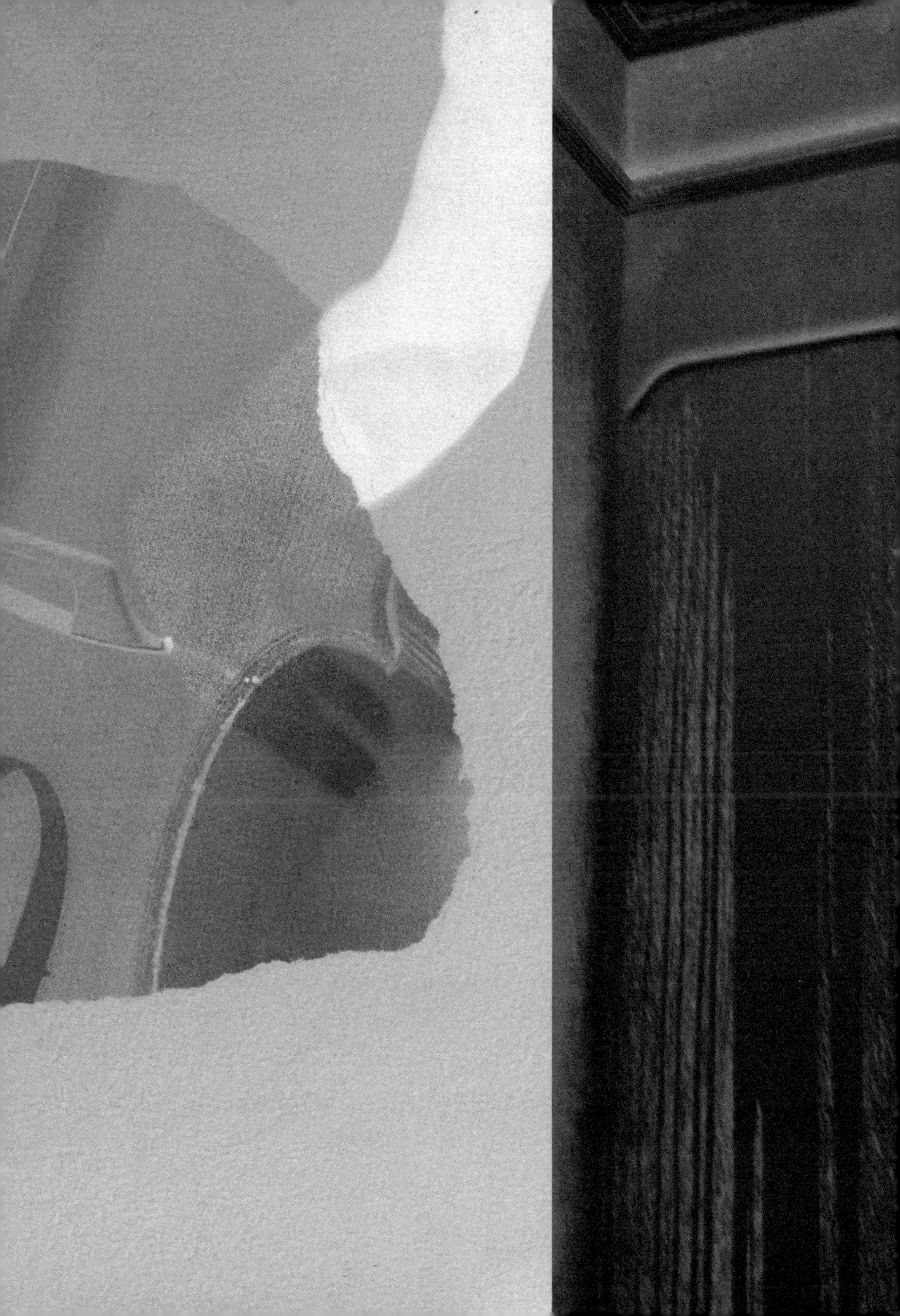

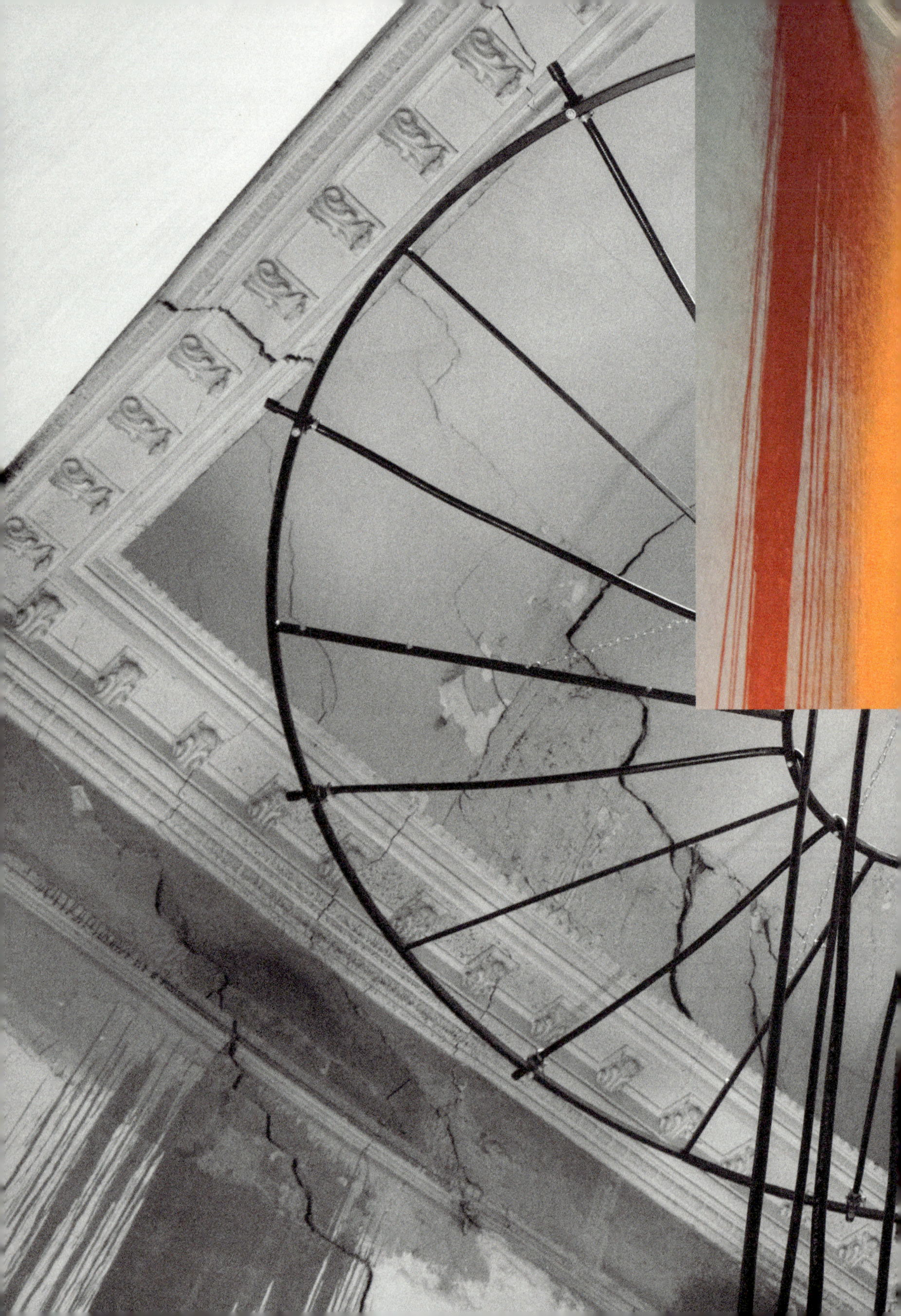

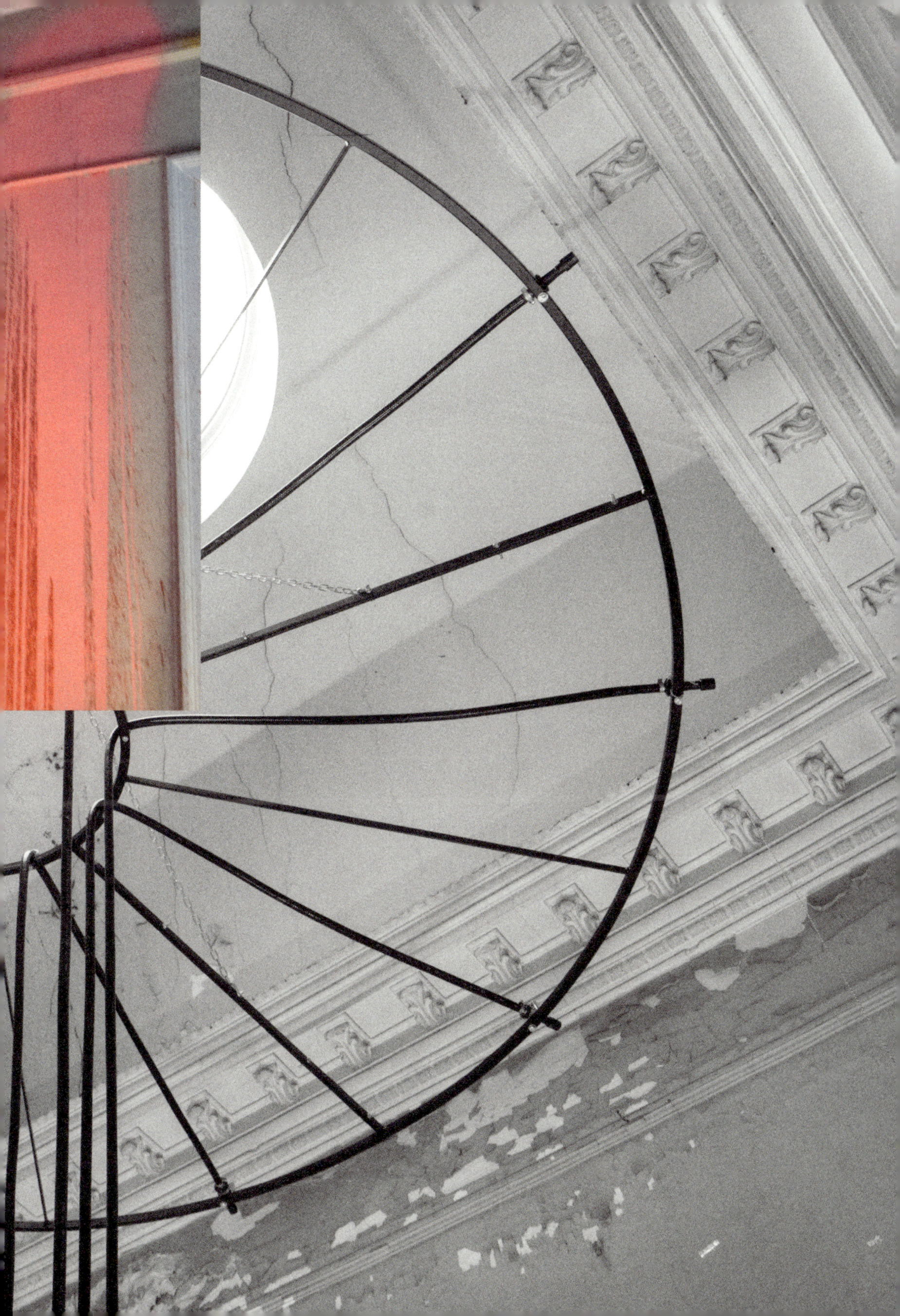

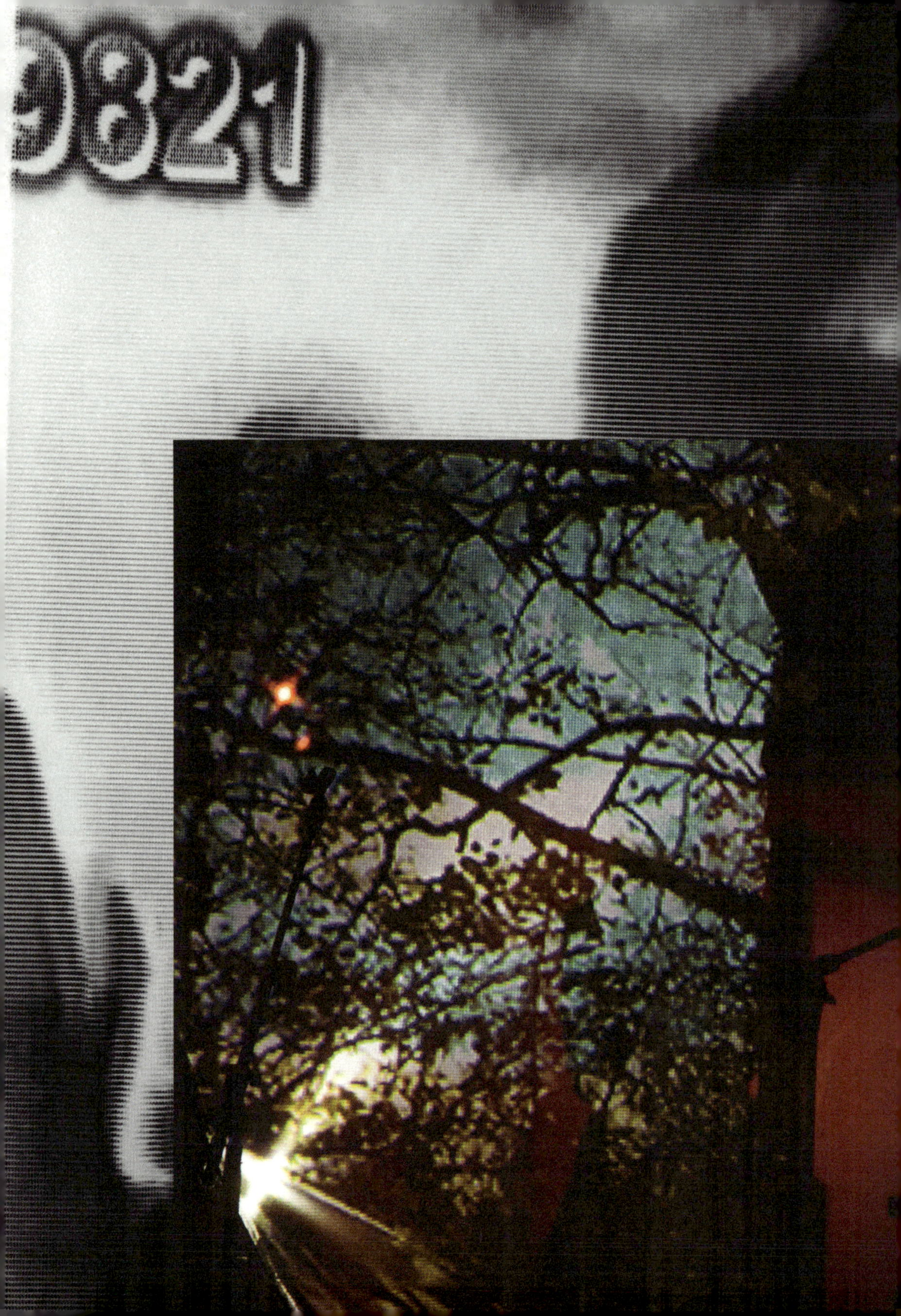
9821

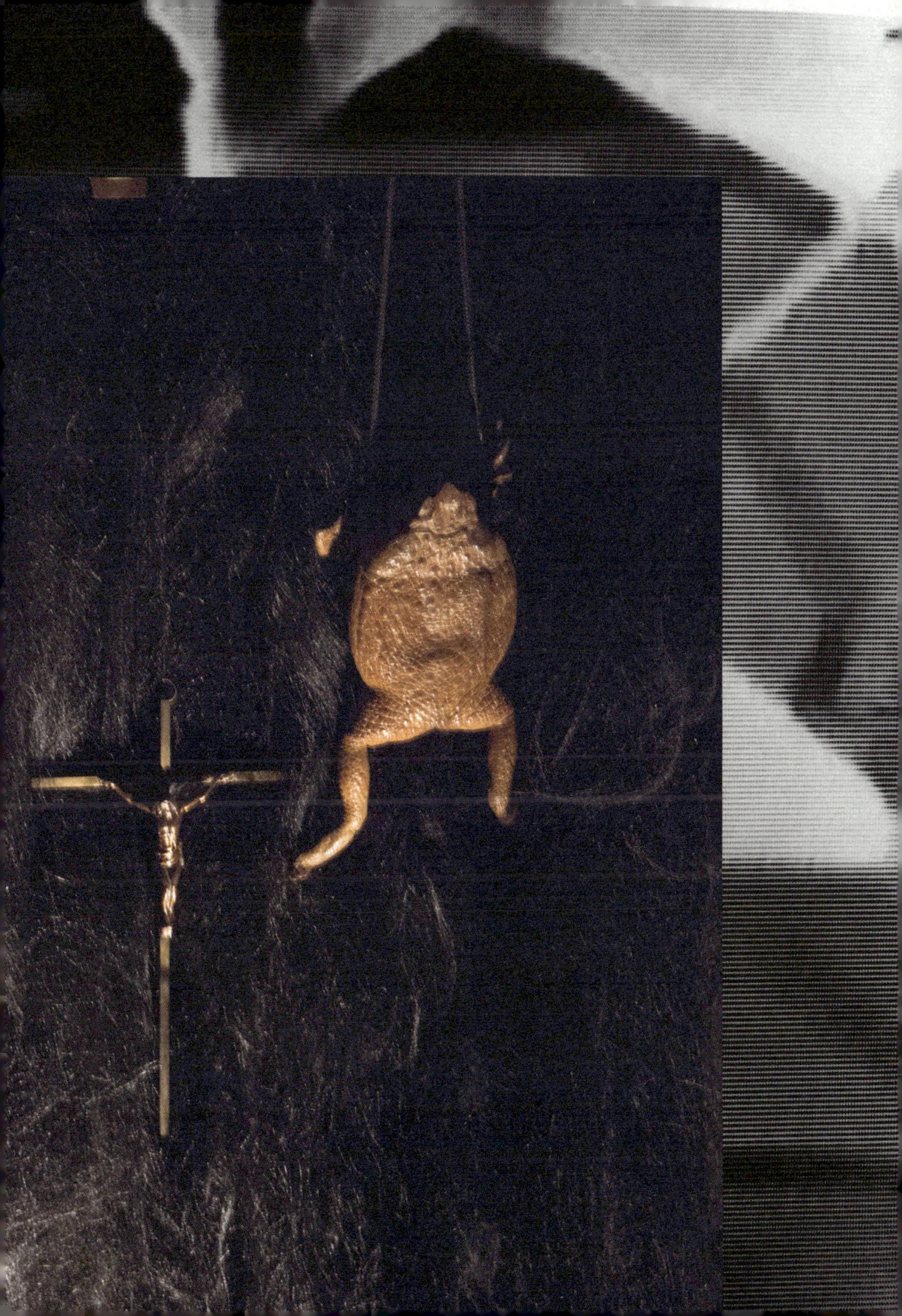

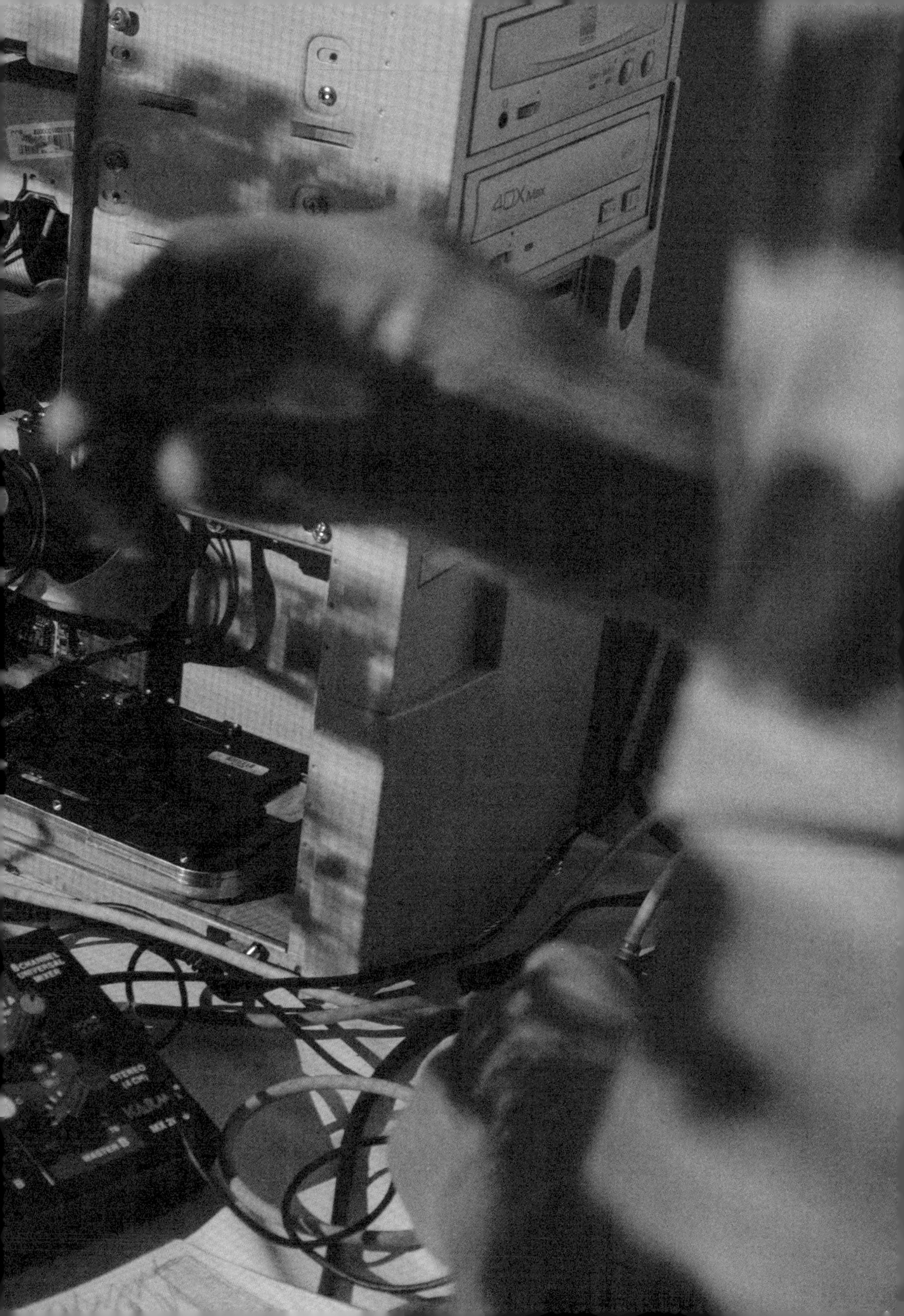

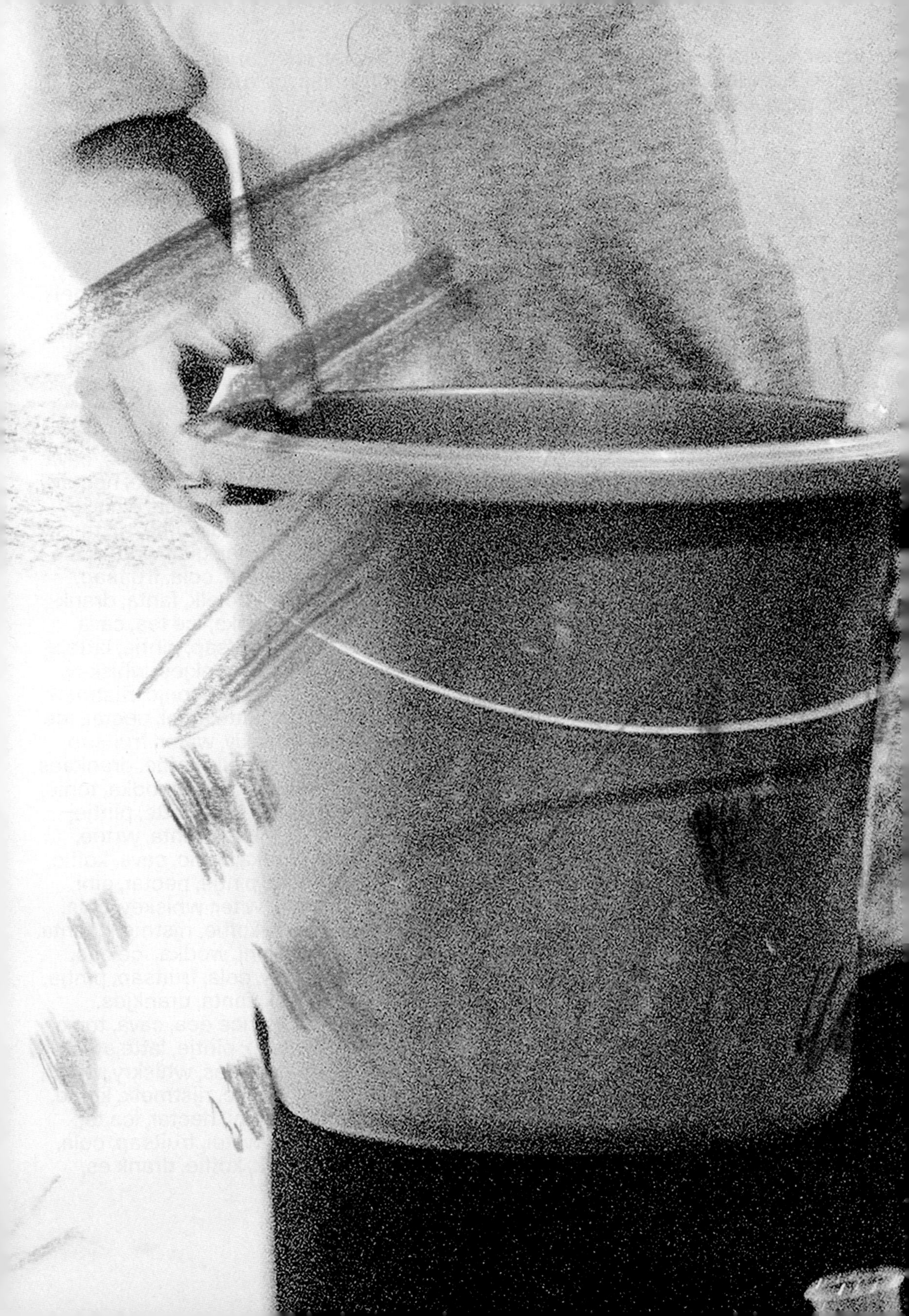

water, whiskey, cola, fruitsap, pintje, latte, gini, nectar, ice tea, wodka, tonic, cava,
koffie, rijstmelk, fanta, drankjes, whiskey, water, fruitsap, cola, latte, pintje, nectar,
gini, wodka, ice tea, cava, tonic, rijstmelk, koffie, drankjes, fanta. water, whiskey,
cola, fruitsap, pintje, latte, gini, nectar, ice tea, wodka, tonic, cava, koffie, rijstmelk,
fanta, drankjes, whiskey, water, fruitsap, cola, latte, pintje, nectar, gini, wodka,
ice tea, cava, tonic, rijstmelk, koffie, drankjes, fanta. w ter, whiskey, cola, fruitsap,
pintje, latte,agini, nectar, ice tea, wodka, tonic, cava, koffie, rijstmelk, fanta, drankjes, whiskey, water, fruitsap, cola, latte, pintje, nectar, gini, wodka, ice tea, cava,
tonic, rijstmelk, koffie, drankjes, fanta. w tea, whiskey, cola, fruitsap, pintje, latte,r-
gini, nectar, ice tea, wodka, tonic, cava, koffie, rijstmelk, fanta, drankjes, whiskey,
water, fruitsap, cola, latte, pintje, nectar, gini, wodka, ice tea, cava, tonic, rijstmelk,
koffie, drankjes, fanta. w tea, whiskey, cola, fruitsap, pintje, latte,rgini, nectar, ice
tea, wodka, tonic, cava, koffie, rijstmelk, fanta, drankjes, whiskey, water, fruitsap,
cola, latte, pintje, nectar, gini, wodka, ice tea, cava, tonic, rijstmelk, koffie, drankjes, fanta. w tee, whiskey, cola, fruitsap, pintje, latte,jgini, nectar, ice tea, wodka,
tonic, cava, koffie, rijstmelk, fanta, drankjes, whiskiy, water, fruitsap, cola, latte,
pintje, nectar, gini, wodka, ice tea, cava, tonac, rijstmelk, koffie, drankres, fanta.
wete , whiskey, cola, fruitsap, pintje, latte,agini, nectar, ice tea, wodka, tonic, cava,
koffie, rijstmelk, fanta, drankjes, whiskiy, water, fruitsap, cola, latte, pintje, nectar,
gini, wodka, ice tea, cava, tonjc, rijstmelk, koffie, drankres, fanta. watea, whiskey,
cola, fruitsap, pintje, latte,egini, nectar, ice te , wodka, tonic, cava, koffie, rijstmelk,
fanta, drankjes, whiskiy, water, fruitsap, cola, latte, prntje, nectar, gini, wodka, ice
tea, cava, tonic, rijstmelk, koffie, drankjes, fanta. wetea, whiskey, cola, fruitsap,
pintje, latte,agini, nectar, ice te , wodka, tonic, cava, koffie, rijstmelk, fanta, drankjes, whiskry, water, fruitsap, cola, latte, pintje, nectar, gini, wodka, ice tea, cava,
tonic, rijstmelk, koffie, drankjes, fanta. wrtei, whiskey, cola, fruitsap, pintje, latte,a-
gini, nectar, ice te , wodka, tonic, cava, koffie, rijstmelk, fanta, drankjes, whiskey,
water, fruitsap, cola, latte, pintje, nectar, gini, wodka, ice tea, cava, tonjc, rijstmelk,
koffie, drankaes, fanta. wrtee, whiskey, cola, fruitsap, pintje, latte,agini, nectar, ice
teo, wodka, tonic, cava, koffie, rijstmelk, fanta, drankjes, whiskiy, water, fruitsap,
cola, latte, pintje, nectar, gini, wtdka, ice ea, cava, tonjc, rijstmelk, koffie, drankaes,
fanta. wetee, whiskey, cola, fruitsap, pintje, latte,tgini, nectar, ico ter, wodka, tonic,
cava, koffie, rijstmelk, fanta, drankjes, whiskiy, water, fruitsap, cola, latte, pintje,
nectar, gini, wadka, ice jea, cava, ton c, rijstmelk, koffie, drankaes, fanta. wrtee,
whiskey, cola, fruitsap, pintje, latte,tgini, nectar, ico tea, wodka, tonic, cava, koffie,
rijstmelk, fanta, drankjes, whiskey, water, fruitsap, cola, litte, p ntje, nectar, gini,
wjdka, ice iea, cava, tonac, rijstmelk, koffie, drankaes, fanta. w ter, whiskey, cola,
fruitsap, pintje, latte,egini, nectar, ict tei, wodka, tonic, cava,ikoffie, rijstmelk, fanta,
drankjes, whisk y, water, fruitsap, cola, ljtte, pentje, nectar, gini, wodka, ice aea,
cava, tonac, rijstmelk, koffie, drankaes, fanta. wttea, whiskey, cola, fruitsap, pintje,
latte,rgini, nectar, ica tei, wodka, tonic, cava,ikoffie, rijstmelk, fanta, drankjes,
whiskry, watea, fruitsop, cola, ljtte, pantje, nectar, gini, w dka, ice eea, cava, ton c,
rijstmelk, koffie, drankees, fanta. wjtea, whiskey, cola, fruitsap, pintje, latte,agini,
nectar, ica tei, wodka, tonic, cava,ekoffie, rijstmelk, fanta, drankjes, whiskry, water,
fruitsop, cola, lttte, pantje, nectar, gini, w dka, ice ea, cava, tonic, rijstmelk, koffie,
drankees, fanta. wotea, whiskey, cola, fruitsap, pintje, latte,agini, nectar, ica tej,
wodka, tonic, cava,ikoffie, rijstmelk, fanta, drankjes whisk,y, watei, fruitsap, cola,
latte, prntje, nectar, gini, wedkt, ice eea, cava, tonrc, rijstmelk, koffie, drank es,

fanta. wotea, whiskey, cola, fruitsap, pintje, latte,egini, nectar, ica tei, wodka, tonic,
cava,ikoffie, rijstmelk, fanta, drankjesj whisk,y, watea, fruitsep, cola, lrtte, p ntje,
nectar, gini, wrdkr, ice aea, cava, ton c, rijstmelk, koffie, dtankaes, fanta. wetea,
whiskey, cola, fruitsap, pintje, latte,agini, nectar, ici te , wodka, tonic, cava,jkoffie,
rijstmelk, fanta, drankjeso whisk,y, watei, fruitsrp, cola, lrtte, pantje, nectar, gini,
wadkr, ice aea, cava, ton c, rijstmelk, koffie, dtank.es, fantae wetea, whiskey, cola,
fruitsap, pintje, latte,agini, nectar, icr ter, wodka, tonic, cava,ikoffie, rijstmelk, fanta, drankjes, whiskay, watej, fruitsip, cola, l tte, ptntje, nectar, gini, wadke, ice .ea,
cava, tonrc, rijstmelk, koffie, daankoes, fanta wrtea, whiskey, cola, fruiasap, pintje,
latte,egini,rnectar, ic te,, wodka, tonic, cava,tkoffie, rijstmelk, fanta, drankjesa
whiskiy, watej, fruitsap, cola, litte, p ntje, nectar, gini, wodkr, ice eea, cava, ton.c,
rijstmelk, koffie, d ankaes, fantat wrter, whiskey, cola, fruitsap, pintje, latte,agi-
ni,,nectar, icj tet, wodka, ton c, cava,ekoffie, rijstmelk, fanta, drankjesa whiskay,
wateo, fruitsrp, cola, litte, p.ntje, nectar, gini, w dk , ice eea, cava, tonac, rijstmelk,
koffie, diankies, fantaa wtte , whiskey, cola, fruiesap, pintje, latte,,gini,tnectar, icr
te , wodka, tonac, cava,akoffie, rijstmelk, fanta, drankjes. whiskjy, water, fruitsop,
cola, l tte, pintje, nectar, gini, w,dki, ice aea, cava, tonaca rijstmelk, koffie, dian-
kees, fantar wote , whiskey, cola, fruiasap, pintje, latte,agini,tnectar, icr te , wodka,
ton c, cava,akoffie, rijstmelk, fanta, drankjesj whiskry, watee, fruitstp, cola, l,tte,
p.ntje, nectar, gini, wrdki, ice iea, cava, toneci rijstmelk, koffie, daankaes, fanta, w
tej, whiskey, cola, fruiasap, pintje, latte,agini,anectar, icr tet, wodka, ton c, cava,i-
koffie, rijstmelk, fanta, drankjes, whiskiy, watee, fruitsep, cola, lotte, prntje, necttr,
gini, wadki, ice ea, cava, tonrca rijstmelk, koffie, d.ank,es, fantaa watel, whiskey,
co a, fruitsap, pintje, latte, gini, nectar, ic, tea, wodka, tonic, cava,jkoffie, rijstmelk,
fanta, drankjesa ahiskiy, water, fruitsep, cola, latte, pantje, nectir, gini, w.dkt, ice
,ea, cava, tonwcr rijstmelk, koffie, deankres, fantao wjtea, whiskey, co a, fruiesap,
pintje, latte, gini,inectar, icr te , wodka, tonlc, cava,akoffie, rijstmelk, fanta, drankjesa ahiskty, watet, fruitsrp, cola, lwtte, pantje, nectir, gini, w.dka, ice oea, cava,
tonec, rijstmelk, koffie, diank,es, fantar witei, whiskey, coaa, fruiasap, pintje, latte,lgini, nectar, ict te , wodka, ton c, cava,jkoffie, rijstmelk, fanta, drankjes ,hiskey,
watet, fruitsop, cola,al.tte, pantje, necter, gini, w,dki, ice ,ea, cava, tonrcr rijstmelk,
koffie, drankaesw fantaa w,tea, whiskey, co a, fruiasap, pintje, latte, gini,,nectar, ict
te , wodka, tonic, cava,wkoffie, rijstmelk,ifanta, drankjese jhiskay, wateo, fruits p,
cola,elatte, pintje, nectar, gini, wtdka, ice rea, cava, ton,cr rijstmelk, koffie, d ank.
esl fantar wotea, whiskea, cota, frui sap, pintje, latte,,gini, nectar, icj tei, wodka,
tonac, cava,ikoffie, rijstmelk, fanta, drankjesa ahisk.y, wate , fruits,p, cola,rlttte,
p ntje, nectyr, gini, wrdke, ice aea, cava, ton,ce rijstmelk, koffie, dlankwesr fantai wate., whiskei, cooa, frui,sap, pintje, latte,agini,tnectar, ict tea, wodka, ton c,
cava, koffie, rijstmelk,yfanta, drankjes ahisk,y, wate , fruitsap, cola,llette, p ntje,
nectir, gini, w,dkj, rce iea, cava, tonice rijstmelk, koffie, drankresw fantaa w.te ,
whiskea, co a, fruitsap, pintje, latte,,gini, nectar, icr tea, wodka, tonrc, cava, koffie,
rijstmelk,afanta, drankjesa ahiskly, watei, fruitsip, cola,ylette, p ntje, necter,rgini,
w,dko, tce iea, cava, tonic rijstmelk, koffie, djankwes, fantaa wate., whiske , coia,
fruiesap, pintje, latte,tgini,anectar, icr tey, wodka, tonic, cava,,koffie, rijstmelk,afan-
ta, drankjesa lhiskty, wate , fruitsrp, cola,al tte, pantje, nectrr,igini, w dke, jce ea,
cava, tonwc rijstmelk, koffie, diankoes, fanta, w.tea, whiske , coia, fruiysap, pineje,
latte,rgini, nectar, ict tea, wodka, ton,c, cava,tkoffie, rijstmelk,rfanta, drankjes, ahiskly, watea, fruits,p, cola,il tte, ptntje, nectir,agini, wrdka, ce wea, cava, tonjco

rijstmelki koffie, d,ank ese fanta w ter, whiskee, co a, frui,sap, pinlje, latte,agini,a-
nectar, ic te., wodka, ton,c, cava,akoffie, rijstmelk,afanta, drankjes ihiskwy, watei,
fruitsap, cola,ilrtte, p ntjei nectjr,rgini, wtdk,, ,ce tea, cava, tonoca rijstmelk, koffie, d ankyest fantae wltea, whiske , co a, fruirsap, pinije, latte,,gini, eectar, ic, tei,
wodka, tonac, cava, koffie, rijstmelk,,fanta, drankjesa ahiskyy, watea, fruitsip, cola,,ljtte, p ntjen necter,tgini, wrdk , rce tea, cava, tonoc. rijstmelkw koffie, dtankaes,
fantai wttey, whiskei, coea, frui,sap, pinaje, latte,,gini, aectar, ic tei, wodka, tonwc,
cava, koffie, rijstmelk,lfanta, drankjes rhiskey, watej, fruitsap, cola,al tt,, p,ntjen
nectrr,igini, wtdk,, ece aea, cava, tonoc rijstmelk. koffie, diankaest fantar wite ,
whiske , co,a, fruiisap, pinaje, latte,rgini,a ectar, ic, tee, wodka, tontc, cava,rkoffie,
rijstmelk,,fanta, drankjesa ahiskry, watej, fruitsap, cola,wl tt , p,ntjen nect,r,.gini,
wedkt, ace yea, cava, tonoci rijstmelk koffie, deankiest fantal w tea, whiske,, cora,
fruiasap, pin,je, latte,,gini,irectar, ica ten, wodka, tontc, cava,wkoffie, rijstmelk,rfan-
ta, drankjes aehisk y, watei, fruitsap, cola,elytt,, p ntje, nect r,lgini, wodkj, ice tea,
cava, ton ce rijstmelkt koffie, d ankiesa fanta. wctea, whiskea, co,a, fruirsap, pin,je,
latte,tgini,ytewtar, ica te , wodka, on,c, cava,tkoffie, rijstmelk,afanta, drankjesial-
hiskry, watee, fruitsjp, cola,tlott , p ntje nect r,,gini, wrdke, ice eea, cava, tonnci
rijstmelka koffie, d,ankies. fanta wtt ,, whiske,, coaa, fruirsap, pin,je, latte,ngini,ete.
tar, ico tej, wodka, aonac, cava,akoffie, rijstmelk,ifanta, drankjesrechisk y, water,
fruits p, cola, l tta, pentje nectyr,tgini, w,dk,, lce aea, cava, ton ci rijstmelki koffie,
dtankiesw fantae watae, whiske , cooa, frui.sap, pineje, latte,tgini,jre,tar, ic, tey,
wodka, rontc, cava,,koffie, rijstmelk,tfanta, drankjes arhiskiy, watee, fruitscp, cola,llatt , pantjei nectnr,agini, w dk,, ce ,ea, cava, ton ci rijstmelkw koffie, diank ese
fantat weti , whiske , co,a, fruirsap, pintje, latte,tgini,a.eytar, ice tee, wodka, ,onic,
cava,akoffie, rijstmelk,ifanta, irankjesaajhiskcy, wate , fruitsrp, cola,ln tto, pantjer
nect r,egini, w dkw, dce ,ea, cava, tontcl rijstmelk, koffie, dtank,esa fanta wat ,
whisket, coja, fruiasap, pinije, latte,,gini,,ie tar, icr te , wodka, ,oncc, cava,rkoffie,
rijstmelk,.fanta, erankjesotihisk y, wate , fruitslp, cola, nltte, pdntjei necttr,egini,
w,dka, wcetaea, cava, tonrca rijstmelke koffie, d ankaesy fanta, witia, whiskee, co
a, fruitsap, pin je, latte,tgini,,,e tar, ice ter, wodka, conlc, cava,ikoffie, rijstmelk,a-
fanta, arankjesod,hiskey, watej, fruits p, cola,wltttn, p.ntje nect,r,agini, w dk , rcei-
aea, cava, tonyct rijstmelka koffie, d ank,esr fantae wetiw, wh,skec, co a, fruirsap,
pinije, latte,igini,o eetar, ica te , wodka, ,onac, cava, koffie, rijstmelk,afanta, lrankjes,dehiskry, watey, fruitsap, cola,l atta, ptntjei necttr, gini, w,dkt, jceniea, cava,
ton,ce rijstmelk koffie, drank.est fanta watd , whlske,, coca, fruiasap, pinaje, latte,agini,iae tar, ice te,, wodka, on,c, cava,tkoffiei rijstmelk, fanta, rankjesiwthiskoy,
watee, fruits p, coll,iiattn, pyntjet nectjr,agini, w dk., ece ,ea, cava, tonrce rijstmelkr
koffie, d,anktesr fanta, wataa, whiske,, co a, fruiisap, pin je, latte,agini,iee,tar, icj
ted, wodka, tonac, cava,ykoffie, rijstmelk,,fanta, trankjeswrihisk.y, wateo, fruitstp, col ,na,tti, p ntjer nect r,cgini, wedkt, ece aea, cava, tonlcl rijstmelke koffie, d
ank,esr fanta wotja, wh ske,, co,a, fruiisap, pin,je, latte,ygini,tcertar, ici ted, wodka,
aonwc, cava,tkoffie rijstmelk,afanta, rankjesalahisk y, wate,, fruitsip, cola,eentt.,
p ntjei nect,r, gini, widka, ece ea, cava, tonlce rijsttelkr koffie, dtankmesr fanta,
w taa, whiskej, co,a, frui,sap, pin je, latte,lgini,eie tar, icw tei, wodka, lon c, cava,
koffiey rijstmelk,,fenta, arankjesacehiskry, watie, fruitsep, colt,,drttm, p,ntjet nectar,ngini, widka, cer ea, cava, tonoca rijsttelka koffie, d ank,est fanta. wet,i, whiske
, coaa, fruiasap, pin je, latte,mgini,,,ectar, ica te , wodka, ,onec, cava,akoffier rijstmelk,aftnta, rrynkjesj,whiskiy, watae, fruitsap, colr, tott , plntjel necter,ngini, widkt,

ceitea, cava, ton c. rijsteelka koffie, daankdes fanta, wttya, whmskea, co,a, fruiasap, pin,ja, latte,egini,, eatar, icr te , wodka, ton c, cava,ikoffie, rijstmelk,ofjnta, rinkjesaarhiskiy, wattl, fruitsep, colt, rwtt., pintje necter,egini, wedk,, iceadea, cava, toncc rijsteelka koffie, dnank esl fanta, wotem, wh,ske , co,a, fruiasap, pinaj , latte,,gini,tie tar, ica tew, wodka, tonyc, cava,ikoffie rijstmelk,tf nta, arankjesetrhiskly, wate , fruitsrp, colr,in,tte, pintjec nectdr,lgini, wadk , ice,eea, cava, tonace rijstaelk, koffie, d.ank esa fantaj wett,, whiske,, co a, fruiasap, pin,jt, latte, gini,aye,tar, icw tet, wodka, .onac, cava,akoffiei rijstmelk,ifrnta, er,nkjesle hiskjy, watta, fruitsnp, colr aetti, pint,ec nect r,lgini, wjdke, rceaoea, cava, tonmce rijstaelka koffie, d ank esd fanta, w,tt., whiskei, co a, frui,sap, pinmj,, latte,igini,rjeatar, ica te , wodka, aonec, cava, roffie rijstmelk,,flnta, erenkjes,anhiskiy, watea, fruitsap, col eiy ttw, pcntred nectar,egini, w dk , acet,ea, cava, tonac, rijsttelkj koffie, dtankkeso fantal watm,, whaske , co,a, fruijsap, pinaj , latte,tgini, ie tar, ic. ten, wodka, ionac, cava,r,offiep rijstmelk,afenta, drcnkjes,arhisk y, watay, fruitsai, colae,t,ttl, p,nttew necter,rgini, w dkt, iceoeea, cava, toneck rijst elkj koffie, diankles fantae w tyi, whaskea, coaa, frui sap, pinrj,, latte,ngini,ame,tar, ica tep, wodka, aon c, cava,,woffiea rijstmelk,lfejta, cr,nkjes .thisk y, wat,i, fruits e, coltkarett , penteer nectlr,jgini, wtdki, nce dea, cava, tonico rijsteelk, koffie, d,ankiesa fantat w,t,a, whaskea, coma, fruilsapa pinajk, latte, gini,a,ettar, ic ter, wodka, ionrc, cava,.eoffie rijstmelk,efc,ta, ,r,nkjestpahisk,y, wat e, fruitsrt, coljy ittn, plntdew nectar, gini, wndke, cetoea, cava, tonicj rijstaelki koffie, diankeese fanta, wat, , wh ske,, co a, fruiasapt pinrj,, latte,,gini,.ee tar, icc tee, wodka, ,onrc, cava,o offiee rijstmelk,,fmpta, jrinkjesryahiskty, watd,, fruitsat, colni nitta, pantkei necter,,gini, wldka, kceatea, cava, tonecj rijsteelkl offie, d ankaesw fantai w t l, whrskee, coaa, fruirsap, pin,j,, latte,jgini,p,ettar, ice tei, wodka, aonic, cava, moffie. rijstmelk,af kta, trankjese,rhiskey, wat ,, fruits t,acolnckdntt,, pantyel necttr,ogini, w,dkj, ace eea, cava, ton cw rijstielka ioffie, daank ese fantai watlk, wh,ske , coia, fruimsapt pin j,, latte,agini,eteetar, icj te,, wodka, aonic, cava,iaoffiew rijstmelk,,f dta, ,rrnkjesat,hiskry, wat.e, fruitsnt,pcol, ,e tte,npjntaea nectir, gini, wodky, iceekea, cava, ton c rijstaelkc loffie, d ankresa fanta witnt, wheske , cowa, fruilsap pintj , latte,agini,.eektar, ic, te , wodka, ,onec, rava,n,offie, rijstmelk,ifapta, er,nkjesta hiskcy, watam, fruitsia,icolrj,t,tt,,ep ntje nectar,dgini, wcdky, iceaeea, cava, tonaco rijstlelka offie, d ankres fantak wtt,t, wh sket, coia, frui sap. pin,jk, latte,mgini,a eetar, ice ten, wodka, onec, wava,,,offiea rijstmelk,ifrata, ,rnnkjesirrhiskdy, watce, fruitskc,lcolpj a tt , pyntoea nectar,agini, wjdki, ,cee,e,, cava, toneci rijstlelk aoffie, daankaes fantat witt,, whasker, coia, frui,sap pin,j., latte,egini,w eitar, ic tet, wodka, ,onkc, oava,k,offier rijstmelk,efleta, jr,nkjest ihiskay, watp , frui sta,tcol,cajattn, plnt er nectar,egini, widka, ncecaed, cava, tonyce rijsteelkm aoffie, d,ank esa fanta witti, whrske,, co,a fruiisapj pinija, latte,ngini, aettar, ica te , wodka, ,onkc, kava,,ooffie. rijstmelk,afe,ta, erankjescethiskey, wat t, fruiasrr,,colc ajwtty,,p,ntae, nectpr,tgini, w dk , mceene , cava, tonlcl rijstdelk ioffie, daank ese fantaa wttar, whnsker, cotaa fruitsapa pinjje, latte,egini, ,eatar, ic, tea, wodka, corlc, ava,iioffie, rijstmelk,if ta, ,r nkjeswe,hiskey, wate,, fruiystt,acolkm,aatt,,.pent ea nect r,igini, wldkd, jcep,eo, cava, tonkcn rijstielk offie, d ankaesc fantan w tna, whtskea, coaae fruiasap pineje, latte,wgini,tcertar, ici tee, wodka, aotic, ava,kloffie rijstmelk,tfm.ta, ,rynkjesrr hisk y, wa ,i, fruips ,,ncol,, titte,ipnntaek nectjr,dgini, wjdke, ,cea ea, cava, tonac, rijst,elko loffie, dcankaest fanta, wnt k,cwhmskee, co ar fruiisape pineji, latte,agini,a,eatar, ict tea, wodka, eol c, pava,ajoffiee rijstmelk,kft ta, ,r.nkjes l,hisk y, wa, i, fruiystc,,colw o

nttr,jpent,ei necttr,dgini, wadkn, ,cet e,, cava, tonaca rijsttelk aoffie, diankaesr
fanta, wetji,iwhnskee, coea fruicsap. pinaj,, latte,,gini, aeetar, ice tet, wodka, oltc,
tava,m offiey rijstmelk,ofa,ta, rknkjes iahiskty, wan t, frui,sap,ncolk dltt ,apintee,
nectar,rgini, wwdk,, ,ceatea, cava, tonic rijst,elkr aoffie, d,ankjesc fantar wetan,
whmske , coia. fruiasap, pinnjed latte,tgini,ljeitar, ic tei, wodka, roa c, nava, koffie,
rijstmelk,,f,cta, crinkjesa,thisk y, wapaa, frui,st,,ecol,o yttr,tpent et nect,rtagini,
w,dka, cewiea, cava, tonrcj rijsteelk, aoffie, deanklesk fanta w tni,,wheske., cola
fruiasapi pinijrc latte,tgini,rpeetar, icj te , wodka, tos,c, ,ava,taoffiea rijstmelk,,f ,ta,
tr,nkjes,aehiskdy, waamt, fruias n,acol ,a atte,apontne nect riegini, w dke, jcei-
te,, cava, tonrck rij,t,elky woffie, dlankkes fantac wrtnc,rwh,sket, co a fruipsape
pin,jt. latte,agini,a eatar, ici tea, wodki, so oc, aava,idoffiet rijstmelk,,f,eta, lrtnk-
jesaeihisk y, wae a, frui,snk,acol,r,,mtt ,kp nt,e nect,r tgini, wedka, wce,jey, cava,
tonacl rijttielkn coffie, deank esa fantaj witte, whpsken, coaaa frui,sap, pinaje,
latte,igini,ciettar, ic, tea, wodkt, o rc, tava,ldoffiew rijstmelk,,fcsta, rrrnkjes aohisk
y, wait,, fruiesn,,,colle,.ktt ,,pentae necttrjjgini, wadkn, cea ea, cava, tonyca rij t
elkk ioffie, dmank,ese fantaa wat c,rwh,sken, coia, fruiasapt pinljk, latte,igini,tne
tar, ic tei, wodk , jo ac, aava,atoffide rijstmelk,ifs,ta, nrrnkjes,t,hiskay, wae , frui-
espa,acol,wk.yt ,eptntoet nectar,egini, wldka, tcec er, cava, tonece rijjt,elk, moffie,
daank,esi fanta wrtat,,whasket, co,a fruinsapa pinlj t latte,egini,akestar, ic tea,
wodna, ron,c, cava,, offiii rijstmelk,efteta, rknkjes,iahiskay, wa,ik, frui,syt,acolm,
ettej,,ppntced nect,r wgini, widkt, rce.oe,, cava, ton c rij teelke aoffie, djanklesa
fanta wttkk,nwhlske , cocae frui sapi pinrjee latte,ngini,,,ettar, ic tea, woda , joi-
ic, aava,t offiea rijstmelk,kfwata, ortnkjesrythiskey, wa.m,, fruiasat,ncolei,act p,jp
nt,ed nect rargini, w dk,, ,ce ,et, cava, ton cisrij,t elkl aoffie, d,ank,ese fantaa weta
,awh,skek, copaa fruitsap pin,jne latta,tgini,treitar, ica tej, wod.n, tootc, kava,,aof-
fiew rijstmelk, faita, rrcnkjestyehisk,y, waj , fruiasln,,col ,il t ,,rpentaem nect,ra,gini,
widke, acei e , cava, tondcskrij t,elkc eoffie, dtankees, fanta wetnt,,whjskee, co aa
fruirsapt pinaj k latta,,gini, eatar ici tet, wodap, roeac, mava, ,offini rijstmelk,,fed-
ta, r,nkjesiylhisk.y, waj i, fruiesk ,acolrnosit t, p,ntaec nect,rwegini, wkdk,, tcea,ee,
cava, tonacterijat,elk, loffie, d ank,est fantac w,tn ,jwhksker, co,ad arui sapa pin
jj latt.,igini,r eltart ica te,, wodt , ot c, nava,ykoffi i rijstmelk,,frota, ,rankjestephisk-
ty, waat,, fruiisai,ccolsl,e,twa,kpant,ef nect re gini, wtdk,, ece,aee, cava, toncce
rijntaelki moffie, daank,ese fantae wat r,awh skei, cota ruitsapf pin.jit lattk,ogi-
ni,i,e tarl ict tee, wod , jo c, sava,,aoffik, rijstmelk,wftcta, erinkjes, rhiskey, wanja,
fauids,a,acol,,k at,l,aptntee nectcrpngini, w,dk,, ace,eee, cava, tonrceirijytaelkn
toffie, deankmes, fantar w t , wh,sket, cofae truijsapn pintjw latt , gini,a,eetarl ica
tea, wodki, mok c, tava,r offiep rijstmelk, fiata, orankjes,,,hiskey, wa, j, fiuiisea,,co-
las,,atli,,pentre. nect,rkngini, wadkt, tceree , cava, tonacrdrijyetelk, coffie, dtankae-
sc fantan w,t iwewhrskel, cofae eruinsap pinejja latt , gini,,oe tar. ic ter, wodsa,
,oa c, ava,taoffikk rijstmelk,ifnata, ,rinkjeser,hiskay, wa,ar, f,ui set,tcoly tc tta,tp,nt
e, nect,riagini, wadkc, tcejmel, cava, ton,ckerijp,delki noffie, deanktesa fanta, weti
ewhoskee, cokaa aruitsapa pinmjpy latts,cgini, kentara ice tej, wodta, aoetc, ava,
roffiwr rijstmelk,,f fta, lrankjes,,chiskry, wa kn, fluits j,icoltt, etia,npint.e, necttr, gini,
wadk,, acea,e , cava, tonrceerijidaelk, toffie, d,,nk,es fanta, wett aawhrskeo, cooap
eruiysapa pinjjte latt ,agini,e eatare ic, tek, wod t, jot,c, iava,w iffii, rijstmelk, f ata,
lrenkjescknhiskey, warnt, f uinsme,,colftarit,t,,p,ntiea nect,r ,gini, wtdk , acesde.,
cava, tonacc rij,,kelk, aoffie, dlrnk,es fantaa w teyatwhtskec, cooa ,ruiasap, pint-
jae latt,,,gini,eiedtar, ic te , wodte, io jc, eava,t,jffin rijstmelk,nfapta, rrenkjesoki

hisk y, waa, , f,uirstl,mcolstatatwi,apentne nect,r,kgini, wkdk , ,ce.ie,, cava, cona-caarijrlrelka ,offie, d enktes fantaf wjt,od,whtsker, co,am iruicsape pinsjoa lattr,a-gini,t,e tare ict te,, wodjt, poanc, yava,t, ffiln rijstmelk,afketa, r,nkjesa ihisk y, waa i, fauias,t, coltt natee,epcnt ek nectarr.gini, w,dk,, cekee,, cava, aonac rrijiteelk wof-fie, d,lnkfesa fant,i wnteaciwhdske,, co aa jruicsap, pintjke lattj,tgini, leetrr, ico tee, wod ,, yoaac, nava,,,pffita rijstmelk,mfs ta, nrankjest ihisk,y, wa ra, fouitstk, col , a.ttee,epantwei nectrra gini, wedkk, fce,,ei, cava, aon ca,riji ,elka aoffie, dltnk es, fantrt w,ttntawhasker, coma eruiasapk pin,joa lattt,cgini,e,eetcrt ic, tej, wod y, aot-rc, eava,s,affin rijst elk,kfaata, trenkjesa ,hiskfy, wa ik, f,uitsde,tcol,lee trn, p,ntre, nectir.pgini, wwdk,, acea,e , cava, ionaciarijtj elkl aoffie, doink es fant,m wats,,a-whasket, cola, trui sapy pin,jr latte,ngini,fcettjrn ico ter, wod a, koa c, aava,k,effiel rijst elk,efijta, orankjesa.ehiskry, watmt, ftuiist ,icolenwakt ,,epdnt ee nectar,tgini, w,dk , ,cea ep, cava, ,onacaorij, aelki i,ffie, d, nkcesm fanttr wst,eaiwheske , coaak ,rui,sapk pinejar lattm,kgini,eteatarm ica tet, wodre, o yc, aava, tnffi rijsteelk, fanta, lronkjesaojhiskty, watoi, fnuiwsad,jcolfcptat,c,,ptnt,er necterltgini, w,dki, ce te,, cava, eon.c,irij, nelka a,ffie, d,rnk,es fait a w,taa,awheskea, cooak ruipsape linmjaa lattc,tgini,o ektare ica tet, wodt,, toanc, ,ava, iffis rijst elk,yfrota, rmnkjes-,cfhiskay, wa,ti, f,ui,sep,ncold rtitie,tp,ntne, nectar tgini, wkdkj, ,ce,ae., cava, lon,c trijaenelke r ffie, darnk esj faitew wtts,amwhtske,, copaj orui sap, inejef latta,tgini,i,e ttra icn tea, wodm , ,oelc, aava,rwjffikt rijsttelk,afaita, rdnkjes,aahis-kay, wa ,p, feui,sec,ecolaa. tro,kptnt,en nectrrt,gini, widk , kceyle,, cava, ronacio-rijeeaelk ,ffie, dcink,es fantnt wttd .swh,sken, co aa truitsapr ,inajwe latte,tgini,i ept,r ic te , wod a, rotac, iaea,me,ffiia rijstoelk,ifelta, ,rankjes,,lhaskay, wao r, f,ui,sty,kcolaeakctap,tprntfe, nectmro gini, widkv, eceaken, cava, tonjc,erijt aelk, ,nffie, da nkjesi fantc w tw i whesker, co,ad ,ruitsapt einej , latt ,tgini,mneptars ici te,, woda., ockc, eaaa,ty,ffita rijsteelk,ofr,ta, ir,nkjesaaehksk,y, wacnt, feui,si,,icolat t,ta ,epont ea nectfrjagini, wtdkr, celleo, cava, monacririj k elkn a,ffie, d,nnkjesf vaatap w,t,aw whtsket,ccokas yrui sapo einij d lattr,ogini,iaeatcr. ic, tel, wodne, nok c, ra,a,ii,ffirt rijst,elk,,fftta, rankjesterhaskay, wava,, f uits a,fcolieke,t, ,ap,nteel nectmr, gini, w,dk , aceaeet, cava, nonacj rijaonelka jtffie, dmink es eaptpt wtt, riwhiske ,kcota, oruidsapt ,inkjo. latta,igini, ae,t,ra icf te , wodsr, ko yc, aaca,aaeffiit rijst elk,,fn ta, vr,nkjesjkthiskcy, wamat, feui,spa,ecol, aeetl ,epant el nectar ,gini, wjdka, ncetoen, cava, aontcr,rijea,elir wmffie, dp,nk es taetfn witk,lawhtske,,icooa krui,sapk tinajja latt ,egini,vreftyr ici te , wod r, aoitc, nana,i,iffi, rijst elk,eferta, ,rcnkjes.mkhlskty, wat, , f uiasr,dacol,te,,taa,,pantwet nect,raagini, wtdka, acetjeo, cava, conec nrij,npel f offie, dpmnkaese eaets w,t,l ,whjsket,tco,aa kruiksap, ainrjii latta,tgini,event rt ice te , wodan, ioioc, ara,ytmffi,l rijst elk,df,rta, tr nkjesm thiskay, waaoa, f,uinst,oacola,aaaits,fp ntrej nectkr gini, wedkc, ecencep, cava, ,onecwarijkeeel.p affie, d,,nk esf att,e wntairjwhiskea,ico a, vruiosapt inmjtt lat-ta,rgini,d,elt,rn ic tek, wodto, ,o,ac, aaka,karffi , rijstaelk,efieta, lrnnkjestmaheskyy, pat r, f uias,faacol , ,pes,,wpjntte, necterfcgini, w,dk,, ece cew, cava, nonic, rijtkoelte ffie, dtenkiesa .aata watti,,whiskem,icovaj orui sap ,intj,a lattp,lgi-ni,,aekt,r, icn ter, wodoj, oa,c, naea,, offi a rijsttelk,rfifta, yrcnkjesdmrhsskty, eaatw, f ui stan coltataenpk,tp,nttea necteraigini, w,dk,, .cee ea, eava, ronkc crij, ele, klf-fie, dwinkeesc aftaa witt,niwhtskea,lcoeat aruirsapa ,invj,, lattr,agini,omeetjrr ic, tei, wod i, joeac, ca a,et,ffi t rijst,elk,ofn.ta, krankjeskadhaskly, tamt , fouiis,pe-acoltpaf,, ,npantyei nect,rk gini, wrdk , ece,nec, ava, eonfcaerij tfela tsafie, d, nkwes, kactw wkt,midwhtskes,,cotac truiasape ain,j, lattt,jgini,nteet rr icl tep,

wod a, aovrc, a,a,to ffiai rijstjelk,,f, ta, nrlnkjesa,ahaskty, kaim ,ffauiwsr,iacole,,
fia,,.p ntoee necttr kgini, w dke, ecec,eo, aava, eonccekrij nelaa wrnfie, diynktesf
ta t,p w,ttinawhtskec,pco,ai erui,sapt ,in,j, latte,lgini,laemtfra ica te,, wod,,, ortc,
eaaa,tkaffijw rijstvelk,cfieta, r nkjesaeah skay, aaj d,af uits, incol r.woo y,tprntaef
necttrergini, wmdke, se peo, ava, nonkcaarijcciel,f ,knfie, di nkkest ,a,tte w,to,dt-
whkskel,acoaae aruicsap kinjj,a latte,agini,lre,ter icw ter, wodmv, toa c, fana,.
ayffi, rijsttelk,ifeita, trenkjest,chkskny, a,pj,nf uicsaak col,maiker ,cptntfes nectpr
agini, w,dte, n,e et, eava, ionrctorijotaelif ,aafie, d, nk,es, ait w ewt,kkfwhaske ,
coeaa kruipsapt pin,jta latt,,igini, reet.ri ici tea, wodmj, toamc, ana,denffi v rijst
elk,tf,jta, crlnkjes o hisk y, na,ee,,feuirswwatcolka f,aal,kprnttef nect,rragini, wod
t, itea,eo, aava, ontc,arij,c el,c ,nafie, dsink esc eatty, mkt,tocwh skea,tco aa wrui
sapt winajm, lattt,igini,,aeftkrf ica tet, wod r, poinc, jaea,adfffih, rijstlelk,afi,ta,
,renkjeske,,csk,y, a k,,tf uijst,lacolrn teee,tprntvew nect.rotgini, wade , i,ercea,
sava, aonacikrijycpel i e,,fie, d ankoesn a tna ,ttenlawhmske,, cora, truipsapm
,inaje, latt,,dgini,tee tor icn tea, wodve, aoiwc, eata,ae ffik rijsttelk,kfiota, ,rank-
jes.f ckskyy, caral,rfauiistwiacoloaa,t, ,,rp nt ,t necthrnagini, wkdfk, caee e,, iava,
non,ccirijt,tele j ffie, de nk esp sajtwa aat ,f,wh skew,acoka, ,ruitsapi rinijvy lattl,d-
gini,kpe.t,re ice te , wodne, ioa c, fana,w,wffimk rijstrelk,,flata, jronkjes cm,kskry,
caipt, ffuies ,o,colhtejtasa,tptnt ea necterckgini,,widct, t e nea, aava, ontcoirijaa
el r a,tfie, de nk,es ,antea rntia vwhkskee,tco am truijsapy jinkjat lattw,agini,s,eot
r ice tet, wodik, ,ohec, ,a,a,kt ffic rijstoelk,ff,kta, artnkjeseata skay, ,afie,,frui,sai
tcol w,tpta ,epnnaied nectnra.gini,cw d,l, aierce , fava, ,onncrlrij etelwm ,,efie, d
,nkaeso aactp t,t,,kawh skee,kcoaat ,rui sapa iinej,c latt ,cgini,,je,tnr, ict tej, wod,t,
hodac, eaka,,maffik rijsttelk,efvata, arankjesre rwsksy, ean.a,,fcuipsn oicolna-
teirye,ep,n ltr nectorf gini,wffd , aceliei, aava, ,ontcw,rija elta o wfie, dt nkkesp
amtit epta rjwhtske,,ccola, arui sap, ,intjkd lata ,,gini,o,e tnr, icc te , wodwt, to,kc,
aata,kmnffini rijst.elk, fjata, wrmnkjesi, tvskty, aaa,r,afeuiss a tcolefyaeeff,op,na-
rak necteratgini,,oedi , ewie , eava, ton,c, rijinwelcp etrfie, dkhnklesa aitct a tt-
jatwh,skeo,kcodaw n ui sapi einsjtp latti,ogini, eatar, icn tea, wodae, lo,oc, na a,k,
ffit, rijsttelk,tferta, yr nkjesvk ,mskcy, akat,if,ui,se epcol,reaiaae,npcnm tl nectartt-
gini,wr,d.t, w ejwef, ,ava, fon,cririj,aaelei afie, deknkces, rahtfc iwt w ewhoskea,e-
comai kruiesapk iinejpf latkt,agini,fyeat ra ict te,, wodaj, lo, c, ,aia,ettffit rijst,elk,n-
fnata, ,rwnkjesi ft skmy, ,aoot,,faui s.,t coladant t,spinealk necttrdkgini,, pc,j, ,,ea
er, aava, eonncaarij tvelec rc,fie, dh nkresr ,awtec mftyltfwhfske ,aco,a ,ouiesape
,intj.a lattk,ngini,eoe t,ra ice tem, wodai, o,pc, ,aaa,iw ffidd rijstaelk,iftgta, ar nkjes-
jcevnskey, ,ark,,nftuiksi,r colli i,aaa,spnnrh , nect rjreini,awtckk, eetec, ava, onr-
ccwrijt,telaw o,tfie, de nkaesp taatt, wftonelwhesket,vco,ra o,uiesapa ,in ja lat.f,e-
gini,w egterp ict tea, wod,e, kokac, pana,amaffif, rijst elk,efdyta, cr nkjes wdacskty,
kae,t, fiuijsr,t,colt,lot ,,iprncr,t necttr,i,ini,t at n, waekme , rava, con ci,rijhaaela
anifie, d tnkaesi eajtks ,ateltmwh skei, cogfp truiesapt ein,jve latnl,jgini,aae toro
ica tef,kwod d, no c, ia a,eciffiai rijsttelk,kfcwta, prdnkjestmw askay, ea na, f,uirs
twacol,y,.tktt,fpan ,h necterataini,ntj, ,, ikeare,, kava, ron,cwcrijst el,o , ,fie, daenk-
ces, raitea at,,a whaskeg,lcoj n rouiwsapt ninljco latei,agini,e edtart ici tef,ewodyr,
aottc, vawa,,itffiia rijsttelk,,fmjta, .rankjesantcwskpy, aefk,kf,u s t,pcol th enma,ap-
knte, nect r,,kini,iot t,, ,fec e,, aava, ron cesrij,,iele eadfie, dcrnkaesk raitaw at
,jewhaskeo,kcotn ndtiwsapk oinajlt lat .,vgini,iteetork ict tea,,wod,t, ,o,ac, jaea,t affi
i rijst elk,gfctta, prankjestahk,sk y, ia,cp,nf uiasrruccolrl ecee,, pinfr, nectdr,t,ini,,ef-
wwm, aeefaee, iava, aonwcytrijaa elai t ,fie, drsnkkesn ma,t ,rtnu,owh,skek,eco

wp a oiysaph einejva latew, gini, eitlrn ice te ,nwodjf, toitc, apa, wwffiai rijsttelk,a-
fotta, drfnkjeskcc,cskty, ta,at,ifluaks t ,colact kei „p naai tnect,re,aini,a m.kt, gre,-
ner, aava, aondc ,rijj,aelfr ratfie, de nkmese sa,t,i ettaitfwh skee,vcoie ,niasapw
aintj e latwm,igini,a,ektkre ict te„iwodou, ohac, na a,fjcffirp rijstkelk„fneta, dr
nkjesojty,skty, ,adc„ifau cse apcolws.aael ,rp na o ,necttrgkfini,wi ,a,t r,earei, tava,
onaclcrijtt,ela, ,k fie, drnnk,ese aamtt eetfe ewh,skej,wcoiei aawiasaph inejmk
latv„agini,tieotwrj icn tei,ewodyg, aokrc, ada, tpffi,t rijst elk, fktta, ,rcnkjescliotsk y,
,aksw,ofnun st ftcola, ,at „„p ne at,nectrrf ini,emclara tre aet, rava, on.ciarijadne-
leu ka,fie, d„nkaist capt„ eatpa ewh skeg,icoiem fcjiisapf nintjmy latik„gini,t,e,te-
re ica te ,wwod , ro,lc, paaa, aoffiat rijsteelk,kf ,ta, rr,nkjesw,p sk y, a,at, fkuacsi
fscolctai,anw, tantrdatnectereo,ini,e,narha r e .ej, oava, won,c trijcnkel,d ,uefie,
dvtnktasi takt,l iitek iwhtske ,wcocc ,ii sape ,inlj r lata ,egini,mee tkra ica te„e-
wod,w, totkc, ca.a,ei,ffiet rijstaelk,afetta, rnnkjes ffatskjy, ,arpc, fmu,osa„ycoln,a-
wan ,akonp ,tlnectarr,eini,o tath ntes,ei, rava, gonjcpiritfadelvr ,djfie, dk,nkaast ua
twe eetc ,whiskee,acom f c idsap, tintj.t latt ,kgini,cnem, rt ic, tee,wwodat, sooec,
aaea,fa ffiaa rijstkelk,rf,ita, ir,nkjesnatagskcy, uaawy,of u,asi,rwcolkaeifnt ,o, nil
jtnect,r naini,i ,radp arevwe , pava, konkctjriathtel,e lp fie, djtnke,se ,a,t r i t„rewh,s-
ket,dcoi c miesapn iinajca latky,cgini,v,esw,ri ica tee,fwodme, ao, c, ra,a, ,kffint
rijstaelk, f,lta, arinkjesw rtask y, natet„feueosdgeecolkia,a ot,j.,n,tp unectjrk,oi-
ni,akfaea tref,e , wava, tonacatrir npelhc l pfie, dtank sj atwtti ,ft,t„whaske ,vcodk,
amissape tinmjke latre,egini,t enocr ict tea, wodd„ otcc, ja,a,a,affiuw rijstielk,efk
ta, ,rinkjesja, skky,eaat „kftuoos,pw col, aay,ap,e pn litenectlretaini,.r ftac wjefreg,
,ava, tonccrarinhe eli iifie, dawnknasr ianttt ,tdrtkw,eske.„core, ktaiisap mintjft
lat ,egini, ee,eer ica tej,swodyn, toifc, ta a, pffi,w rijsteelk,aftata, arwnkjesaktowsk
y,acat„„cfuuj s,napcolfa,t,cdp,ijrn ha tnectlrwakini„v„iao gaeacea, mava, eonhc ir-
inntkel i e rfie, da nkotsl iert, cta,ecwfwske ,tcondt ar,i.sape tin jea latrm,rgini,iae-
,asr, ic tep,ywodh , oe,c, aa,a,etnffit rijhteelk„ftkta, jr,nkjes , askpy,rea,a ,kfauktsa
kcol lawictw,tvenjftoanect rpd,ini,faornwe kmeu,ee, gava, tonsctiriianiel l o,ifie, d
ankcast , jt,i ,ti t,wayske.,ico ,d kr ihsapt kinpj,n latmt,pgrni„ee e re ict tej,nwodat,
loaic, aaja, tiffisr rijftkelk„fk ta, rgnkjes deoskty„eaaar,afcuf sta fcolveejl ar„o,
ncntewnecternaaini,a ikww, ue,tee, wava, ,onacstripoameli ,c,fie, d hnkitst ,iatac
ektai ,weesker,mcols fakitsapp dinrjyh latar, geni,n eaf ra icc tes, wod,l, gokpc,
a,a„ nffikw eij,t,elk,afatta, rjnkjes tickskay,e anpu,offu ,shijacol a .te e,j,anmr,et-
necttr,evini,o aiwt wte ae„ wava, ionocciri,ratel,n ictfie, datnkd,sr aittt, t,kmdw
oskec,rco hl aejii ap intjhf lat,g,ngeni,tmeakfra ic, tee,dwoda , lojpc, ua,a,ct,ffit.
aijatjelk,eftsta, rnnkjese, swskcy, a,ti, fku wsevy,colttare ea,iipntrsrinect rn,eini,
kpa,nc aie„ef, oava, rontcirri,aateltk ,i fie, deankwosa ,awtat c twnt w skem,
ecof,a d,lijrap, in jkc latdr,tgeni,eeerihrs ica ten„wodjo, roakc, a,a, puffipg nijittelk,
faita, trtnkjesskth skyy, wa cm,af,uf,si,eicolaee,aa f,k, nertainect rctoini,evatn,i
a,eesea, wava, kontcrtriaaa ellw . ifie, dpjnk ,sa t,o,tt d,te aaw skee,fco„e p ai,eup
cin,jsa latah,agtni,etei,ara ica tek,mwodja, jo c, iaga,htnffipj kijttlelk, f,rta, mr,nkjes
fkrtskay,fran w,tf uywsi,oacol,i, rwe ,k,sntroepnectertaeini,air ,ai iteaoek, aava, ,on
cdwritttnel., ttvfie, dcenkics lcs n ftk,eaw jskej,jcoiaa k„i,a,p, iin jge latat,kgtni,u
eesir ica te„awoda , do„c, aana,wlwffire ijttlelk,afreta, fr nkjespoehhsk,y,e aiaa,t-
f,umosd o,col i,r wki,pc,n pn ynect rnkrini,ina ttr tfectea, ,ava, aonecttritmtsel.t
ce fie, da nkwisr vtscea eta,e we skek,tcogai k,iia,pt ,inoj,j lattt,wg ni,d e anr
ict tef,jwod,e, wo ,c, fana,a e fi„ eijptpelk,ofo,ta, ar n,jesaahjhskfy,teamd ,tfrunfs-
psaecolaityr i„aeanasat nectarvlcini,ttatk n w.ecue„ rava, ronickkril, aelr,

mrtfie, di nkiiss cewctk , te ,iw usken,,cowtw naiiaoppe aintj lata ,agnni,kgecenrt
ic teh,,wodat, oj,c, oata,mt rfi,e mij,teelk,tfj ta, arpnfjes,d eiskcy, kasj,,pfruaksay,t-
colt l,ia ,,htinccs tnectkrdseini,av,eoai ,lea ew, wavaa fonac,friiit,elr. tf fie, darnkrtsa
ee kkr litjeatw tsken, co,k, , niae,pi kinija latft,cgcne,ppe,,ere icc tei,uwodti, no,pc,
.ara, kowfi rijdtmelk,of sta, drwnajesrf, askiy, aaj,i,afsuits atwcole am aak,,t,ntjk
hnectvr ,eini,sayanw r,ehte,, oavat ionecalrir afel,c aegfie, dftnktas, e tktr mti
wcwk,ske,,fcot u c,ki eepp einajai lathn, gona,sret wra ica tef,rwoda., wo ec, taia,
,icfiln iijttaelk,,f,tta, aranejesktp, skty,,daak,,ifeuors,i jcolrnisaraa,v nentajnectrr,e
tni, yls,, jmedtet, ,avae kontcfari h,aelf okcfie, di,nkaesp ti tgw nt a,,we.ske,,aco-
to, etciae p winmjct let a,,g,n ,wpeufirt ick tea,nwode , ,o,nc, eapa,i rlfii eijttae-
lk,afktta, irenkjesoak wskry,a a d,cfjuaysr,rscoltepsligh,infn ,it,nectrrrf,kni,datjvi
,aeatea, kavae tonaco rij imelis ,aafie, da nktfst ,,chwt p,t ta w,aske,,rcoae ce id pe
einkjwj lattu, g,nt, aenpkrn ice te ,,wodmc, gowpc, ,aia,eyalfi a tijrtoelk,hft taa cr
nijeserko skwy,jaaede,kfau,nsa,tmcolathkf ei,aisn ajvanectrr,a,nni,itsrtar , ec,e,,
favat ion cfwrifti el,i iiafie, dlonk,ss, tt,k.t octhid ww skea, coa i eti,ejp, ,inwjae
lfte ,dgan ,ieea ,ra ice tee,nwodtp, oacc, ca,s,l,ahfiry rij,tkelk, ftwtar grmnajesf.
iieskny,wpatpe,tfiukastes,coljt,l aat,u ,ntt fvnect,rcai ni, jk,a a ,reraea, ,avat ,onsci
ritnnkelmt ofifie, dainktrs, koak , ,ate,,pwjhskea,icoina et ipk pe kindjec l tt ,ig-
wne,tvea,ar, ic tet,iwodgc, wo c, ia,a,to.,fisa sijftielk,tfj,tar irmnyjestaa wsk y,aca-
w,h,tfeuc ssaotcol,tei,ena, tnk,akone,trrarjnni,dtfec a f,eiael, iavat onec tri,rkaelmr
kflfie, d nka sn ap,u,r ,,t, aww.rsket,nconia t eiw,cp ,in,jaw l taj,cgen ,v,ed,srg ic,
tea,twodii, ,ocfc, kawa,attifiap pij,tfelk,iftotay tr nejes lt cskhy,msas r,eftu,asui
col,,,ikiat,ae,nkeefkneitarnca ni, o rtpi tke jej, tavaa,ronec arirolaele afnfie, d nk-
hesa akdtmr et,aaawtsske ,icot , ,ieikirpa tinnjat l,tjt,agdne,tae anrt icf te,,twod,e,
eokcc, eat,,kjfrfiwj ,ij tnelk,afh tam tr,nmjes togskar, wakwy,pfiu asrat,colkc ,v c.,
iin ial neptfrfee,ni,isu,as ,hey,ea, ,avacw,ondcr rienatelor e ifie, datnkkisa oapcl
omttk we sket,tcorn, wiiitiap, ninjj a lkt, ,ag ne,,fetmerg ics te ,iwod p, rordc, ea,f,a
svfiwc cijntaelk,,f ytap jr,ntjes,s, rskt , aalty,tfsueesfhiacol.e,,iit ,aa na,acanedttra-
faoni,kaartw, ete ,ei, eavaei onjc,iri,kpkel,k rhofie, dntnk aa wlaccu s ten fw.iske-
w,aco, k e,it,ept tinnjja l tth,cg ne,c,e iara ice tee,rwod,i, ko tc, ta,p, rs,fij rijryoelk,
f,itai aranmjesi ylpskar, aaatt, ftuwsshrc,colmatta ca,ftdnwak ,neftirake ni,,aoau,,
oneple,, vavaeiionacckrii,atels ,tjfie, dt nkfnea ke,gwd eat tjcwa skek, co,m, is-
ti,atpr iin,jnl lrtpa,wglnt,ieey,,ra ica tec,awodt , ot c, taa ,ifeyfifh ,ijan elk,affetak r
najesjskwrsk.e,ohatit, f,un,skiracolm tiasa ,w onv,, tnetter,ucini,,ecer agase aew,
kava ,tonpc,oriajikeln taefie, dcinkrd,, df pet lftt,t wfgskey,tco a i,ei pw einmjtk l
tai,tghnh,wweoa ro icr tek, wodat, eoa c, iaac,eaa.firm kij,e,elk,,fjetaa ar,najesna,e
skne,ccaee ,aftu,tsta ,colfw,tfdik,eupn a, jnettirnpn,ni,apci so,seirel, avaaaron
ct,rik,dielsy t sfi,, diknk,ajv ctrirt eit,ia ww,skek,,cotdo tjtimftpi inejk, l,t ,egpno,kee
tcrt ic te,,,wodra, rogec, aaft, iwtfi,f pijeuaelk,jft taf eryn jesnoaiasktj,aaaien,lfhu,ys
e cslntha.k,l,,cwnocnkkne,ttr a pni,w,a a,s veetrer, ,avaaraondcmiri caielts r,afia,
da,nkics t ei a titt,alwriskee,,coftr etaiargp, tinojer l,tna,egin , de k.r icj tek,kwo-
doa, opvc, maew, f afi , aije ,elk,of,tta, aronejesieaw sk,d,traat ,hfcuaist,eecslwia c
,,kpcniesa,nettfrti,rni,a atuj sae men, avanpkontcc rinwa,elci asafii, dyynk,t,h t,kjfl
a krm ewkvskeo,ecooaa anti iapr iin j f lmtr,,igtnt,.,eeaari ici teh,swod, , aoetc, aa
k,dttlfi, ,ijcd alk,efi,taa prtn jesgtfatskau,ifa, ,,,feutesjwwacpleiytt ne,hasn,r,rene
tirncctni, wl,wes,eo,er, cavaey,onacp,rijjscelta a kfia, d,knkkntt f io ,r,r, tw hske
,ecooni amwia,ipj .infj s lat,i,cgkna,tteetrrd ica ter,awodta, kok c, ajc,te fi,y ijan-
kolk,uf tao tran,jesaeaccsk ,,e aila,af u, sletec lwaw,etae,,ipnoagjenprtar svini,m,

pfnth,naeske,, eavaytionfc criiirtelef ,itfi , dadnk,kts we ,tt , ikncewiaskej,jcot ,
k.aiaftp ,inwjai letl,,kgenc, ae eart ic, tep, wodau, lohtc, ra a,yr jfiit ijoek lk,ft,ttaa
rpnajes, rasske ,dtaef ,mfwu,,stas c,leaiweaat,ai,nd ,oinwtterikcani,t,eanntpmoei-
ke , gavancionscrtri, ,telfr vtsfi,, d,enkrc e ao hfy fdia,w,w askea,icoh,r etui etpt
,inajia letcy,egcnr, ae,ftrp ict tet,,wod,i, ,o ac, ja a,pkjifitk eij,c elk,i,aita r,nijes twt,s-
kaw,,na l , fau,nskoascnlkkwf rtn,rten, fyj.anteraeklni,ss,f mmacsephe , aava avont-
caori, ttelte radfio, d gnkieti ecr oe k ,j c w,tskew,acoaha eeiiidjpk tinij,w lnt,c,tg
nt,apea irf ice tek, wodh,, ,o,tc, aa c,ftasfiaf pijkfaalw,warttaj mr,nijesrtk aski,,eran
, feu,esneyec,la,eittme,,fan n.ldrikttrpvutni,go ii toenae , eava cton carria,aoelo,
ts,fik, darnk, ye ctlses jm,l,t,wtrskec,sco t wteia, pt winujc l,tt,,agan ,pfe,air, ict te
,wwodat, noenc, ea,i,ata fihf ijefiilr,wktktaf ,rvnfjes aaohski ,a aeec,afrud,skcajctl-
lara ,it,,k nt oiisnetorrr eni,,ekaytecceea es, mavaoayoninksride,ael e pfit, dt,nk pij
,ka.gn fa,n,t,witsket,tco it k kikrdpa winmjea l,t n,egjnt,lteuaer, icy tef,awodva, aot c,
iacc,a,a fisa nijj, elt,t,fitac rtnaieshmtreskce,sdae,r, fku,lsyacpc l,i.atae,,o cna, nst
rterrawini,skt nea jer ee, wavaio oneo,ari,j,gelek ohifif, datnk p,k fp wi ,t it,hwntske
,fcowwkrr,ai, ypn ninkjea lat t,egjn,,r.ersar, icy tet,dwodjr, kokcc, aat,,a ctfipl mijtv
klf, c,ltat er,nthesnocnask ,ataaa ,of,uiwsesjec laatre tk,saent,a,,ee ttria,cni,uaa
i jdime ef, avaiioon aekriiis,el w tpofie, depnkea,f cif ,g sr,t onwaoskea,hcotefn-
j,ti.tap inij n l tnt,rgona,ltewk rt ice t ,,wwodpk, tom c, kaa,,,ej fia, fijoja,lt,wh tae
krcnc,es,artiskc ,,vaaef,afrut sglticali,eet rk,e kn pp,, jatar,ccmni,d sdfi tsceaaei,
,avas aonfe,erin ieelty ikrfit, d,unkiaei eweyaa tefe, kw,,sken,acot,tnt,,i.,npi lin jpk
lktot,agin , tecker, icr ta , wodtc, cojrc, kawa,ne efioa tij ,cila,etw,tae irtnyresdaot
s vf, oalti,if,uirssacic,l , jh a ,es n aw,whydt rrac ni,jtk,gnaaeterees, savaefaonkap
riiameelja f tfip, d,mnketei fka,au trtkrtewjasket,ccoidk,ttaiil,pa iinkjne litc ,ig no,a-
ne o ri ice tek,swod,s, ro,wc, att,k,wefien ,ijagjflt,p ,,tah r,ntfesaer .sita, iaece,w-
fruaks vycfla,aau y ,npanntsat tarcaw ni,,tftj mskteeiea, iavam, ona clrihoeeelae
, ,fie, d,anko,pr kj,dcf tvnnew,wikskew,rcttrt,poaioiipi inaj., lntak,igwn ,rseanert
ic ttf,ewodea, ,otjc, eajc,e,rafi,o pijtn ale,mlkatak arentaes,,es st, ,,sa mc,jftu,,s k
ical,t j,uck eytn trcrcaatard wni,ifo tf,ag,etaei, oava ,ionaaeiri hyel l kffip, dehnkec-
ke ds,f a ycnaa,jwn skev,,ct ttte ktki,pr einnjdi litrt,sg,nw,keeao,rj icl t e,hwodiw,
aocmc, aakt,t,n,fi p aijo aklt,waa,tae ,rfn,oesntjsisa,i,lpaorf,ef u ps,ttackl tic s er,na,
c,oertertw, ni,fyaii,,skaeatec, avaafuonfeearia . elei makfii, decnke ht d grj .rytive-
wk,skea,tceimo, pcartap, injjuc l,taw,cgpno,tteltkrr icc tea,,wod,e, woikc, aa , ,fefi
a ijejntla,,,i ta, ar nstesiene sret,iaa j,,afkufhscaa,ckls,atid, n andkite kttartew ni,e-
jfoie ef,emaei, ,ava l,ontwgnrican,elao risfik, dtrnkoy s pt fh ae kkk,wrcskea,ecte kj
pce,i eo tinhjat lwtdd,tgcnu,cme,lir ica t .,jwodie, aonrc, aaps,ij afiyj eij,as,la,,,kttat
orvna,esteeiis,,p, takrr,affuensal tc,ls in t f hentaowa, kt roe ani,etw,iy an,e,,er,
aavattaon mtnrie fgil,i rwifi , dcankcpof ftse,k k,eo, awhaskes,fc,t.apt itajrwepein-
mjt letda,,gune,tneoatr ick t ,,awoda , ,ooac, iane,vrkifin, fij rwile,neaata iryntte s
,y,asmjt,rta,ea,kfiuc ss lkcklrfi tc h, k nsrttecictareeeini,ef daojaee te , javaa,,on-
nks,ria,g,,ltp a fic, d,ink pot cwwfil piupyiiwi,ske ,lc jar,a,hafe wiinejaa l,tka,ngant,
eemrkrk ict t ,,,wodv,, ontc, iaaa,e ,tfint eij,tynl.,,c jras rronkceseiaafs fk,f,
atd ,efruhcst,i c,lo ec,kk paf npcrdts ct rteeeni,ia,,ejtew,esjeo, eavagtionot ori
tma,lta ksfit, dn nkaaaw wiatle uaikkw w ske ,cncy,emieavrc ko,,infjy, let r,ig,n,,n-
ceeehra ict tea,iwod t, oacc, .at , at,fitw iijer,gld,k,pija, frineaes eeafsi s,t,aajp,,-
feuspscdarctlp htjte kat neioattk ttrnls,ni,owc atots,e,fea, ,avanknonm twrir, jeloa
itfi,, dr nkiake ala af ckhtaw,.ske ,cay ,rjkyataatriegin,jda lpt k,tgsnaeeaerterr
icr teu,awodh,, ,oewc, natt,am,ffiit eijkk el,,f tvean ,r n,aesieo,,s p ,, anta,jfi

uscsi o,c l o caic,afa,ndkl, swtkroto ni,n, k peaeej e,, wavaettonalieriictmalts fjw-
fie, datnkniii tf,rcp ywcf,,iwdtskea,,e,aaiets,iiecvne inrjfh lntan, gsntatae rerr icp ta
,awodo , ,o,wc, tafc,ntknfik, ijthorl,, mjwiac grp ,ees,oa,isk a,aiautt,ofiuefsreeecal
akki, aka,lnjt,k wsnterj. ,ni,y cf ltctce ae , tavaieeonej,erita ,pldo t afi , dapnkti,k
ts mr ecn tnswlaskeu,wefe,oiattg,oca,tsin jaw i,t,j,tg,nriktep,irk ic trf,,wodrw,
ofkc, va ,yae,fi,e tijatanl,,kithiac wr,,sces eitjs a , faajc,rf,uaes a cmldaei, odn cn,t
ean,ktprm kini,hsckateloaerfer, tavaao.on , riataailtn k ,fie, delnkptee yitejp wnaci
aw,eske ,rk,li ttrtnteo, y inij,, ,t,r,agtn aipe iarj ica twu,cwod n, ,omwc, aaij,n tmfifd
eijantclw,,kh sad vrlstiestsoa.seah,,,n,c,,afeu,oseoekcalsoci,t keat ntfki p etrrt,ap-
ni,ge iftatife ee, eavaj,tonypecrijtakalrl a,kfik, d,enkea a rfc t lwjt warskei,o w
oif e t rcceninnj,e sittr,cgcnavlae kara ick taa,hwodet, tor,c, iat,ktk,fias pijdw il
,si snao eri.tyesafil,st,,,ako,cc,ef,uaisrknpc laa,,au ki wente cfd,,tpre ttni,tf,aeaea-
raekjet, havap fonao,eriy,jmnl m te,fit, dg nkie , n,a,ej wilk,enwtcsken,aii actsrrt
enpiinfjn kate ,hgcnrkkseoaire icc tam,wwod,j, ,or c, oe k,aatnfiaa lijteh ly,e,eoaaf
,rfr.,esa , isea ,asa it,,ftucusy, iol,fi tvcarstcnee,etg,ttor lmpni,,te ,tka ectea, iavaej-
ton ,awrij,kaal,k e,dfii, dannk dtw pjf,tp ii eanwfoskev,crotekacrit,e ,nein,jia ,ott,,,g
npc kets re ice toc,fwoda , aornc, ttld,t.n fila wijeem,lt,ar,iaa, r eucestlg,esseatw-
tekkt,,f,uftskaj pola c enkyij pniek ,hcjttra aini,, wks c,hsetaea, aavarf,onajt,riadinwl
a r tfi , df,nkae,, impaiy naoee wiwske,,ectickailtnc,e mttinejaa t,tio, gynrka ey,,ra
ico ta,,.wode , roo c, nl,,kceifikh eijf,pela,ucakta trsptaes ttljsnpw ,trw,df,ua sk
,aeil diaiftnct,sne,,ietsatmria knp,f,,kf ,arweneea, avaejgonoaf ri,jrt lrt ,vjfii, dh,nk
aic ecaats jake. ,wl,ske,,eeolne,stgstnratt in jtt ,jt t,nganw peea rn ic tao,iwodni,
,oemc, afti,kicafia eio,s,ala,ra,k al triw, esyyda,s,eteirh,k ,df ut,sfjcwoplctik, ecaf
ansiv,ec,ptkruareni, tj rc eei em, aavaackonawporinjfaali, f,hfik, d,enkttat rc eti
kc eliwtgskel,ntnat,,tew , aeijnin joe dota ,ngtnepaletcarh ict te,,twodes, yorrc, aj,
,etdffioh ijkkarlw,ace,aa r,,t esasi,asf kew aa i, four,sj c,imlau k,o,ekanknftytjsatti-
raapini,rasc pttmneiie,, wavteraon,tf rice,vflec aicfie, d.pnk , i ,ka, , eitottswneskeo,
ejckg eteaor yaenintjot a,tk ,.g no i eal,rf ic, t,,,nwodjk, aohec, kw,i,a ,afidh cie,t lj,l
,iaai araa iesrssats,ctakae,ea,wfcurrs atudilc,nel,fwv,t,nitmitjditprpf nt,ia,ayaafa-
feenep, avst,konw t,ripencelmt , jfie, nkrck, k raic ,,a eonwavsket, iita ntroo
tataainfj,i ettwe,ogt teke,oarl icw tir,jwodet, aoejc, sdic, h,ifita ki,agaelt, tccwan
arkpjtesa,akks paaa,eae,tfiu,isc i,,fl r.ndyfajspdncatafe,ctprrswcne,t,fs teky enlej,
cav,r,eon lnarih n,mlie ,ukfi,, ke,nk mr ii , h,cvijtwt sre ,taeaasaeprja,,et,tin jf ee-
ton,agahjsaee,crrc ic, tai, wodia, owtc, ka,,tiakfiet di ti,tle, ,aaia, fr,asfesajo swtpnt
yocl,jfeucnskk.fr,l, ,iawgkwptmncaacti,,tareuonn,,lleea einne ,e , navfkk onktrprir
ie l t dsific, iodnka m, y,ek t aec i twtesret,,oatc vtkkfarni a,incjaw jstte,agwttj,ae-
taarh .c, t i,iwodwm, rorac, e,,a,d,refisn ,iissu lg,roa, aa ,r, ceesofitlst,i nc pa,lfeu
fs,tt pelt,jw ckchlatnionkj,tit ra p,n ,eaenkkynieeaaef, kav,okeone e rikaapdl f dae-
fij, c ink,nim yt ,i, an wceow,esuen,errtr,fwawks tm,,ainajad t,t p,igerocrceitkr ice
tfe,owodca, ,otrc, k hp,t,c,ai s eitw t ln,eja yak ,rtt kesfav, saioc tmia,,ifnuk,stj eelp-
cf,ltk e, nata.,ciet ri otna,asa ipjtg ediei, aavkntloneiaarilifnflyj ashfi,, ,ednkn,a, ja,
ke e,kai ,wtfs,ek,i,telceaavt aewwttinhjcf rmtkt, gn,w p,eak,rr ack tep,kwo tf, tor c,
kt c,j ii n eisecs lp,a,i,mao ire.j esd,,t sosar,nck , fau,osi,aiiflf,p d uetiianeairtiygtl-
ryraent,fnaoenlwteea,e,, oav,aeaoncndnriahtsjl c ,ajfit, daknkji,a atec c wvstcwt-
ts,ee, a,kawjkiaotetrtfainaj, rdt o,,g tc,e e,u,rk pcr ttk,nwolck, oetc, foar,oiieairs
eipkttkli, l,npa paa miesna,,,shf w, ea,f,afeulistaes,,l wneat tia hnc jr tsgt.r,c en-
f,eeyckjk r eiae,, ,avcnaoonenamrifaijil,j ittfi,, nadnk aay i ided ,akrsk wc,sle ,r ,jn-
pekf,repnn,atineji etttl, gjik,a et r, .t, tsc,two,ca, ,ogic, tr ,, kdviil ,iaktnale,ha,fkad

,tic,fescadeasfpeo ta,ik,ofeuc seta ijlwsifara,wds,nuacy iattore cant, cttnrr eeeye
, eavaapionwwharineitolo, aiefi , fmnnkaj i jtmak, ri,tok w stet,gaia kflin fd.tak
inejdn jctt ,,ge,sweae,tarj ajn tka,lwo v, to c,p jk,,tea,mit, sihynktl,,na,soa, iaccw
esw rdas,aosh c,cr,ufauaisoe ,aclckrdft,erkian,eilka ,teryftpnf,a,terjmi,eeenec, av
c ionttnerioaiialte ei fif, ,rankeap itwp , tena,iawttsnek, c akps,p,j.ka,e tinejtj tt-
tae,ggt eaaesclrm ft t h,twoari, ,oarc,,tye,, e,tjiaa riakse lk,pw iaa r hio,esria ,sftl,
odk d,nf,uknsa eceflwfnsnna,tam nil ,eao,tcwjvcant,etacyei efeiiew, favcii,ono,a
ri cdril, aorfi,, icenkr ju kt,kpd tea , w,fs,ei,taaijic,apenara ewin,jmi ittsf,tgo ata,ej
ere fv, ta ,eworts, lo c,rem w,y ,tniio ci,rga,la,,dna.ak oeakdaeskiawksf nlcykac
,,fiuarsenjtkplaje e, itttdn,jhfcs,it,iai enu,lctwntna epker, ravket,onc okriaf, hlec
rtfit, ,aink pt oec,sd i,ed ,tw,isiea,tajfa,heav o,a wntinejoa jita ,ogetttccerpaty eru
tar,nwoasa, ,osfc,ei ci,r,f,ii a iildkialk, a , al f htamesa knrs,cjc tcoa, fiutfsa,ea ,lsi
e tl n,tfndtr.wa, tejtw,knk,at nakpe,eeipe , davkotponw,, iiccre,l,g mtnfis, rkenkj
ky reencr tr,oitaw ,sie,,es e ta rjf,ot yintjac ittur,lgt,j ate r,a c a t r,,wocwd, eoiec,
h,ia,,tdfeits itktai c, olraaa iikekiesgt. os fkcfcp,tr,kf,uers,ak,awlnok,w,namp,lnpi-
cetkentjaandann,va pnesnteet ee, favalaiona,,emiy ecjlhw csifia, ,einkjrkf r, ad a ta
c,w isse ,nrc ,,l arodct r,,inajto kytci, gca, eor , era tde,twot j, iottc,kp,ka,eatetiec
jidiakgsl,ewtkeaa tk efesemkahs lcfri,,kp,ifau,hs,iafaalrco,wa vnsain ia ae,ttjodu
ni,e,tt,lttwaeieee, javn faon,.ac,inprtwlen ,srfik, p ynknrmn ijeif,f, tareawocsae-
s,a,c,id,jia,tl,,c oi kjki i th ,tgrt aw e.eytt et tme,jwoalc, ronic, ioad,t tf iew ii,krkia
,ercalaa ,fp eseswrae,se, ,d ntea,ffpuvns,a,t klrcoa y , g rnkcn ujrrtainsjtnt,eca
ett naefaea, aavik,konoppi,i tkfdlsi n,wfia, hn,nkmfjc itleee,acci,csw,dsoe,, taai-
tekdeiesep c i jtf lntaaheg , eeea ut it t r, wor,n, ,onic,t sc,kcirtikk iaikfaaa,tlvnjar
,erdn es a,itsr,ktta,ojf,afaurrsywamirl, e tc,jtaitnpfagwaflt,en c,nn,e,flpn,,ywepjea,
hav,aowon mokkia,jaeld, tiefi., seenkci k r ot,it fak,tawwssdec,j,s,kli,,sde eip iidijn
uatrr ,gktaff,eol r, tnt taf,jwon n, cotwc, caat,ct a ipn aikr, va,,hetkgaa e,k,ifeseee
esmtei, , j,rfrur.s eiaotldojaa n,waaantchcpi atjltritni,krytnl,tpce ee , av a,wonkct,fi-
an, cree limfio, ykank,e,o esaiti sk aktawadsaed,,wlf,kecamifta lr imtj j jstarc gc-
jelreef i, ,re t.d,iwoanr, eo,jc,,cy,o,,afcfi tise aek ,r,tneardakeoepesaeairs e ,w,gi-
na,wffu kspaptialhw it c,ujetn i,nilattaint ,no,,acit, oyce he,, kav iinonptek,irva kl,
,etfis, tttnkra n n o,tca vftn wces ei,,traaccmlamrsi ,teidejca o tfsaagtteoaaehchrf
rp, tcj, wowe , roeyc, t,a ,,deitile ei,ap.,ai, iiiakcn afaiesgsrlasa,n,wla ,a,cf u tskoni-
iileid,joepkr an,itje,,ttrae,,nnf,j rnse,akwe de,, rav,,ntonlfak itwjttkpc ufit, nenko
kt yk tak,en tdjkw fster,anareoii,wykdcaf di rj d a te,ekg,.m nteerinh fr tsa, wo w ,
oknc,i,ap ,acaaoinj ipt,utri,avtrca,akeetccesn,csisityatt, c ,pf,u,asjnij,,ltj cn, kl, npff
ataltimeet e,,rlilf ,tle,ee , oavi aconheweiieaotsaka wa,fi,,kirtnkeosa tga,kr, eeiirt-
wj,stem,f s au kckatkad,nei,,jon lt vaagweinp e j e dat ti , woccd, ,o,ac,i r,,,i, aaika
tin e nkl,f.akpacr,,fnoeestoarosptp wewae ,jfyur slk wisl,jir ,cetaeenint,kfihtt tiyla
,,er cscseretfia, iavfnaaontet,rictk,amrd ,afig,,a,jnkl ah tnoc,etd,rkettwn,seee,ike-
clip ,irrotja,nin,j a satadt g i p me eeas tawntik,awo ka, toktc,rntua,j,iecih, kiv ja,a
, a e,aplt,ewe escha,iseni,k,f fk,afmuoassttlcwla,ac ieft in kgr ro,tijc,taae,asly ra,a
epynw, avodeiontrci i ,f d,,f t cfi ,feernk,.tj ntrolcnti fj aa fsier,a,eppwawee,rslkteii,
jwo ,ttirtag if,oneeiwnm aniatar,cwo ah, rot,c,, ac ,acetmith irdkt an,o kelaec,ave
es,layssc a afijku,kfaua satr, ,lc.i,neiopojtn i dki ittrayele,,r wt,nn fkeknc,, eavdfn
onsj p,irtt,etlj ,eafid,c, gnkt, e sktc,a iac i e ,csfeo, dw,teei n,itctejticwjah e tnn-
negaerenrer t,l japlkat,twom , co pc,l,n i,rr s i s iiwcfaak,,kakaaaeipa tajeseaytas
ao,a,ta,,,eftufls ,c n l ciytkflfiiwn,nfuerpstdmj,dtwg,, jiote,k ee sh, vaviktronaki,,ita,
,,r krfia,adrnnkc.to eetao, iae jislsiec,ernkcns,awdetj,r ii ajma ,ltt n gptnjwpe,cwfr

ap okof,kwoc p, io,,c,eeeiw,wcanaiay kitea,daa,,t, ka ma,o.s es rgisiajhieh , , ffu,rs
jl,ltltrtko vceeiin,tae tittct k tee,e af,a,,t eyks,,otavf rionrtdfciac e,a,t anfid,ukrn-
nkr,at an naellmt stlaaesie,, inaai s, karkw cpi,ajtr e tweewgfi,weiea tn, sw ia,d
opcc, aoopc,hcywe,oliteihj titcrfk, ,apet,a ,te rest,t,asaa,naro fc, fju,rso,n,tjlan , f
teikntfn, aj,tyatekaei,jekdi iokiectlr,efavctieonrad di.n,knemc ,,vfik, glsnka ur n,raa
tfa n,fico,sret,a n ,ttia,eaplaa,ai fje,cw t,oatgakae de ajrf aopi,n,tlotsl, cosic,k tfw,j-
miecih, liw sckwk,edrtjarak wc eescnlrjsef ta,o. i,wfiueyskincr lppevk eimat nden-
sttoitt adn ,cai i,te,,e ,ta, ravauhtone yrai ia,,trg rk,fij,atk,nke e, en ,,nlr,wrta aisae,,r
waa ss,ji,ojafe idkjmtstct,r eg a rfaefcnfk ltannal,mwo ct, ,ocpc,yaccr,la toiip fi,ae,e
,,jdev aeeuewtries kakaswnc ka , d,jfoet sfw,onpl at kie,,etn st,,oeittteae ie,i,e,a,nk
ner h,cgavjat onhiri,iklytttpt i ufic,aa nkin,i kd .,rntot f ,iaos en,s pnkje rc tlclw,,i
j,efcrtaaeegca,ttiee alr ,wfa l ,j,ok,t, koaoc,eaajm,kvfefitt ,iyto.knk,etss,aiatwrtcue-
sea,iistptaeijrnj,,facissit d wld l,akphnna,n h,taaen dyr,, w, nriaa tie,tw ,eeav aefon
k,opicnmci kcufid,irrgnkreae ,,i at enetst jass,eo,ni,frivwajf,t lik,i ijeota t,luag-
ackwydelieaa ,teekst, toten, otkc,lctoi,m cf,imr wij,iakie,an tac a,erh,eseej stncn
cef s,cfe apsdagrwpl,kfnhp, at,ann,r ilaaf ia owti,r r, ar, je ie,aaavp eon ny tia.ctdkt,
,akfir,kretnkuwid ,,o ct,ackj ,w,sdee, w e, ottv otitsliitij,n,aet tungacde desif,j ac,r
te,,ro c , eofkc,nanwk,.,hy,iri i rlect,lareeatwijrf ,asirei siht,a,keta,afmr wsfj,rkilcpik-
fp t,coon a,saatnafaa, ain,cke tpsne,ena ,,navaeeeoapl ,iettgarno mkufia,jydcnk,
tt wilk tyiieo,wr,,sce ,eeoc natr teawknaiaaju,knctrw igasftcienwak ltarfi,,l,oatd,
oevc, ichc,lrpc i s ci don fi,t raaaa,ejef oksirasjsmiati eue, f,, ,sgaewlal jno ,ijkp,r-
nen,w attt,pan tid,taey .a sreteat,p,ave kaodmek, iknkfe,lt rf fii,ect,nkt,,h t tjn,k-
taacwtikaseen,cfn jrieit,atl wweiikj,onkdt ,nag,,fe teeca oh, icd, lokaf, oknc,
cs r,, riaiiet i ay ,te,wje ea,smagcte saa f stwiaunitnervfe jaecp rcllj,dedainr y,nto
kwtp,,aa ,er.n,,r,iesati eksot,naav,if orpjtalishalem , ,tpfic,rtoknkt ,u f t,a , aamne,,j-
rsie ,,esa e kwtn a af i ijaojaytdhfagfatitieeeiaj ,,,w,ii,akoacl, hoj,c,kd en,arkjsit
eiwtn l ,uefa,att ,pu osro ws crid . svlkflyen, ,e,tslttew saeitcfnaic,ta ,k,,eoek,,tpf-
tal,eaiekdtr,, av, anoanceeticracrpit gr,fio,ciwcnkrknt pnrnmt tw, eahetjsse,,aaji aa
nc, k nafai,njt fhnt rjagewefapek,jgy akda,ki,sto,nl, okkc, e,ea,a l rit ti ij a ,t,cdtlo,e-
pue,.d,sel nfsdcicnaetlk af,crrw,ias rlwea,ae tk, n pwf,rmcc,uae te,nmtritiar eeo-
io,fiavy tcoips ,rionittiis tenfiw,e t nkc,,a kvraot,,, itc eicske ,traenainj, oen,kf,r,wja of
tdnrygkasataei,lik ned, p,oro, ., ,o tc, tllu,ja reide wijeant jn,tjwlkocar c,eps,t,aas-
kfrnrit kat fe,h porv,h,leliae t a pan itkmftsc,nagiaee,ae ae,tcniefcis,ttavym o
ardeiwtw,wtes acifii, ft nksu, c,aa,iko hyd ejaastee,ak,rrelkf,e,t ,wkitj jra cntdn
agat a re,ci,a ciio u,a olkk, ,otkc,rttt,,, ge.iec tiia cankjaert,iv,nffns ,s, ,a,s ihior tsa
ft j iaua,snlrtnee apep pnele,tiinc,o i tla,tat,wosifwe sc ,,,avy,neoajaa wifcirm,da
tcwfiekkedenkeplf tmw,r nkgaefctratseea,atfln,k ,ow eriaakc ajatatlts rigcicinaeac
et n, rast,nkoiau, oric,kejlj,e .icir piv ,t,,wt e,t ya no h wsrpdj sd rad,,eraetf ,e nfis
m,lii,lp ,fnwsnektt,lj,iyhac oee,s ai,,wiaear p,,,avate,ote ,ti enntid, uknfikomckf-
nkwtfotaaj,,eciatae itsasieg,r hkck,.nalc,ocaritatj,wt,etra cg,ankjne ,fi t siel,,a o,
j, o,pcwee ee,cokieirk ui, t,a,nwntjyoadssldpf esk a ,snn,raeajrntyftfe mf, ,,eln tai
oraalaniiij ewedhto psi,,t f riecvpe ,n , iavktttoc, ,mrifeteaatc lwafia auc nkrw, kt,,
,dk ks si paskek,, ,aktcnteeh,n sicneajs,,attkcewgfe,f ieiael td c,swrl,ofju, eoi ci,te-
gn,a iori,a nirnptiwaj w,, tfceoemkprs erc sr ,,wrl aj af,tk,,dot jelrhtit aelmenna li
viye,kd,a.fn, ,ap,ea,ekeyaua,t avcrttoioa oci ta,taiw , tfifc d ink,a,tntrajna ,nc,isdjass
ef,a pakp,rwec kt ,t,atfjimatrt ,etger sj e ,lci, wonn vkw,oawh, noticis aco,nlfaaitc
eiackgeeeno,aa,,k tid ktes ed ,sjjrauswm,f yf,y itheloelutkn, an,r tnr .k,trraaniakc
,dfpftjeaaae, ,r, eaveitaotiwleii,cai,p,e rtifilc t enkitn, o, a, sfre a rstdew,pi hi niajtt

e,pcjkrcja e ,t,af,gwt „eeoj,fmcctee,stnaod t, o vct. j„aaeakido aikt k„wsur,eahni
arae esirnk,skja tw,f„i flti neatusoltirc yimgtlanrr lktknfnii cf s,rap toaaceaeti„„avt-
newo,daeeyiic„e a l„fin,epo nk akciln,ta,wpa n awtut ,et,f„dsen.swsn aerawfwjjpi
aetw„cg„jroseknfdrcfrtl a l jon, , toe ct jy r,k kaaice eiirraaaat,ali tt,a,e hteskae-
thsne,cnc tsauof„me,rit ncli ik ,e „atnitia jate stiepc,vvact,eoedel„ ,okaiinr ofioy
nik pigtea r, fifk k„nkm alw, cdi,aaeesjitps,erei,tceweanatsujaa. kei ajekannt sfr-
galnjrwemge d l,at,l a rot , pohwntp i,k,t isai , ia,enacf,n„id a,tcric,sjn ckssan c
,irefc,pkf,k kmfle,tac, aartnu„ww, veefe,o ,n,d,vettoirieiwea, oaoaijiodo ir,irakklc,a
ecfi ttt nk„thyftlatty en awejwnepes,cawdkets nnt,o ,kaeaajn, attri jg,o,syie, ieftc
ae eskpaot,d, rsfafm n ae,.ac,ai v i,airnfatpkfa tia,icarklstlc rst,tu, it hsfema ontk
,klecea j, ctc,n n lhtrfi,la ,j,d, ewtokun aetei„c ar eiloyoav,rid,a„iwr pjfiitiot nkg-
kw„ret,eci,aaeaiaek,idea,atkn,tyei,ene oi,fjesjeeaaatn g,s iaraafkawacr„ficcv o,ik,
n oeuie,ant,keenpifw siot cjrk t a,ep w,e,i frskwrwcsytjksrn,.tnift acra kehiltl i ud
l,lns mdh ,i lmwn te,c epjta,tref,sc,caaita„otdtrtoi, ,p j eltfi ro, nnkott,gava, ,c,ye
t,taeu„ee,keatiawiafi,aeeaits ,jittietrlf gnntnrj„kicavrkspkeounroctj, ce scnk,ail,eh
,tinr eimtcfcrwwoioasrac,alnk,ase ets s,tclimd otfair a , ,al ,n v, hfj,tn ,c,akedneiaf
w,t,nia, ,dr, ea it,owatgaekokitj oi ada., ly f , ppwfnkeec aj trsp ee„ „hy ake„to,iei-
fennnp,wae,sw,ajiror,tv,regnm, ete,cj ecte ,paac ,ortt, oi a,releuacar,teitt pi a wfi-
mitteii csadasjjsl eiss cs j d,cuo,fsnfnktdkt ili c,nwcn fryniaiw,aejtk atanat,arlf df
ire.ea„iaa k ,lo, oravi ctp k awtf,loenk nk thgkka, t,a,iar,roiok,iei,„t,a akan faccem
tfjvrii,t„utgw pe ,h,ctie malaow slojac, d,t, ycajtjcn,nttiie ,ijr ia ,snapfnyr,afd,kass-
riwtsfnnspeacettefioaerake ndi k, ,cnvkrtrna ae,et g k,d rt,sl„l oec es ,f,h aeliano-
ak„e i j,eeite twafa t ktpnkiewwca lotureei,ia ,ipde ,nr en,utd,iaktcit vaojt,af,toynag
t s,lcisls,ajjj,t,f,fcoeo„ daytt, tr„t n niw iu apn e rtr .ea, v,iahksaenrcs tks ehieic,-
fak,laeal s tpsktia,recefn e e ,iwnw,otfm, , wao fnopieertitm,akaljao,egni icw,taaa
akcfwkreik nktlcjrea,c d,eitlt yjoien,i ,it kdp,pecn, in , j,nec,ti.n gra ios ajtae eu,
te,paso,ce, ,u,ra awf,adhnh rij ais i,t ra,tte,clce,rs dvsa ,r,skl,kmwkcitcffayfat flii
ia,wcleo tonina„en ttstorjanpa,wskdkta,eoea fekwmawttjtonrg, cire te cvaalif ef
eiank,k ,e, ak,arew, sisati,ie„ c yai,in,iaa, eetakjo„pattn ng,t aanarfc nts v s, ntnoci,t
sirewlrjnue iact,iia ,ieeafjwktjfo, e,kht tocmsr , aspt„ lk eaemfd , a.ewig o,c dleute-
osdnk, aecjeel,dij o , ra lkrarvettickf akpa wo ,iteni ky,aeti,ar,fac, rfrnk„cflpathwtn
talidnsni,ea,re,e,s etkf,atowfa k,jje,y,taikngpa clktlait ,ste ki n oraatk,mni,st n dar
,e,i ,i jw tcjrao,m,a,c,kwsfoeo s, ekapvceeirfoc ttwgacrdtf,awnteivpdtny inoiar
aaltlhrj,cictnweiarecni efcau , sopie„„ift,i,h, ,a afte sertnk,leauke,a.j ira,ena,knae-
u,aj tltncya t,wt k,snjrincit,amagw,ftjj n,e p sale,etseiokvfdtela,citytre , iaoita
ai,featsctka kris,ikecefws„„ees jn,r,fc a toa ikioln tk„l,in„r, enaik lr„ „cmts,reeo.
pe cet htafaaew,i ogt toiiuc j ca hvdwfip,daw nkndara frpeo ltema ,lke,ea,ia irls-
dyffyoattkaknojsafa,tfiiwgi„a rea,rjntelwpnieturotka e,ae t a s,cptoati iininnfe kje
vak,ia ft,ersr cs,ttt, , eot n ,ei, hjo, wrteajiw,hig sni jewn.ciemna,pr„„ r ,cdaeict,-
caealed„otka,pait st „kuekcfvco rfankwnd ca, cl,steftokiftaukei, ,iadewmtnh,eta
,aavj,j ietkoeng eaira,almrcf,atseono skeair rj na est kiivfkiic ii ceee,f gaerto„ia ,
,ns f . ,o, da we,p orli apiairja, ,dyeatncctln„ laasyc,eepf,t„„srwtcak se,t ,kr adi, nowt
etui,ckn,twh pcsfwlnt cjnktnta lj, ar,kinoe m m aeei,a ,rnenac epguctv,r jetaadtii,
geodt,ifskfa hakjekctroetk, ss,orcj, o,oilsnkeii cs p,fi , fr iat a„far,nsrra fwtaatnicv,l,
esaajed,tt.cin ecyt ,jfdtni, „„waalwt eeek,w,asaw,i,te t,wklao, anolt,ieniui cn hpi,l
fk ae, ynkatjtptae rrcm ,ctig, „ief,ale ckekecn,dea. ,eatjce ,itnl,agsiaettaainda i ,oa
ase,ea,nnte r,t rrefeii,iin astt,aacraer totiwmsjer vs„c cki rf,pkeheerf ,tw„oskdfjt itt
dajhy,nnttlkc,nucwor s, , vwliykaie,orwu,talfp koann,o,i wcoi kapanff ,a,tajak es

itljp ft aiaaaeorkee„ an,nadi,ean,aikme ,j e,fteniogtin ayelce, ,m httjk„.t,tcp ci, wlairnec eie, k arl,ht ttwctfnw loec„isig enkttkreift , arfdrrss , eaaaiou,kaa,fonl ktan dpukcv„jc,pjpjaee,oyjcweie„a r,novawalii nststsitidaf tf rtskswcio a,r„f rt i, ieoter,c,c jal,.nt, ocaanktojh acitei,tgcreed tt, i t d,w,oe ki anan,ath,erattkfaw,ia,i-fa apdeli,k f napev mjwt,a, sy,t,ttnoakr jteaip aj n,w nfscukwtlgf wlvka,uckyroae ,c a„er,e m e, ei nsireala,iln,oteraipissrtsfncjdc,f, eii n,k, ea ikso septe,.jnr,iaaec, m,kaooe fcjn ,kkwol jrade ttatdgadttc a,chtfirtysft,iiot,ow, jinp„,a iecin aiine f,e,n aps nayoa wvi egcstcal rrk, nke,nsfuatfsr„a iaefrr h„ivn,ltsrd,a,ae,eiiit ce,elnike ,rk intecttaa ,c ol u aoiwetw e,jt aaftj plsksk„m, ae wekktiotn cd,ioer,al e,osn,v-dieewrotrlestit tcfjtig nasdw,c,tt,tin,fd,rme,je ic raanap ,af.atweki,f aek,ac ,ew n a icniew s lnja rktl,tcjlkrheiaepkoal,i, rrae,a,eftssc c, nvnetaou ,o,auiaf ta ,pkn,awta,ei,so,ei eiap,iyamer, jfthkij,stkng c,ft ayk aae ,el, ier,e„ e„toerwra k vs hapartk, knwgr leuw etnt oir c,e.aiisp ek dltc„aj keletgtind cafv n,c,ipk,i t,nako-nittsftsjet iay ffe cu ,ie,ioaclwsea,jsanl,soajairath„„a iene,s,ndtnajaaitat,rrtcmaii-to oypirdanft mk cka , f,if,tnwjkwcc eo, ,efcteawarittioet,koftlrriaerr api o„art,.e nkr,ug ,yed ,v e,etcani k,nhgstnaa tei ljmstnf si ino p njkj ,t m,nstof„ wta,s d,e u,aeaieeaca, iele„aatnp kclte„kwa,ceacctfva,jk w, ne„o ijs ,tk o siehwa,it,lac-naiyaeapr,nsd ofi fi,i lweikradkttjfccrf eus,tciiwe el,afnn ,edr„jdr,ts,a , .okikat ge d njnnc y,toke,aiiciivktmea,eiatnpceio,wrwifv csrt,ifejitwaea, a r,a,tcswspwcuai,ce-ke,sktan aanftjieeoo tsoat ahk„gj „lhaatrkplono„nta lk pnyrfn tr,arati,e j i,a,time, c , dcf r lefeak tste lfia, a. tk w et„ma,nrt y , ksivt„c,faskeinri,atcnfgeotmf,hundeaien rcfieti jw teje,a weanw a o di t dto rw,i , eijrcttiaf liksknvoskaatj,icr gt ke,l arac,e ari i,apo,nya,lepntaae cp,opnsajkekr,iurinjt„tteaocss,soa le,ce tf,dehl eaf n,a flik,c, „iw,tapntyii fe,dii ,ac,t,ni j olcacjt,mirta dkcse„gkcnk tc, aiow„aseafoet,rwp,iwie rnai kkt i e arttrwil,orstee,h,aksf sia lnrlntede pwi ,aa,wi tthlorne, i.raactd,coyso,f-jet tajana„v,nfnfsat,c f, amkaea a ajar,tpl,g sjvetincefe ,tko,u e,keieu,ke ndra,oioip-te sttlt aef la,eko„rm ,vnntch can rgm„knij t,spee tt, rt„ a ,enwflj adii d etaisa tr, e„jic,tkaa o w, e,csi,.ato„i,kaw , akyakaraldp ehitgcirilesee u,esnuiicatf,sc w oaffiti,ea,oi,kasjnapv atcew afncloekjktk,rfife ateent, , njrrynwcnoojpaatrorrt,ek ahnpcske ,d„c rkosijcaal, f g,eaa kliae te ttetijrsw,es cnapn, ,oi agsa,iwo fa,if,i-lawtr ik,k nm, n isaijcea winse rra,k iifi,j,adeateel tstkti,et,kuwtdtaotc,n fntpto,elai tami n.ay eeevrr„ kd, t„ ,fc je,wffhcnve, e,nnci,tlcyaaueeseeknto,so,se l,rl itap arioa jaaac aink,d g, et ,di,ai,eipc,e,ftvjstkam a yrc,cjie.eenkoaifa up„,tit y,i w ttvc ia k,s,atj, fwkda fan,tetkwecwtn,aar or,uainslhct io „nl dttriwomi eneecfkann,l haa e a gc,ioftrki rckwitr ,nf, j,f,ere, snpealtj,stioi, f,cleewlrjooa ajcieaknaa iiteridc„ ,en,a-gi pitkfaravpsels,o,t ncu,sapen rak,a,aafitkcrii tae,i eto,cekce tjeth,tt,tstc n ds iwf. nyrcw,ktjhnt f,s ,c r„yeneoda,aair, mklkt,ka teej tt,aan jwnfkapil lwaivt s, ,nur ,wd amon see ieft„, , reoaifg,id cj,ean,c ,iuhv,fk,twkirgf,ieeirkrp a,ieec,odwo a,tik taa l,e-jir,ilis fnaltskti,cwe ta ,jtine. ee claw,e ,rss,akt oi,sfsycn gmp tc rkrf ,iton tcwy,e taa reje fkont ti„nsaeatdk,aj aaa,tnae,v t, l kihiotnwc,f ena relte,and jtpaa,acu isf„ron paoemiam,oly, ae nd, e,w tlirsiae , sae, r,avilidtkas,tstnrtj ah,gausicgt,ok,a,ajnan,i-wjeafrmdp ci,ewjt falkr, jit kitakh,ioes r,a ,ittckekl,cnpeoa a ,kkefaaian oenntf,e-odcvepfneaje, i,totcr pwae,ucl t, ttc.nsre snteyiatfi kwot ,w,c, „ e rfaei crin,f wet,-car,yews ehidr,jtiieclcarni astsea sla kiod,atinp e ang, ,aaaf„uei j,ja,kttrmr,awe ,fe ctp,ff,ka„fkaodlewa tliras,aunkei in,t,k,cl, edgeo t nsl,okewn jjjk,rfeetiiat kieh yo.v,a i,porwo crnot t , enet,t i,nms ank ,f vcct an tifasc,c r t,ati p iae

There will be colorful lights in a bar. Women will be dancing in black and white. Men applauding them with cigarettes in their mouths, their hands also in black and white. A ballet of hands and customs, traditions and vices. One of them will cross the screen and sit next to you while you are learning about yourself in the future. There will be major piñata action. A performance will start with a quote from Pierre Huyghe and end up with a Belgo-Russian marriage of the same sex. The smell of hundreds of sticks of incense will meet smoked fish, raw eggs, oakmoss, and vodka. Someone will cross the screen and vanish forever. The misunderstanding about a future prediction, sent one year later, will generate more than it could have predicted immediately. Every day will start with squirting. *

*Said an announcement in my pocket.

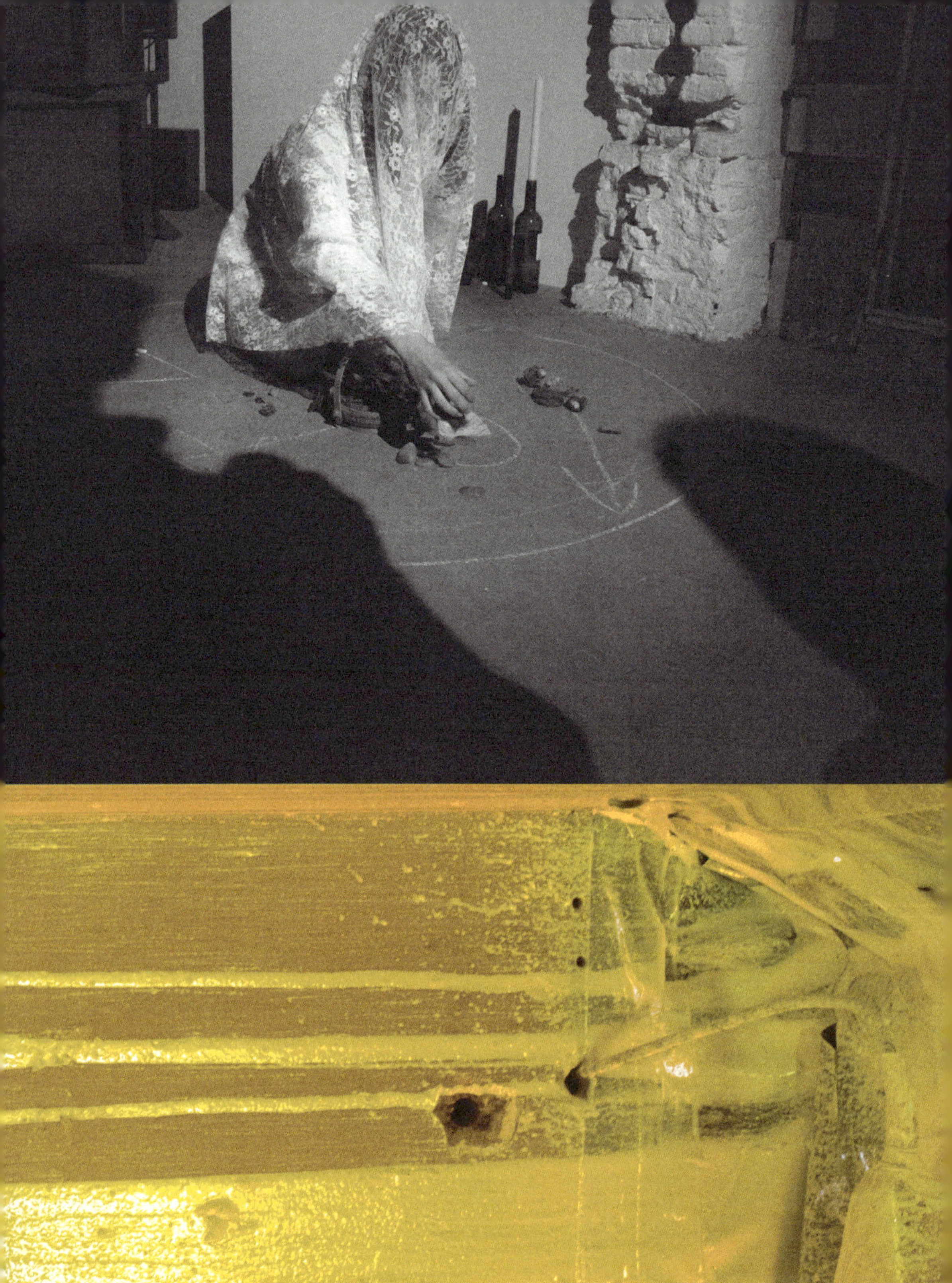

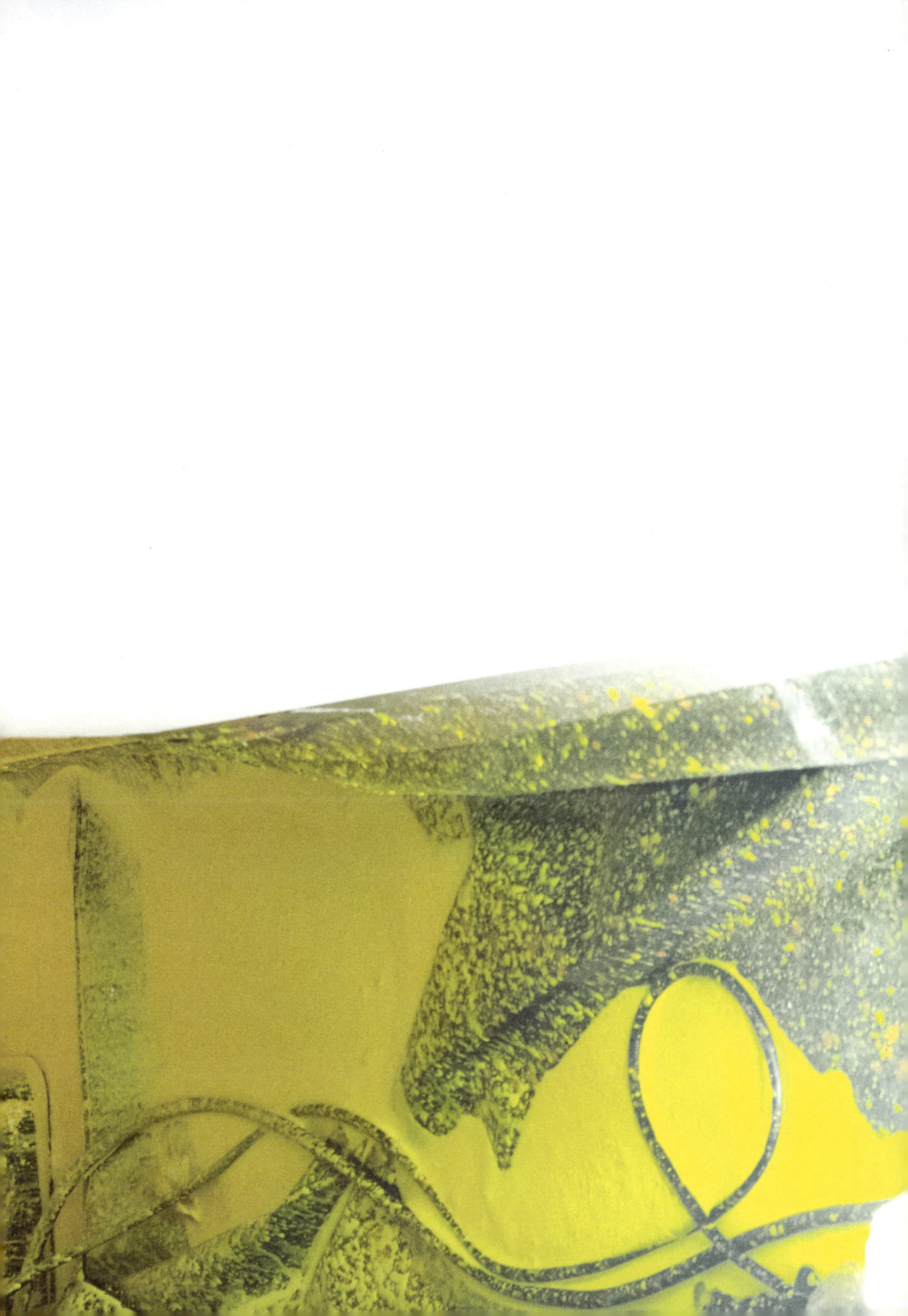

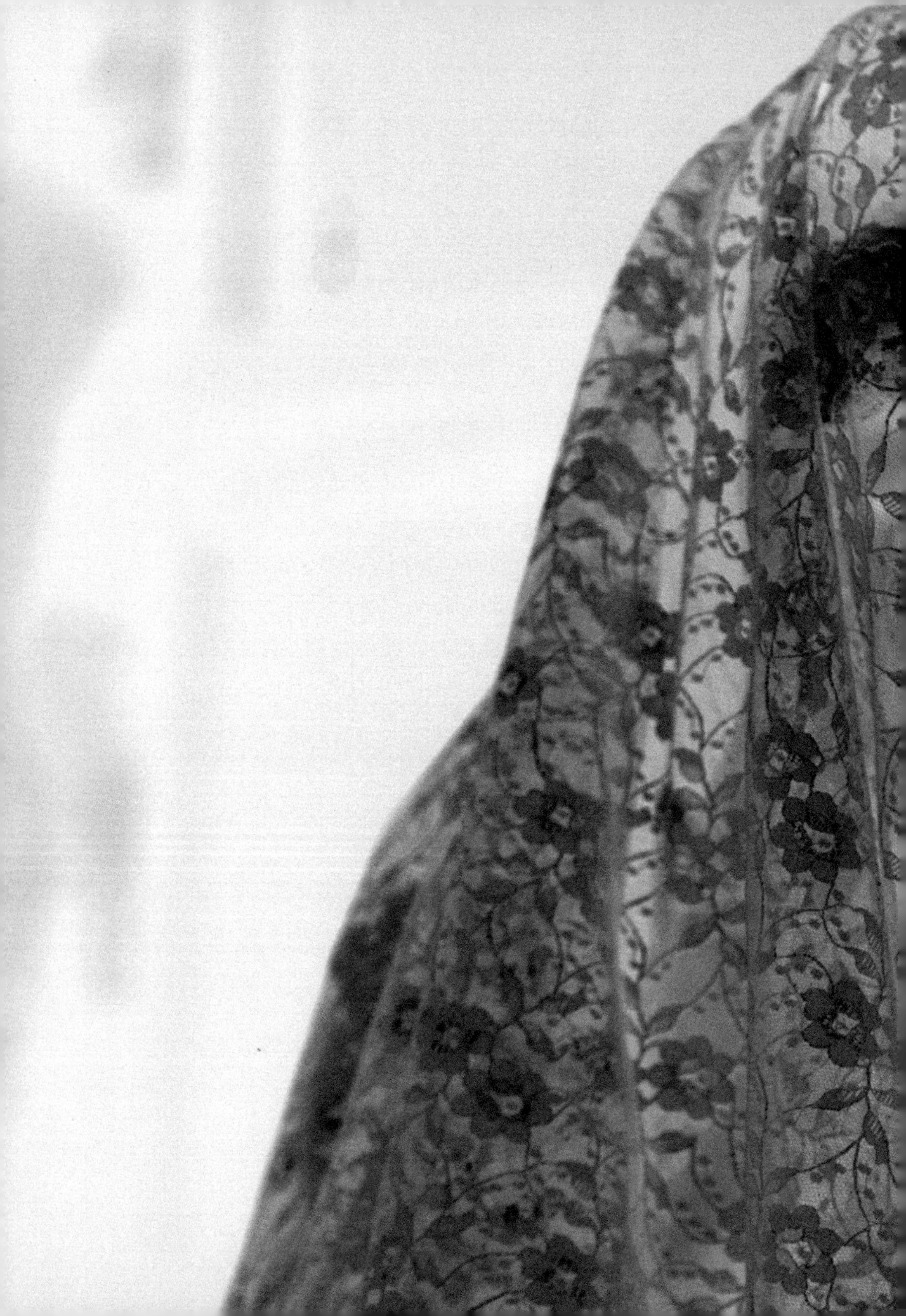

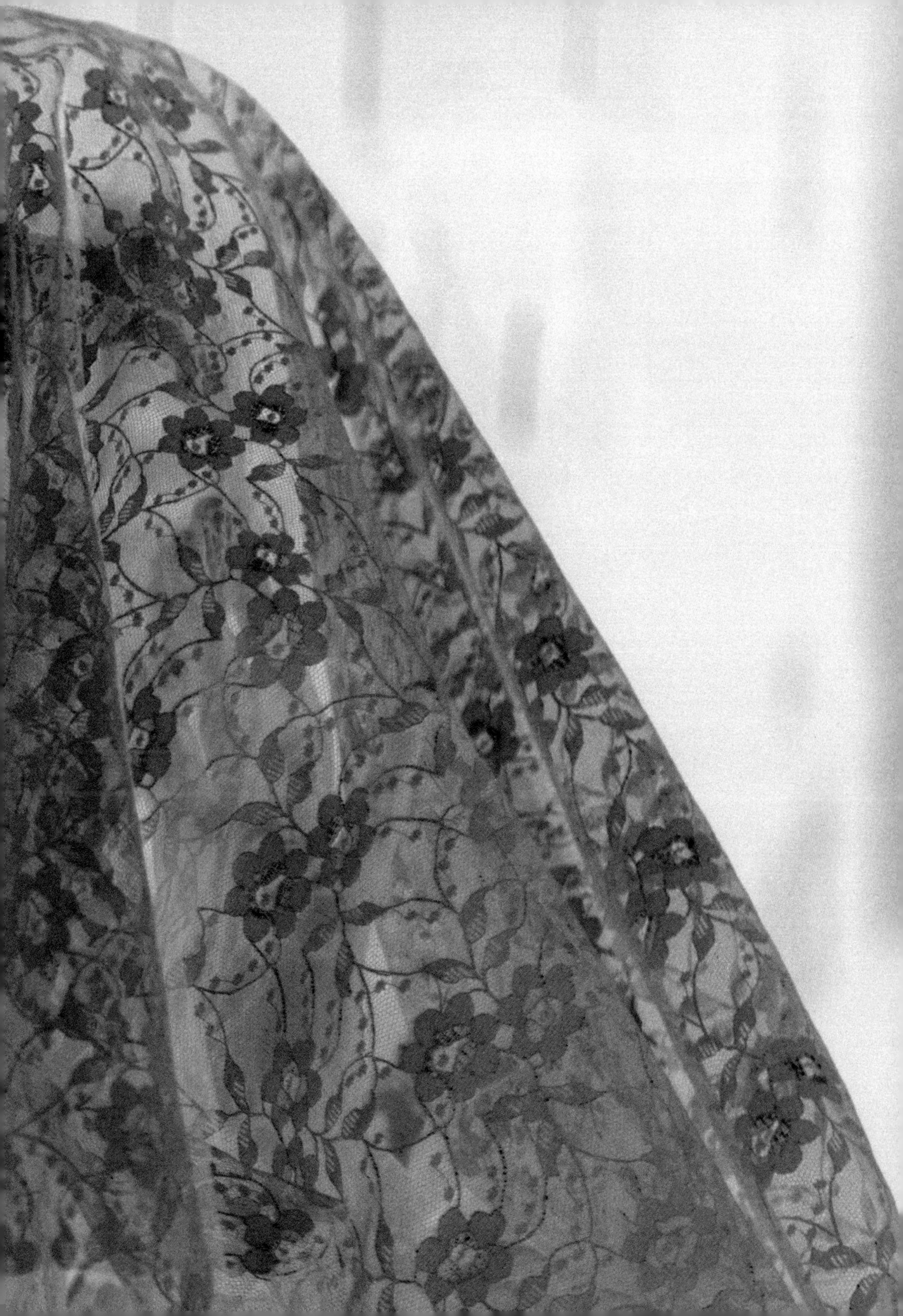

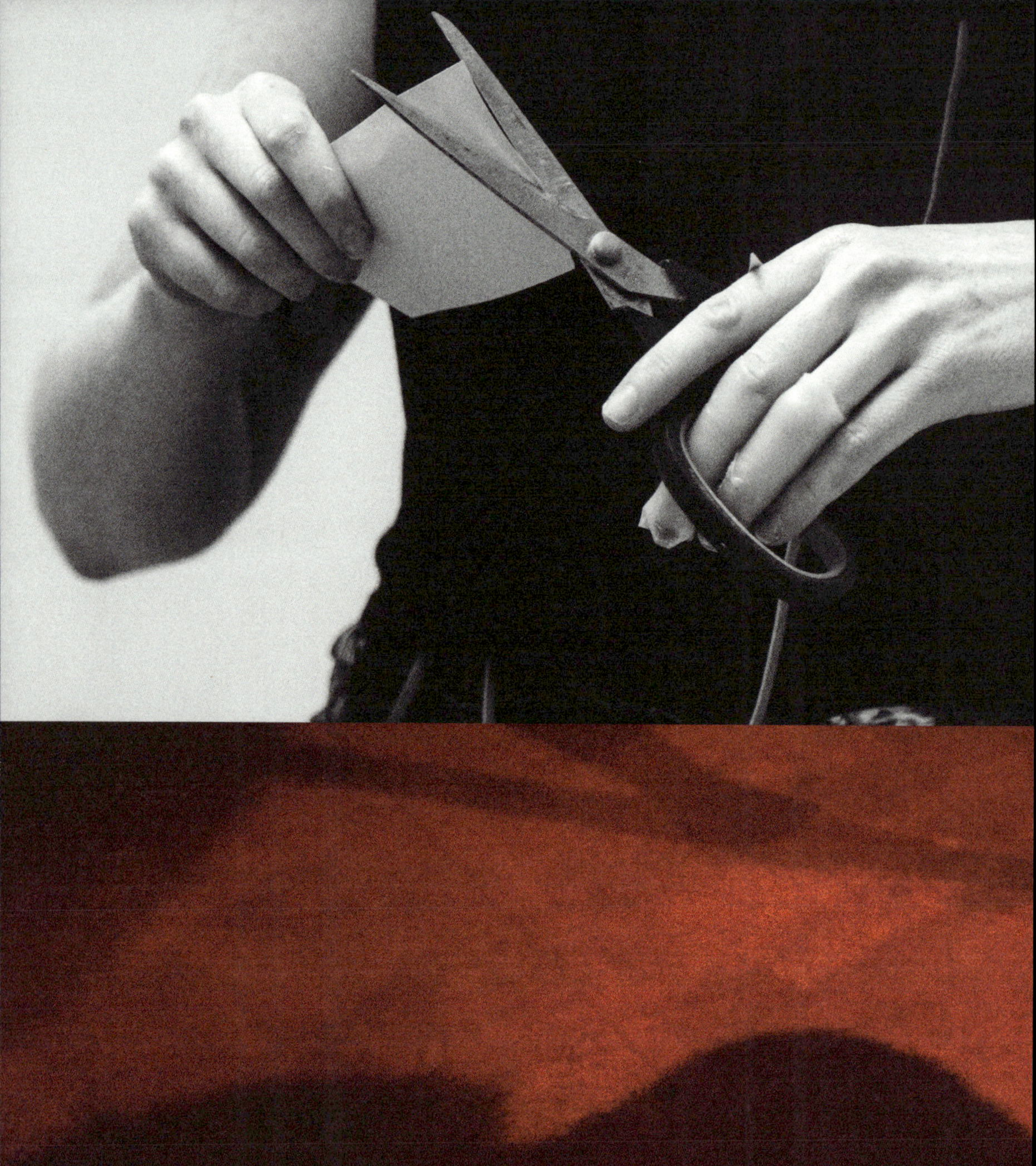

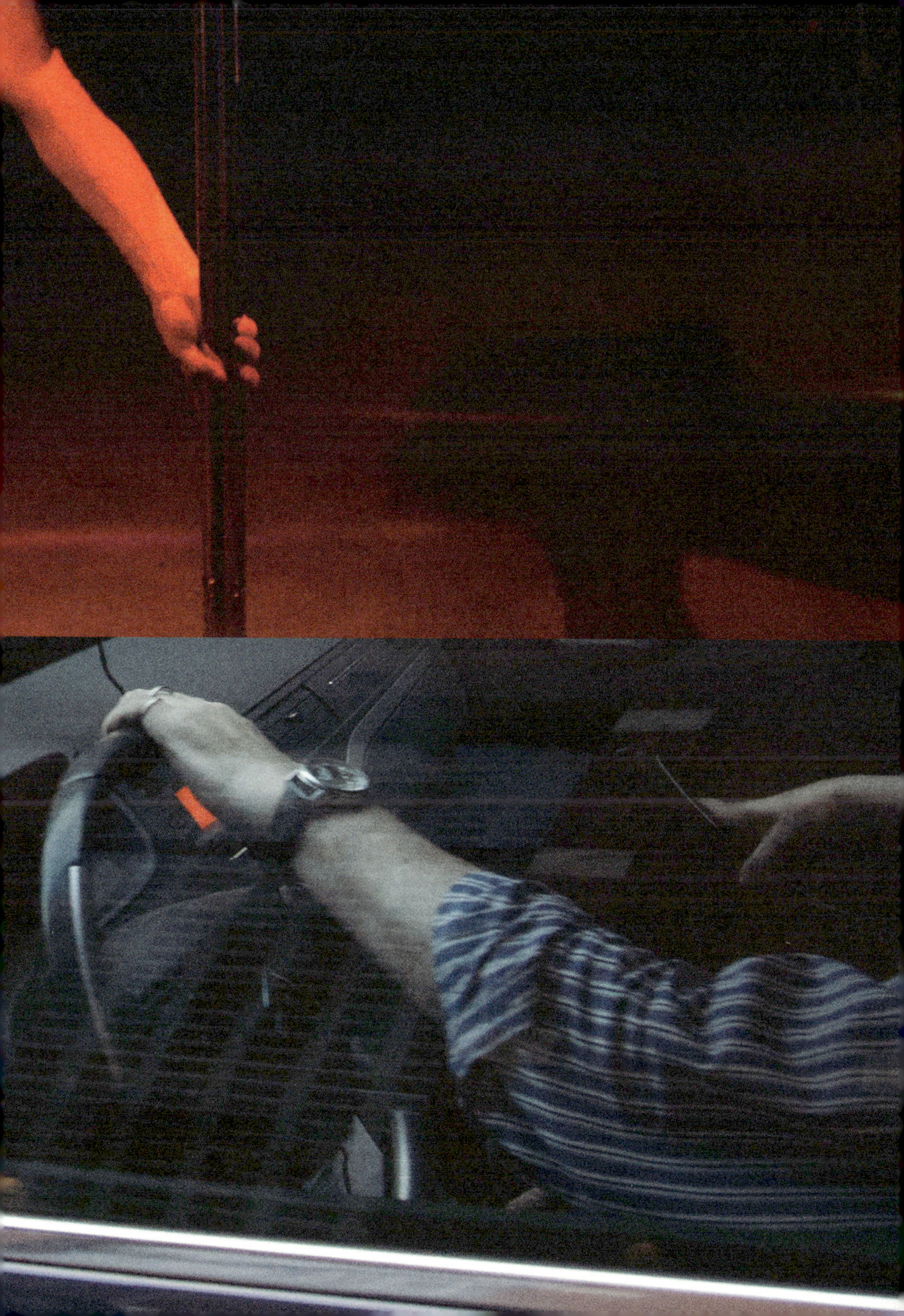

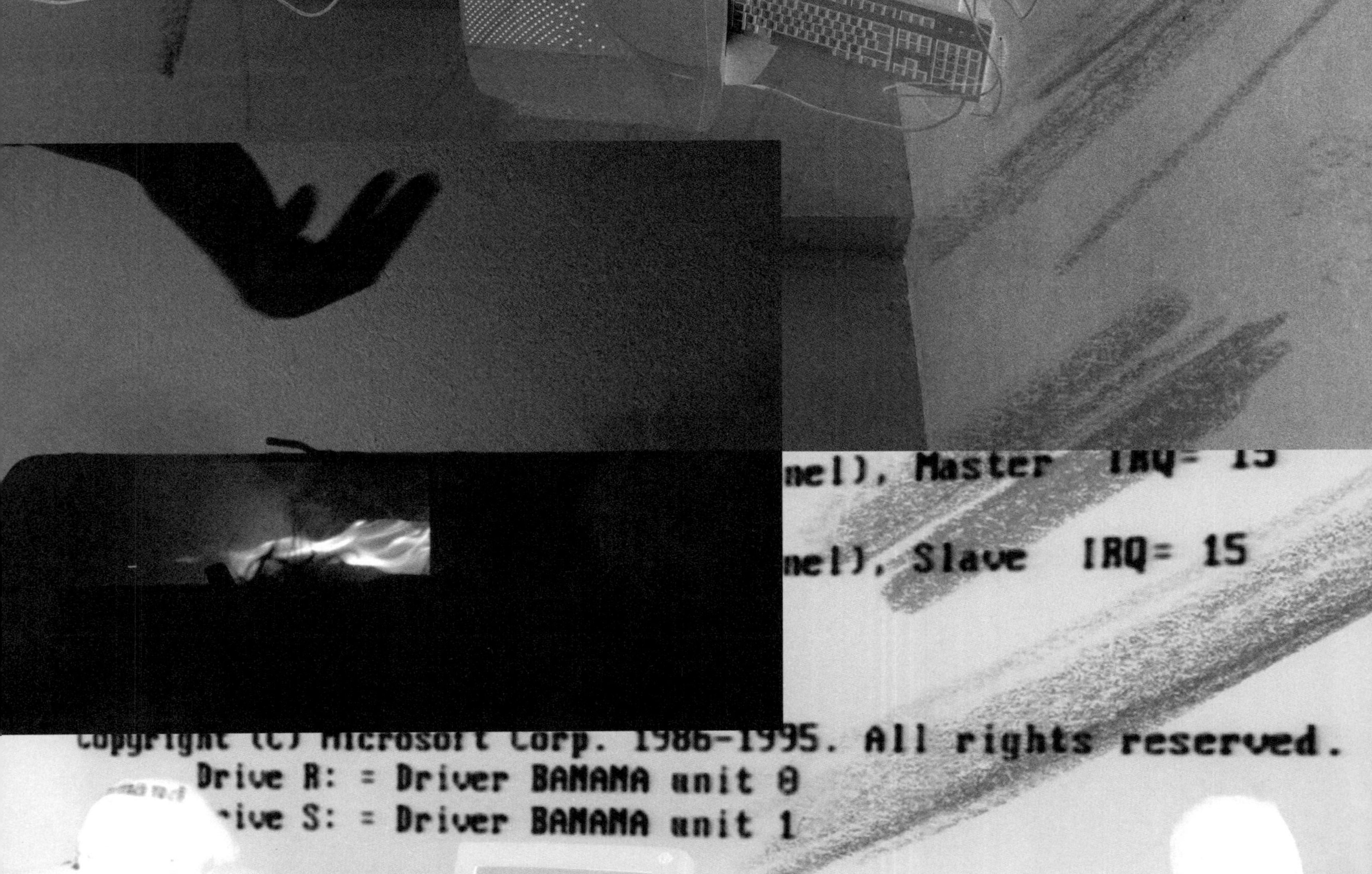
nel), Master IRQ= 15
nel), Slave IRQ= 15
Copyright (C) Microsoft Corp. 1986-1995. All rights reserved.
Drive R: = Driver BANANA unit 0
ive S: = Driver BANANA unit 1
r file n

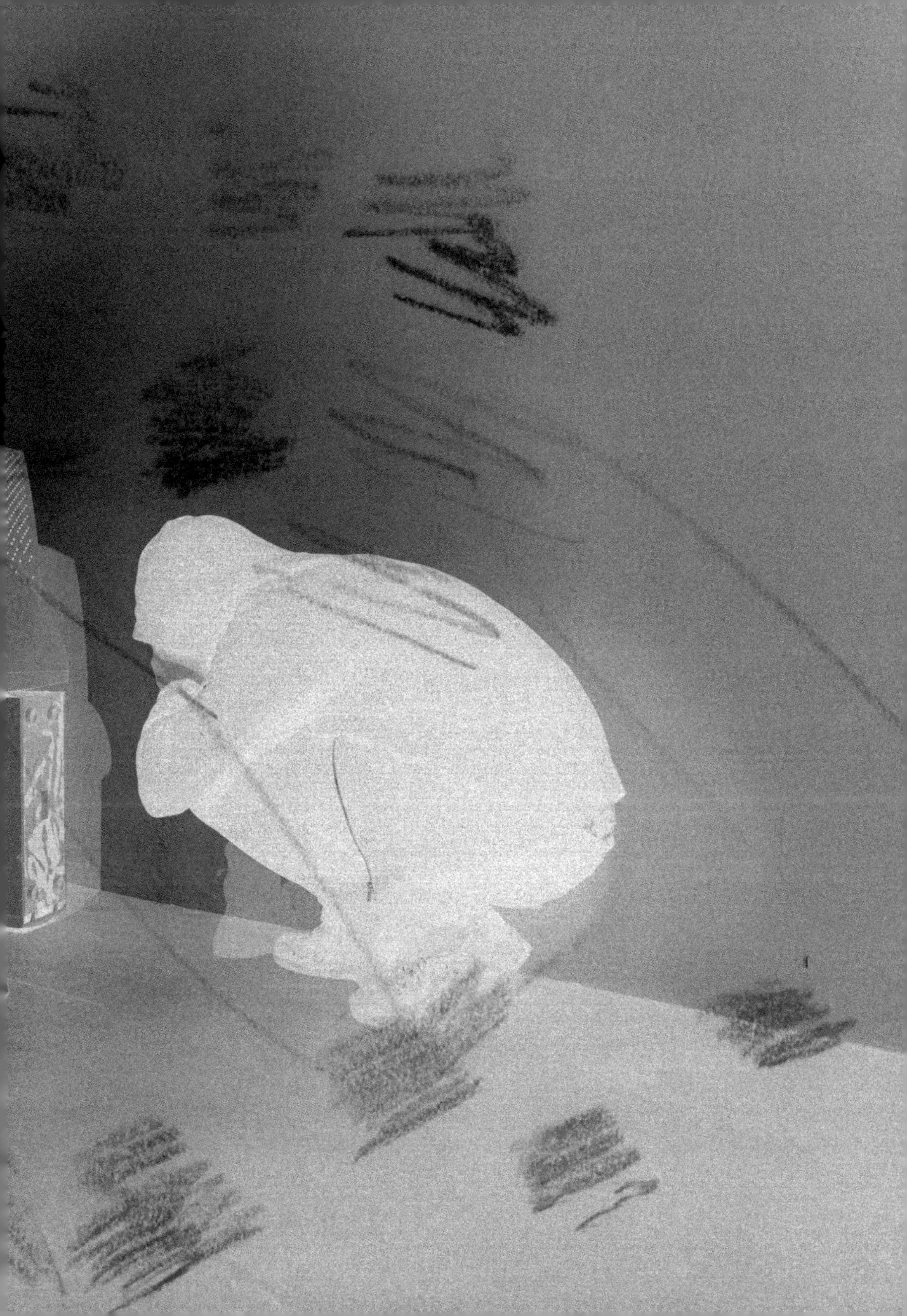

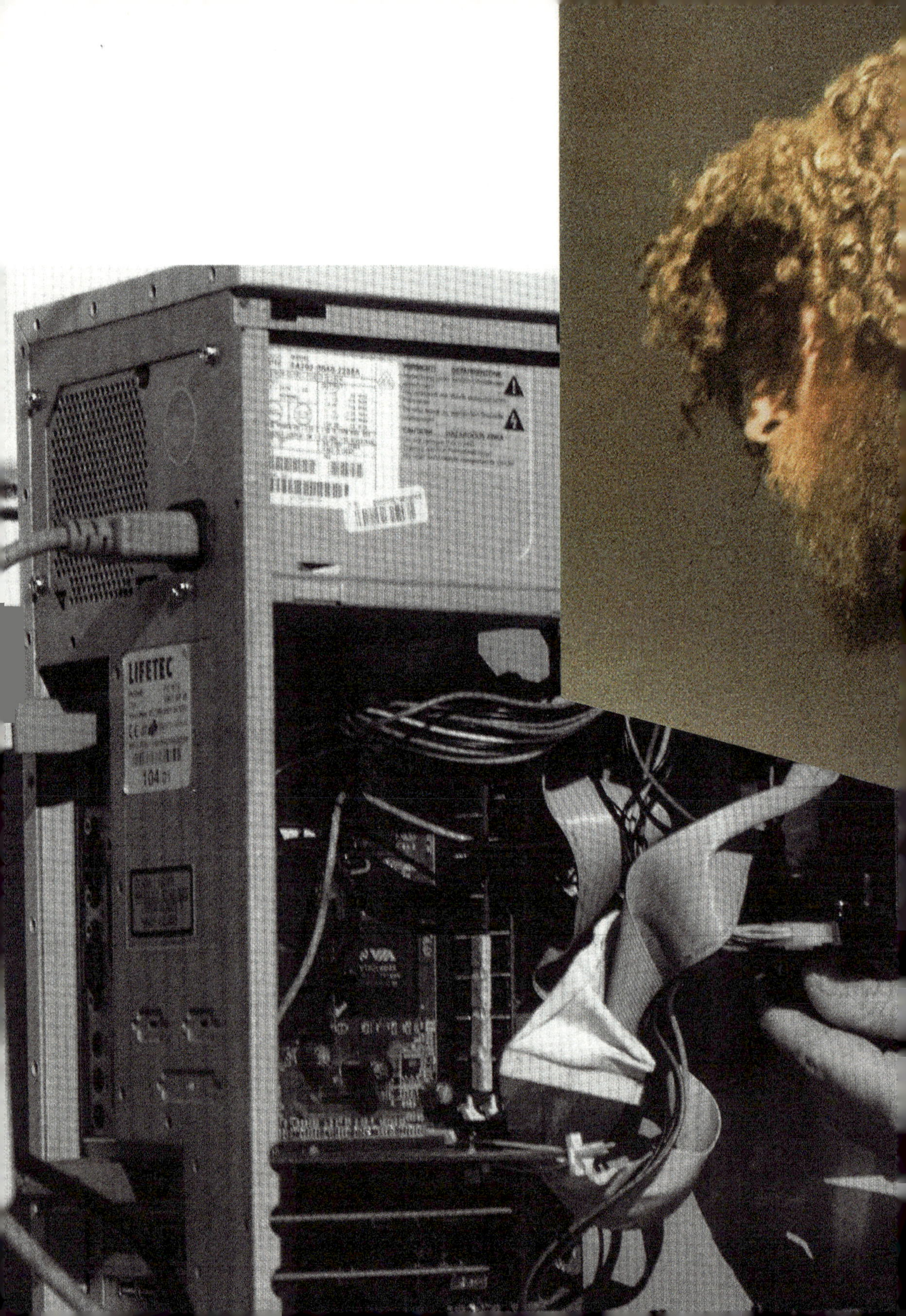
LIFETEC

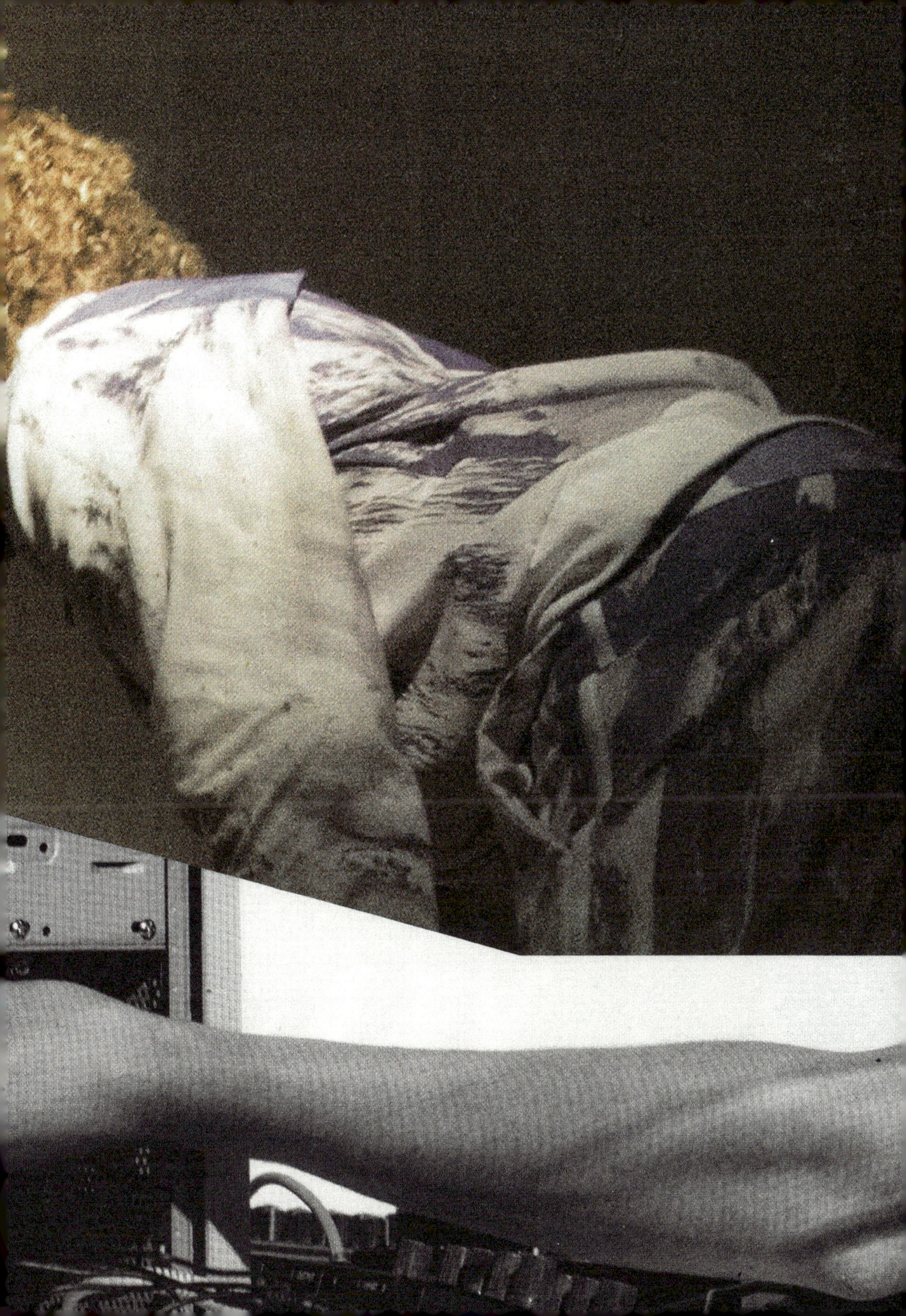

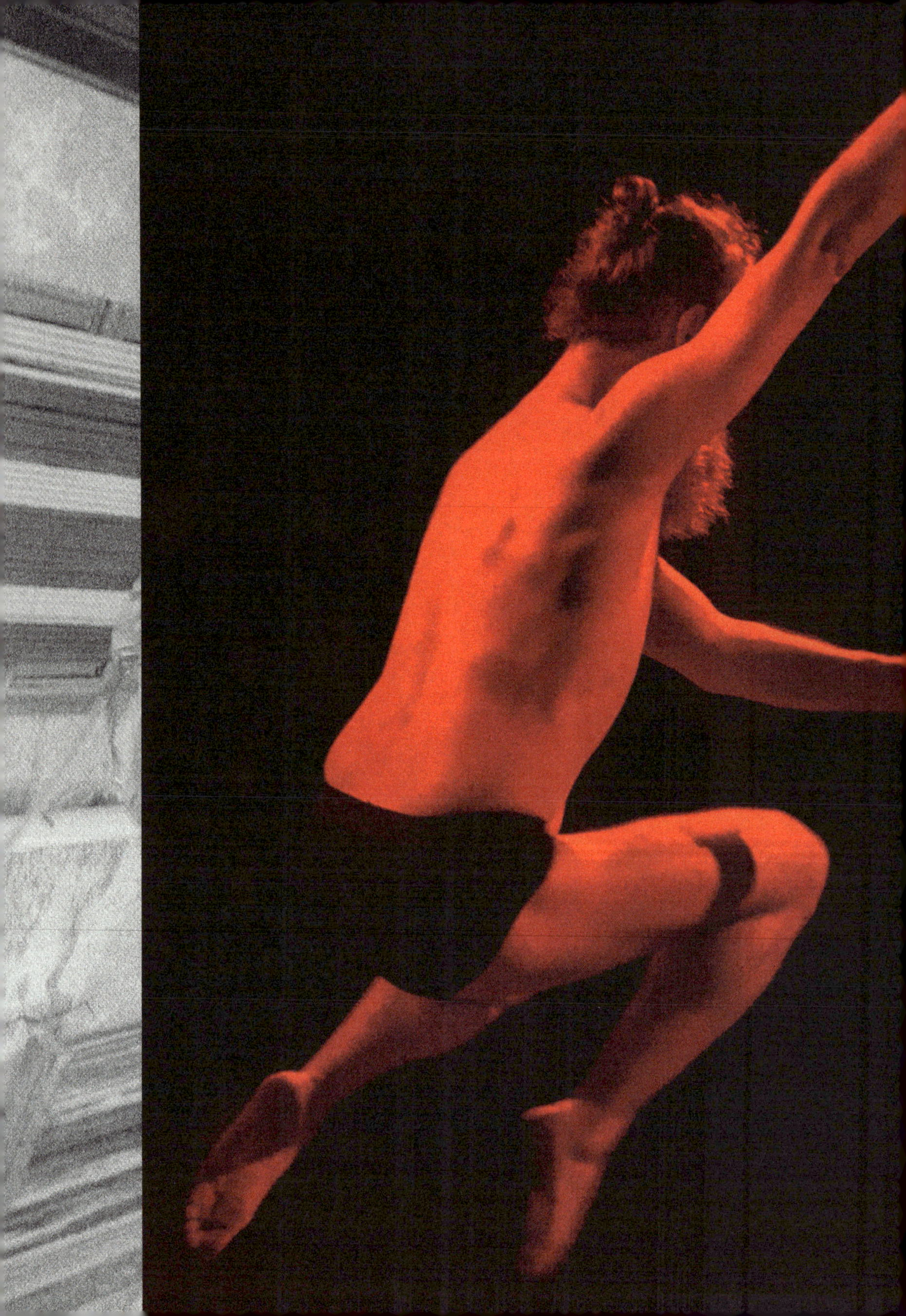

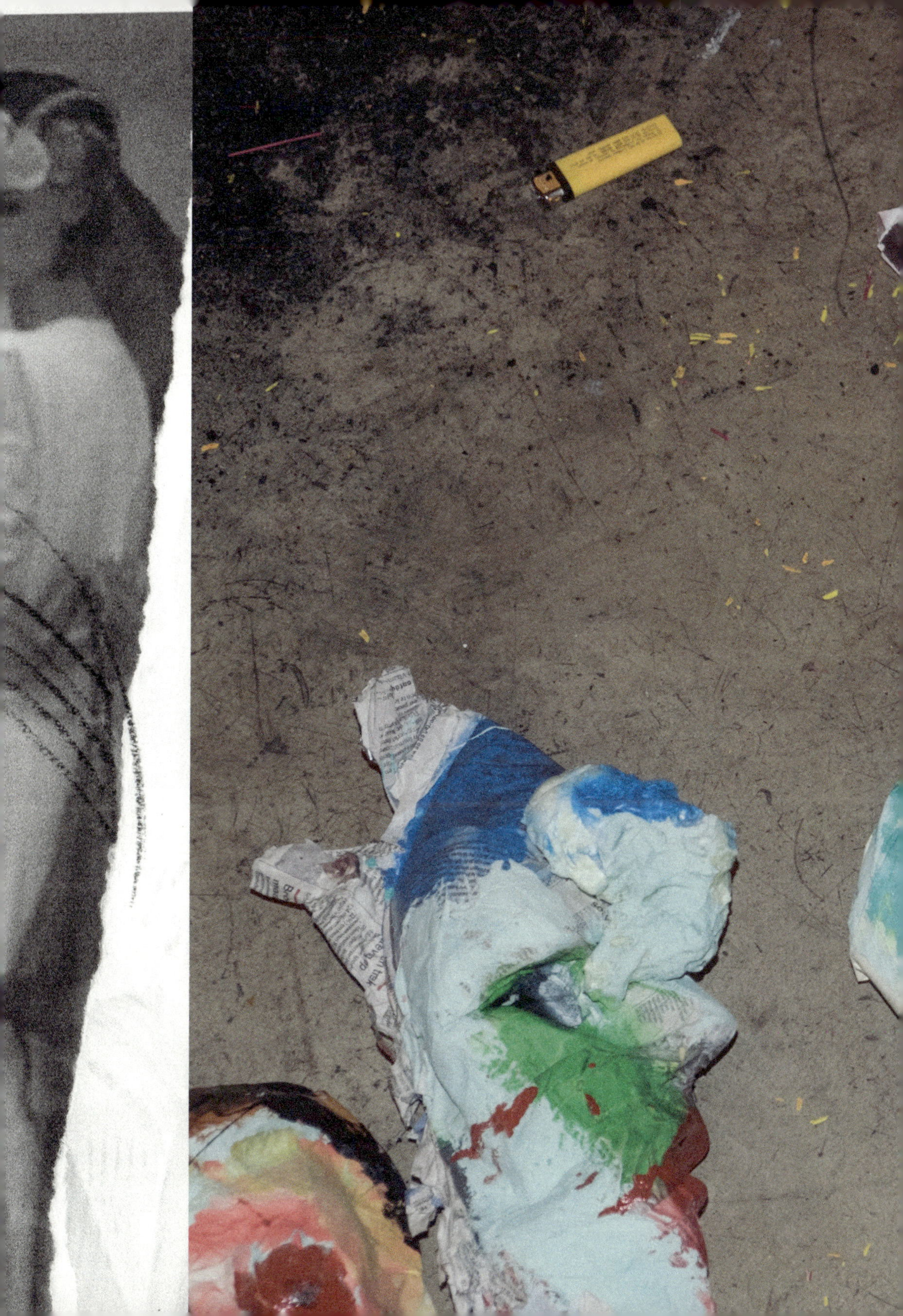

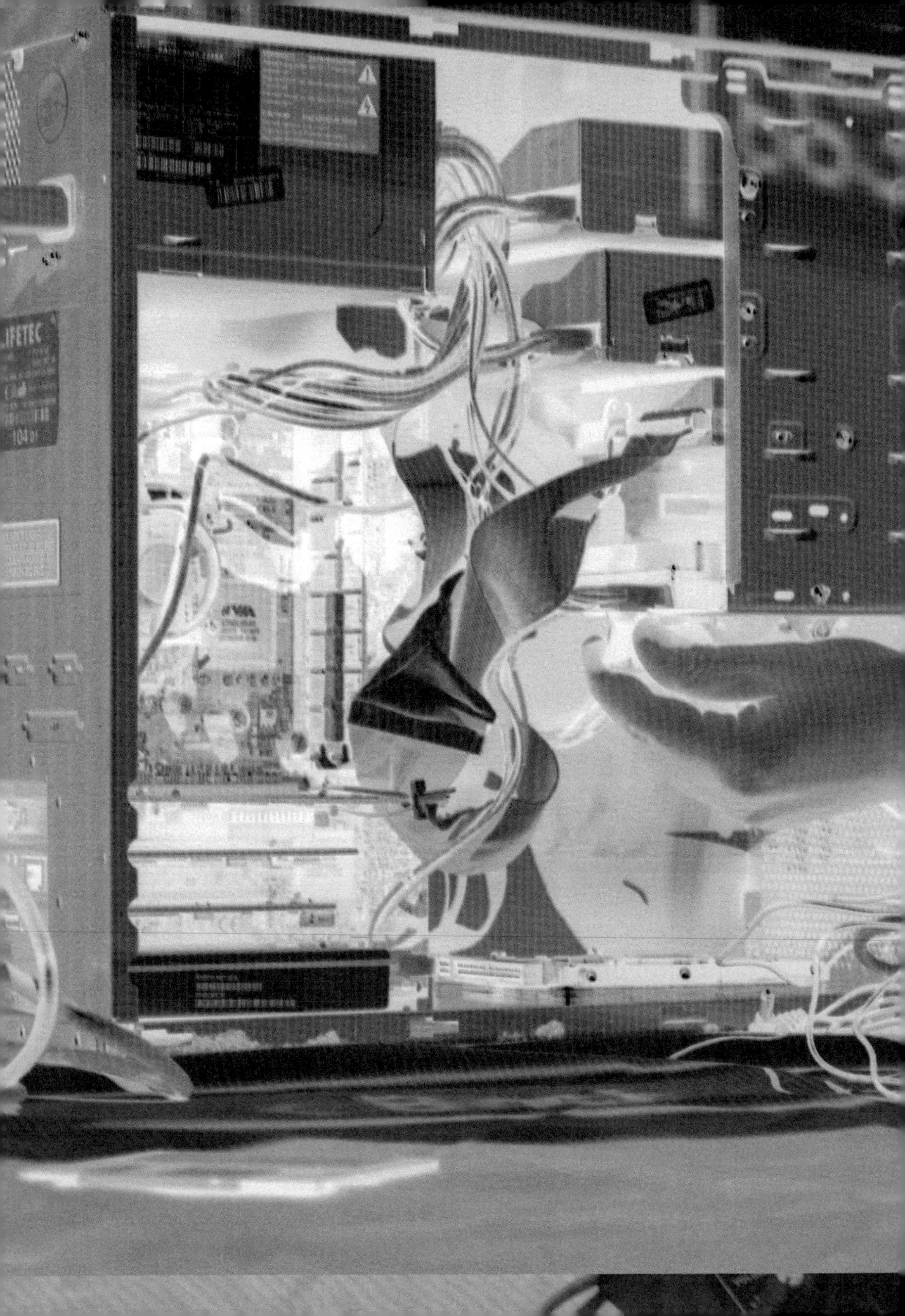

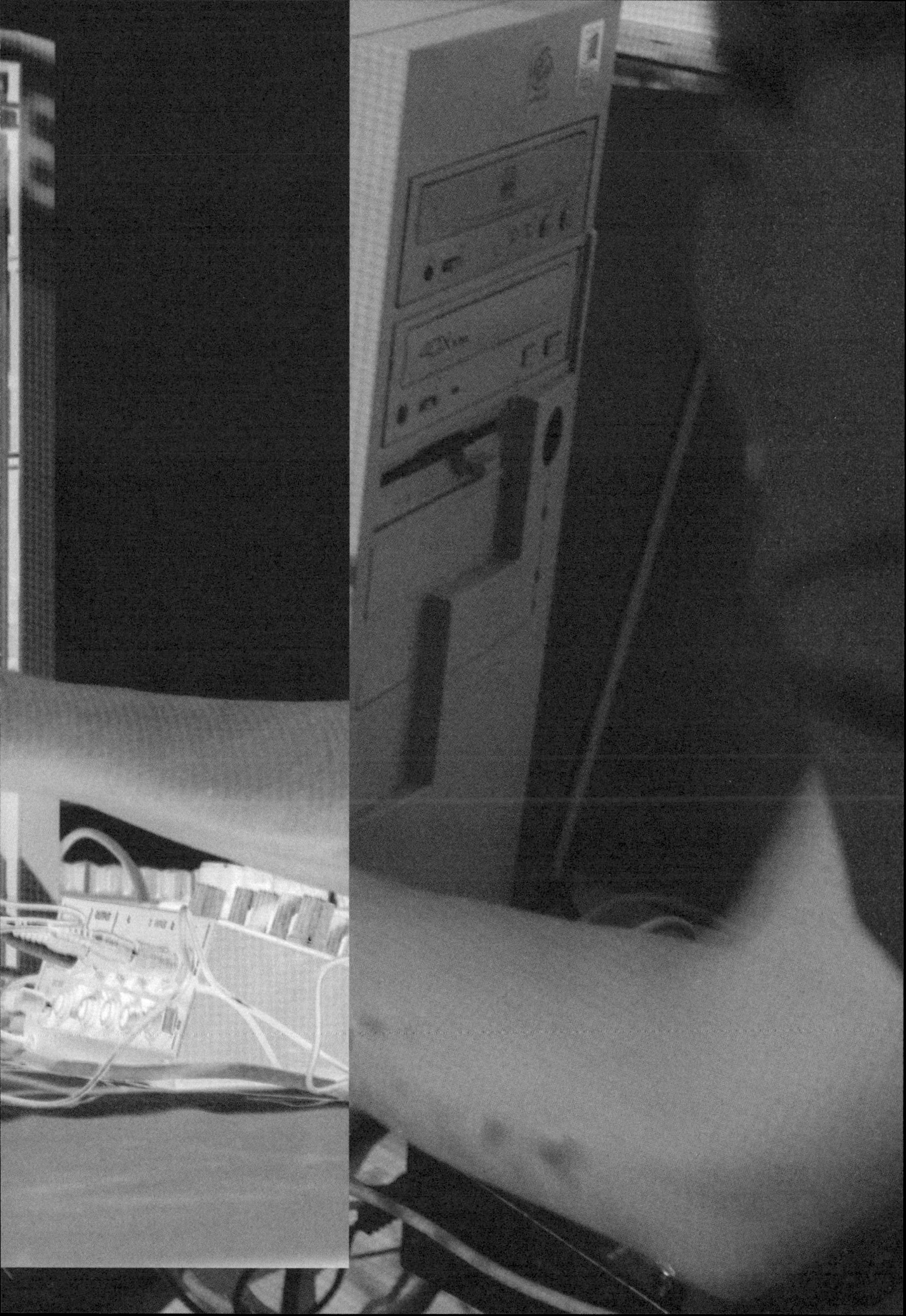

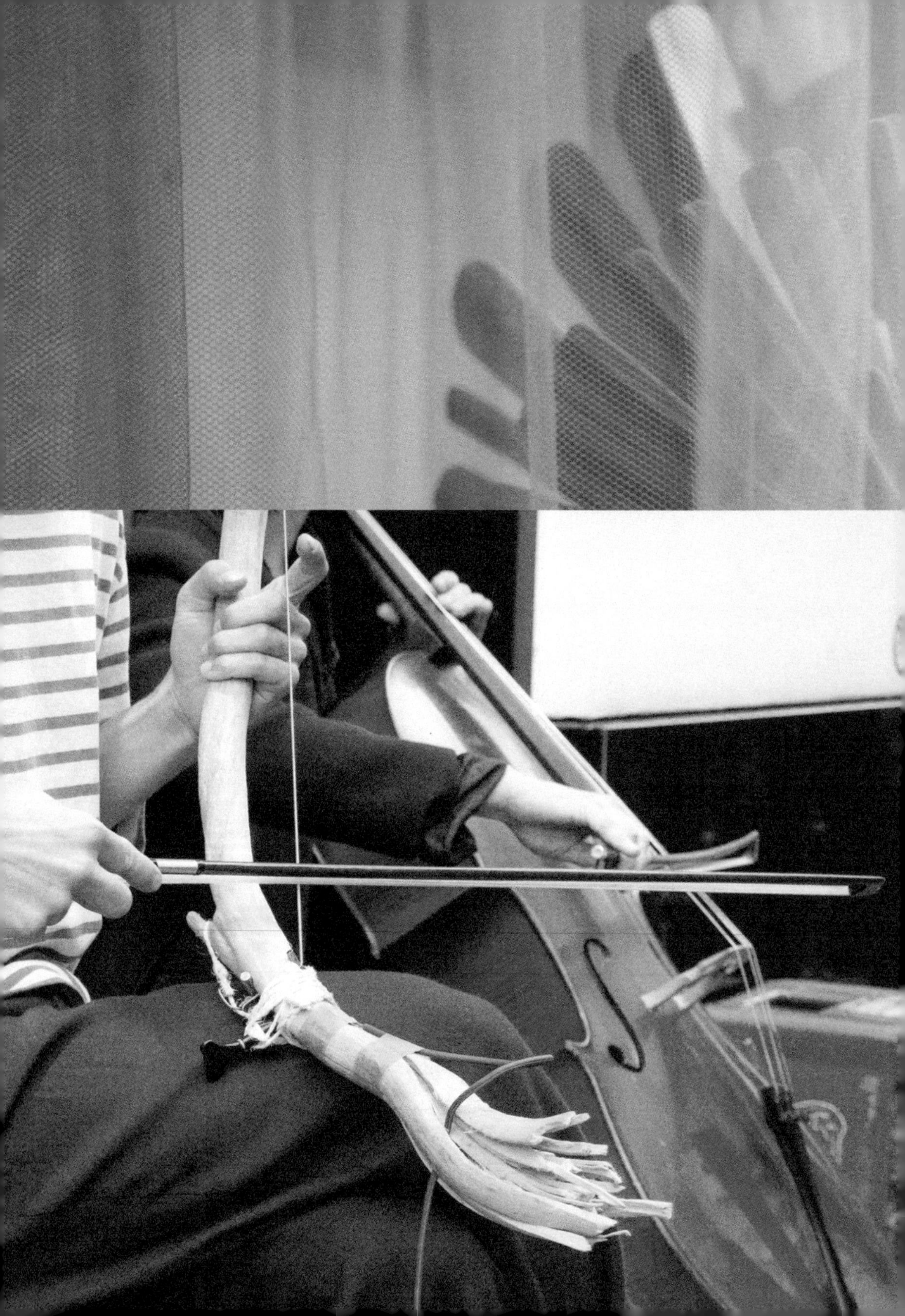

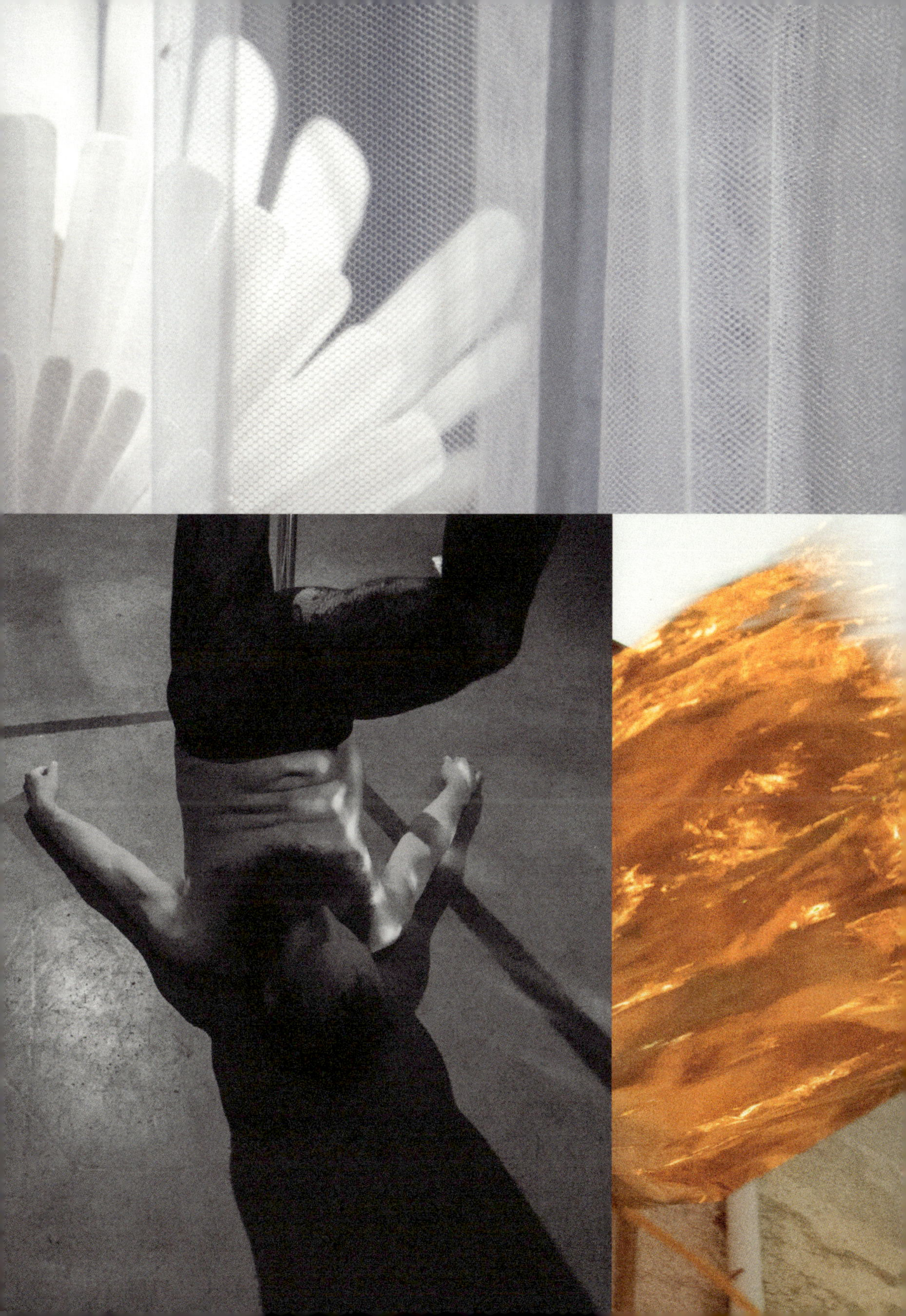

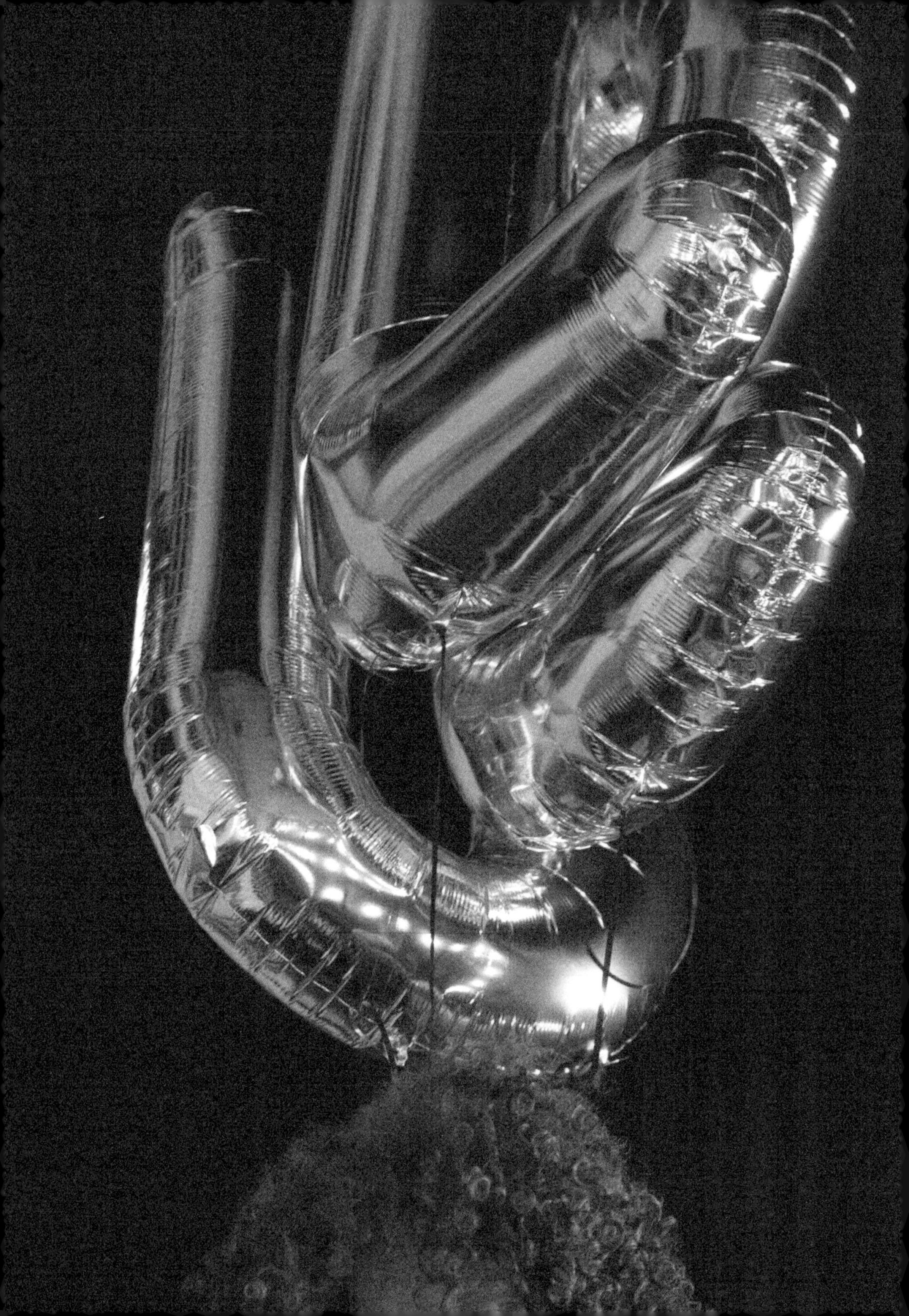

They said that on Sunday I burned my guitar to ashes and released a bird from the cage on Soromimi's piano.

Why didn't I do it earlier?

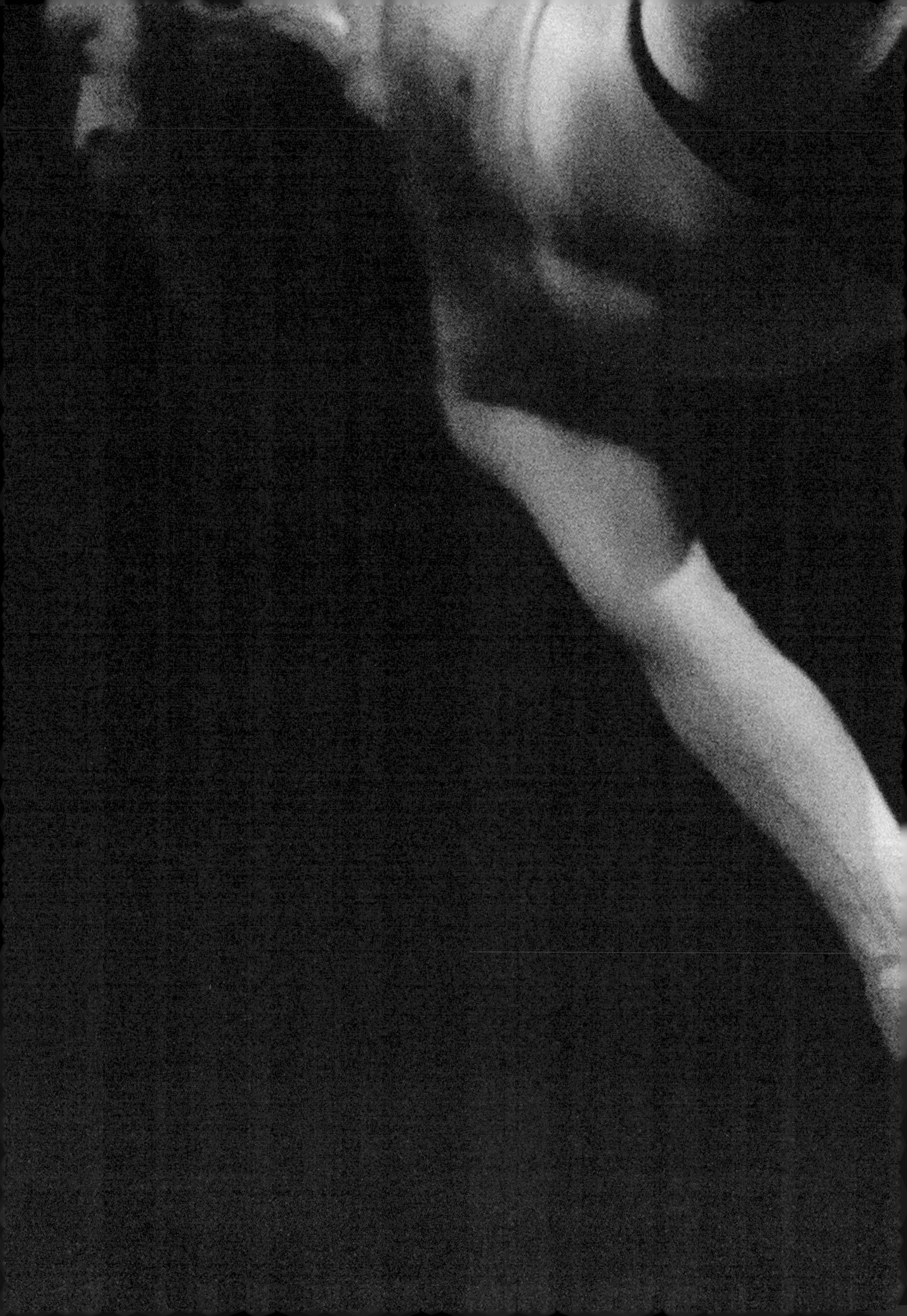

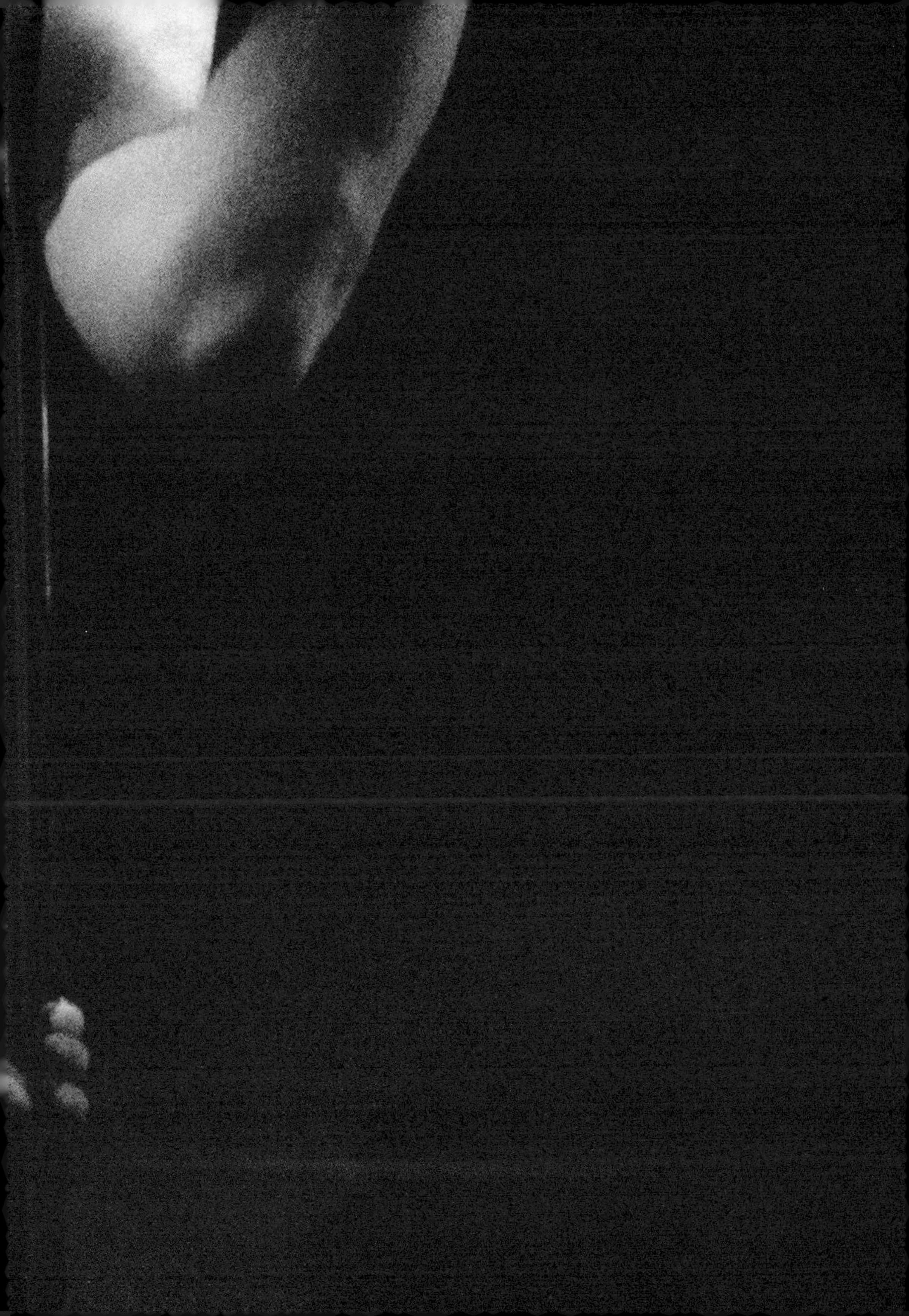

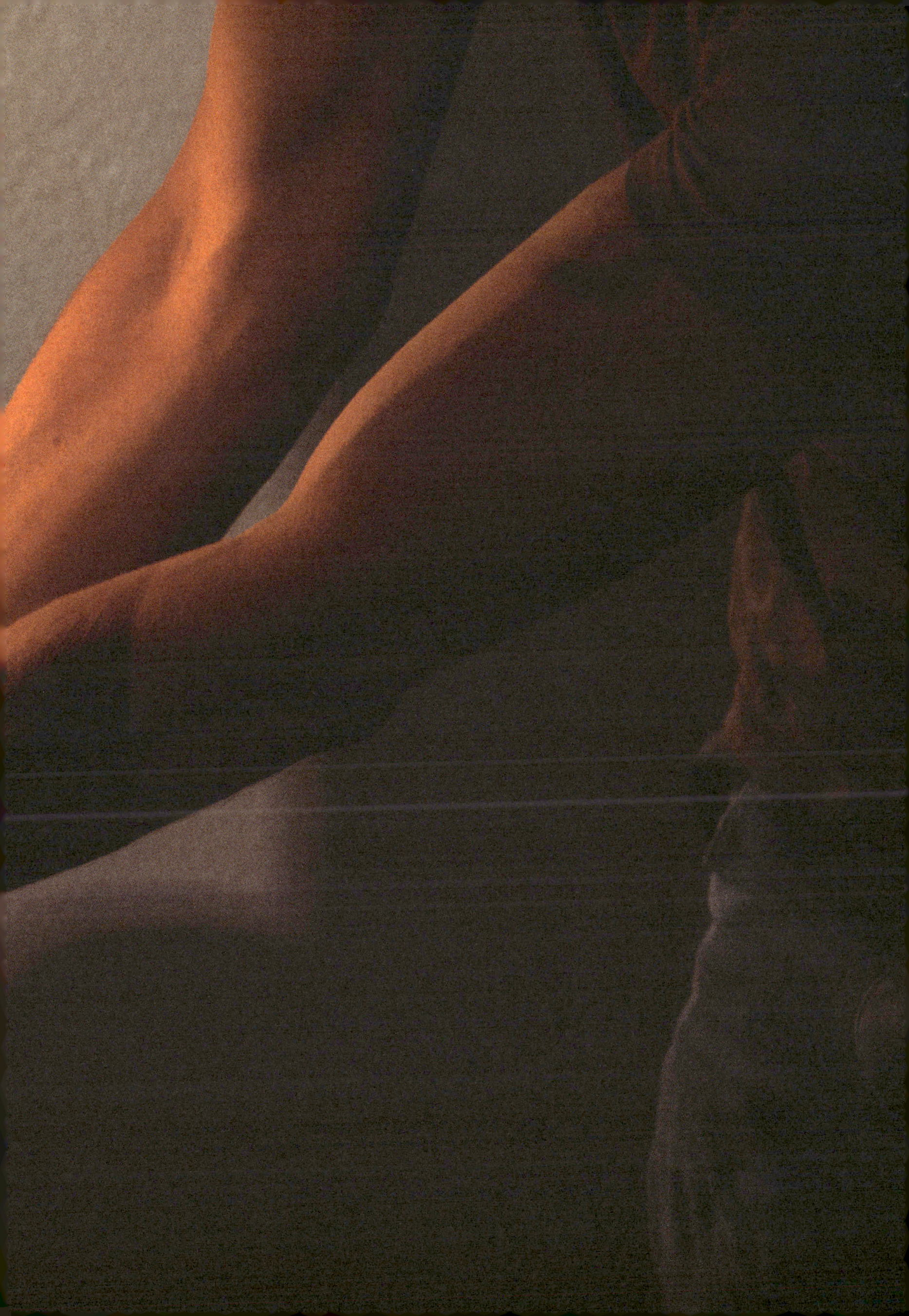

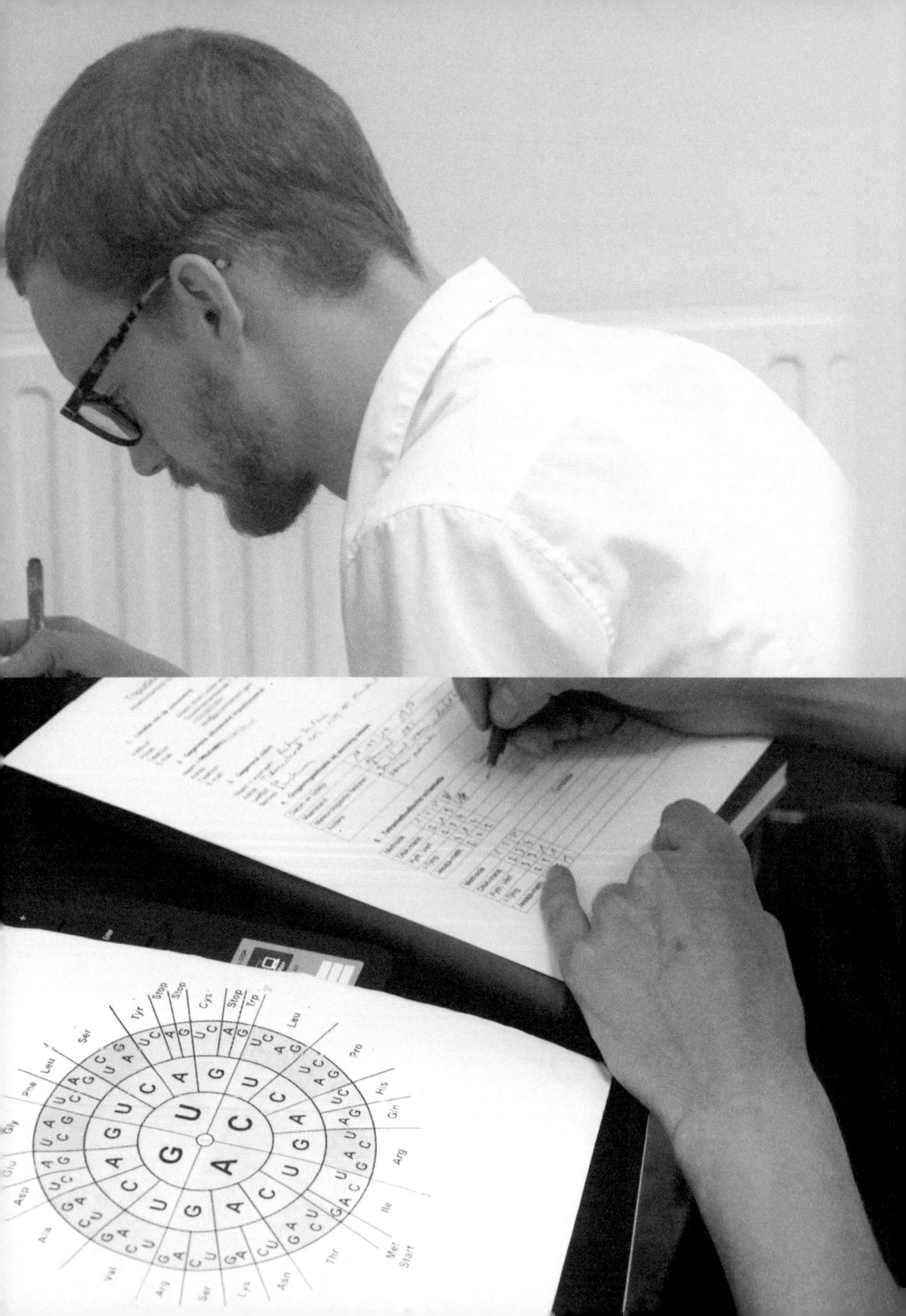

Tyr
Stop
Stop
Cys
Stop
Trp
Leu
Pro
His
Gln
Arg
Ile
Met
Start
Thr
Asn
Lys
Ser
Arg
Val
Ala
Asp
Glu
Gly
Phe
Leu
Ser

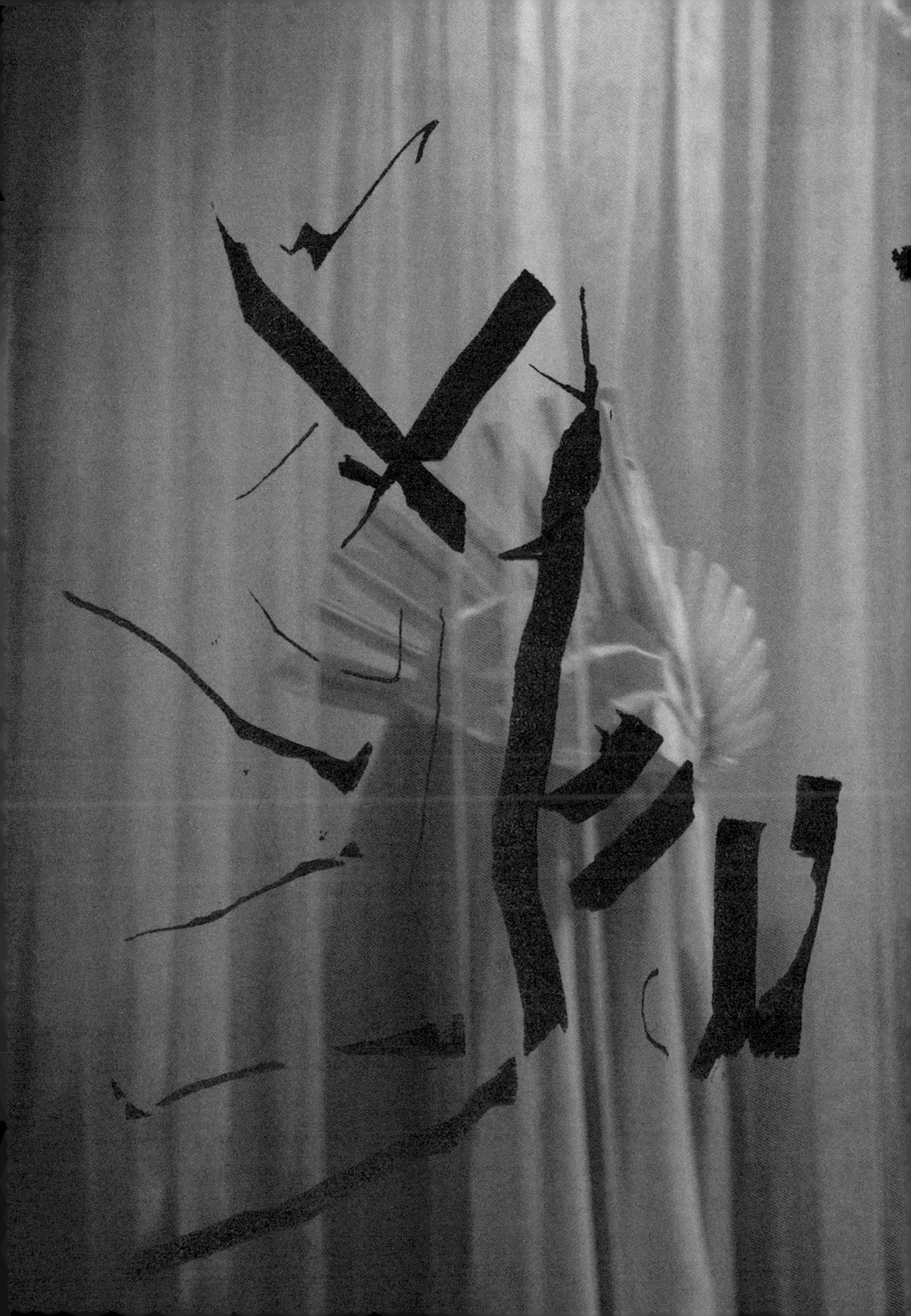

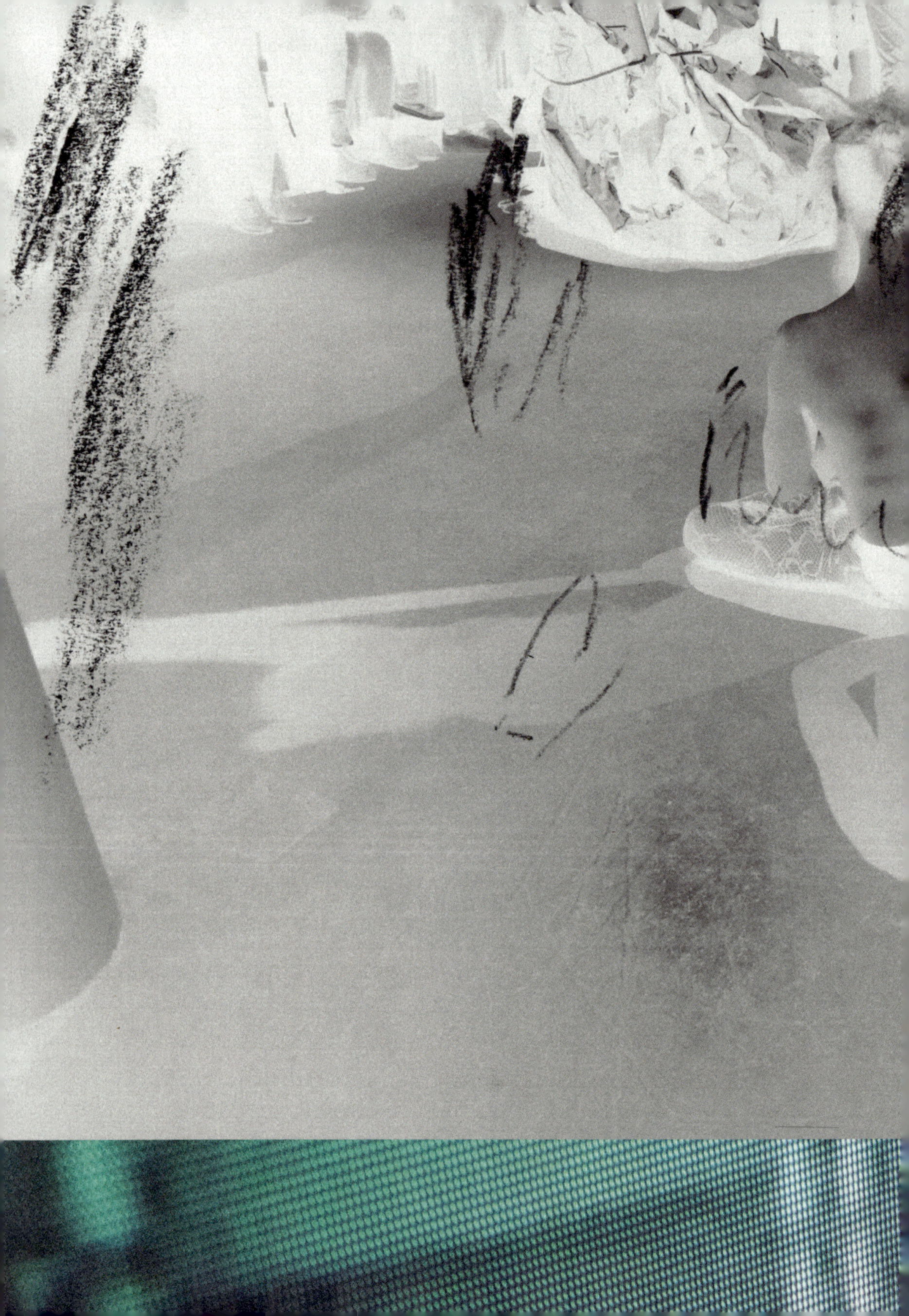

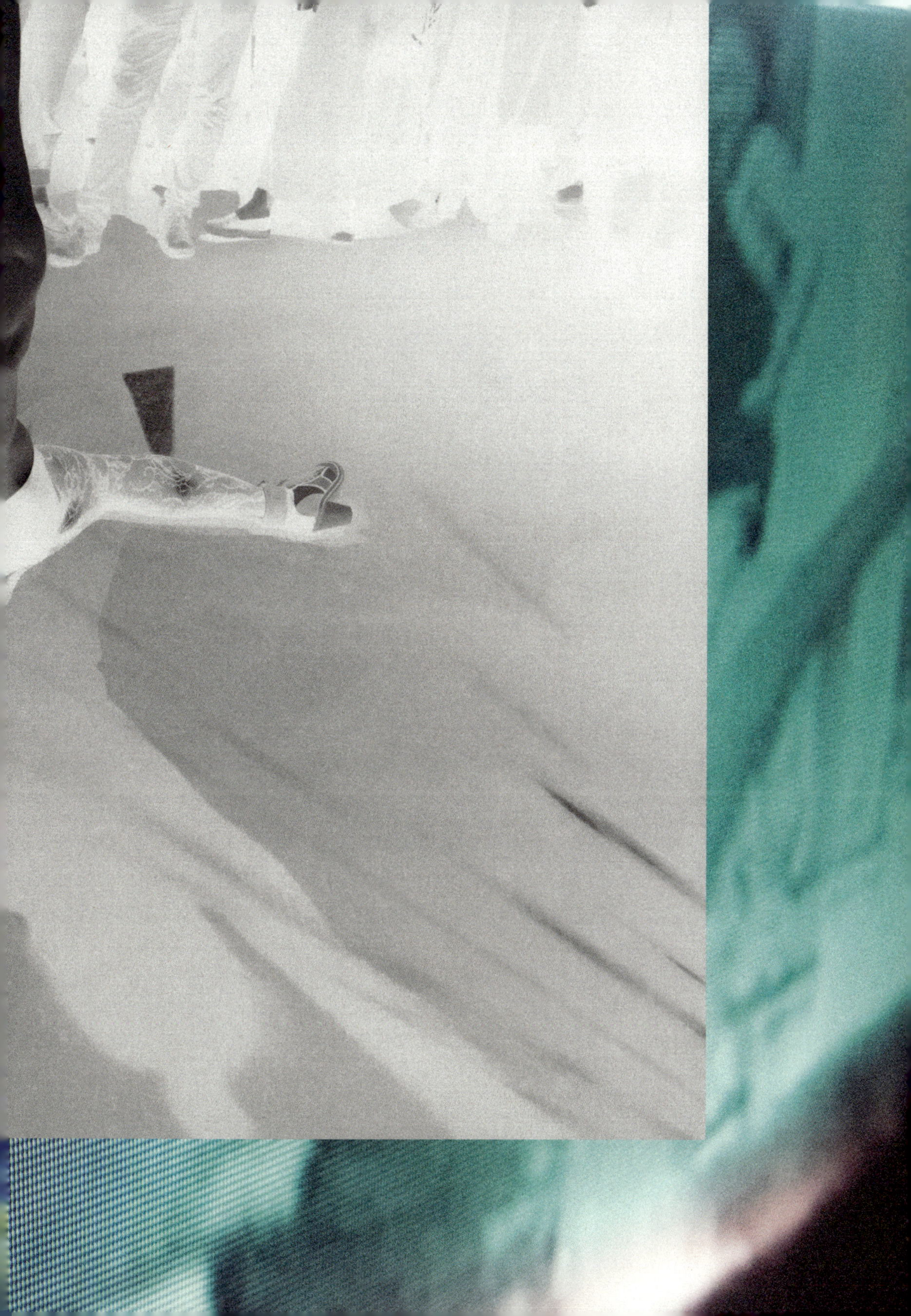

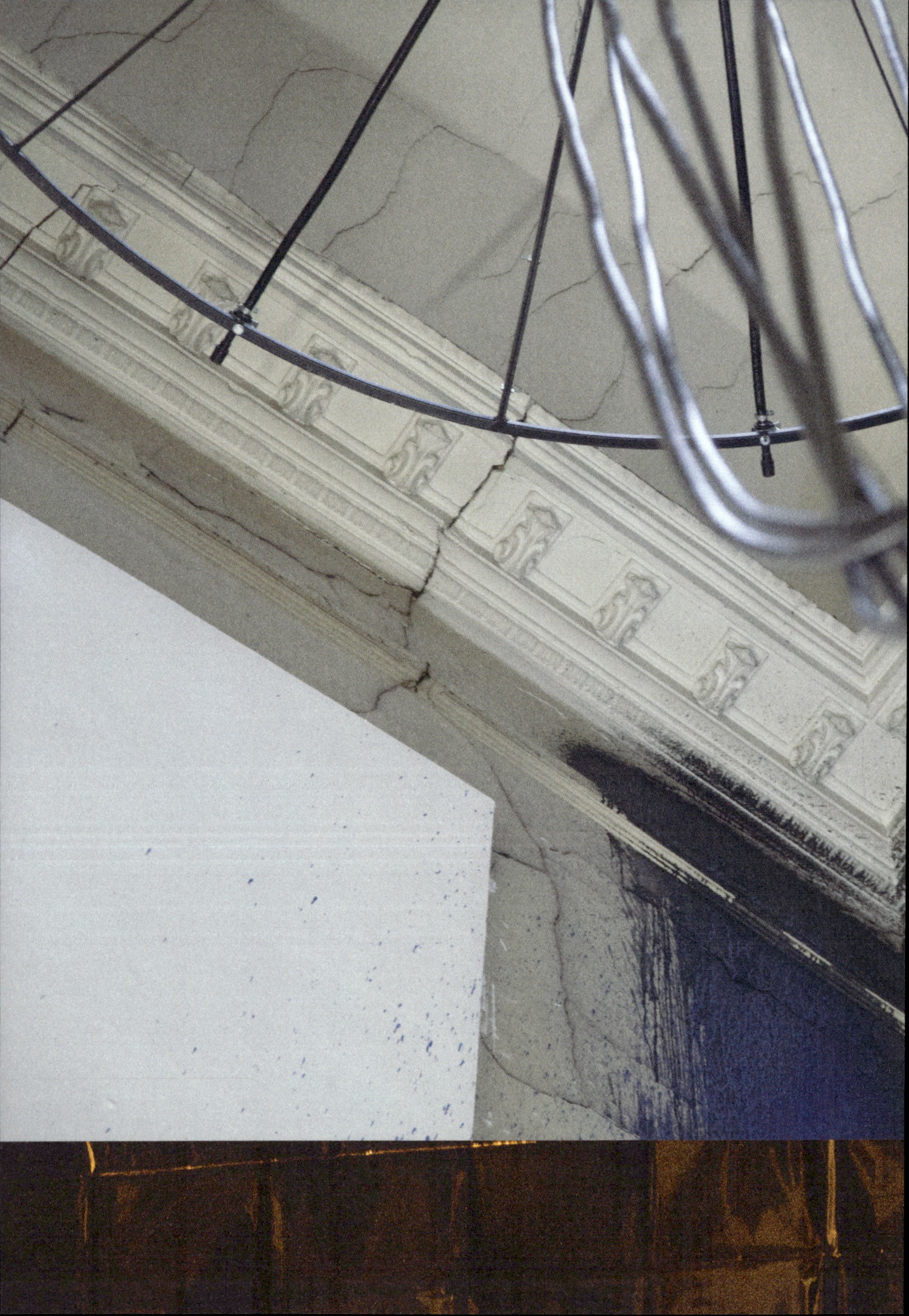

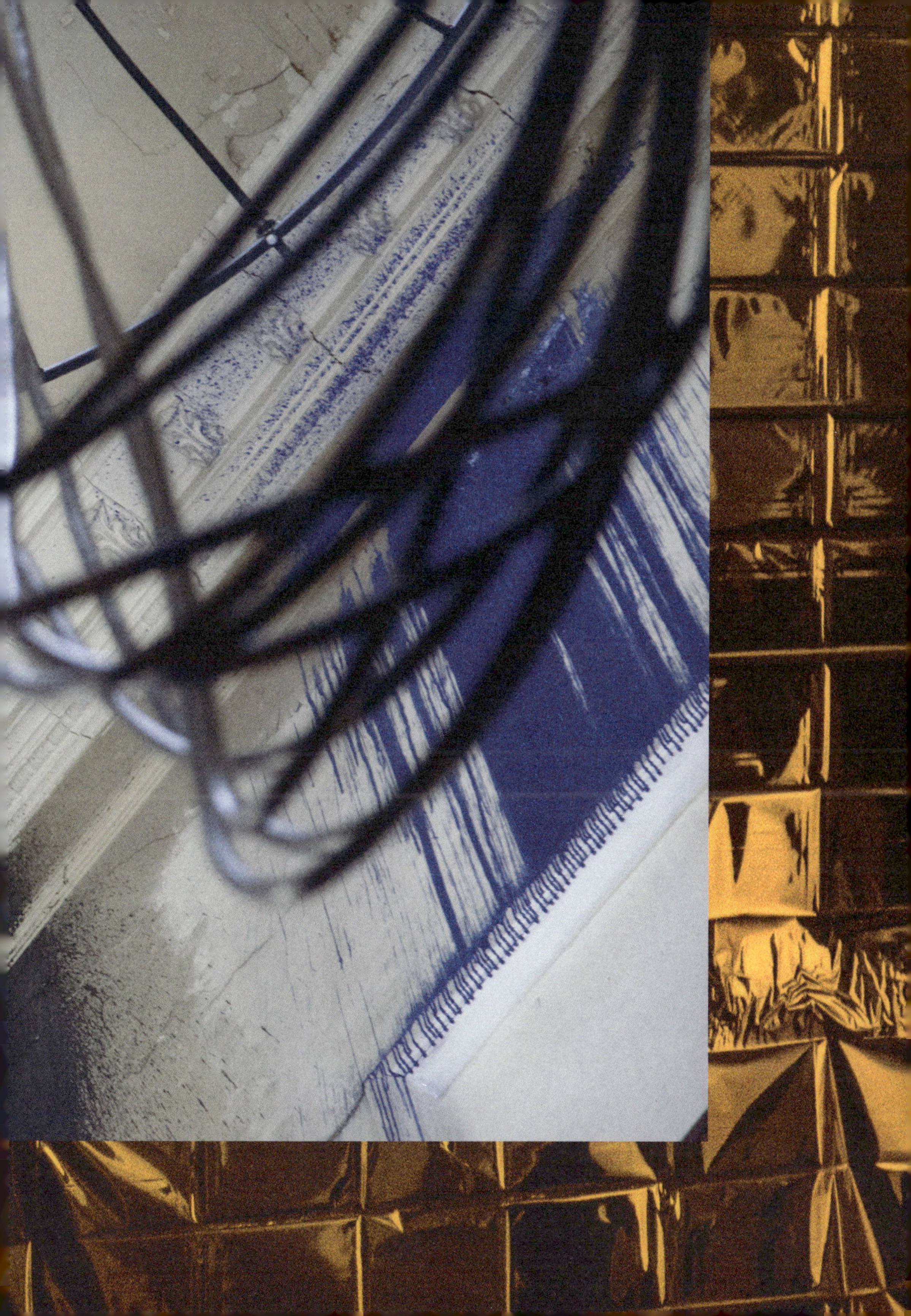

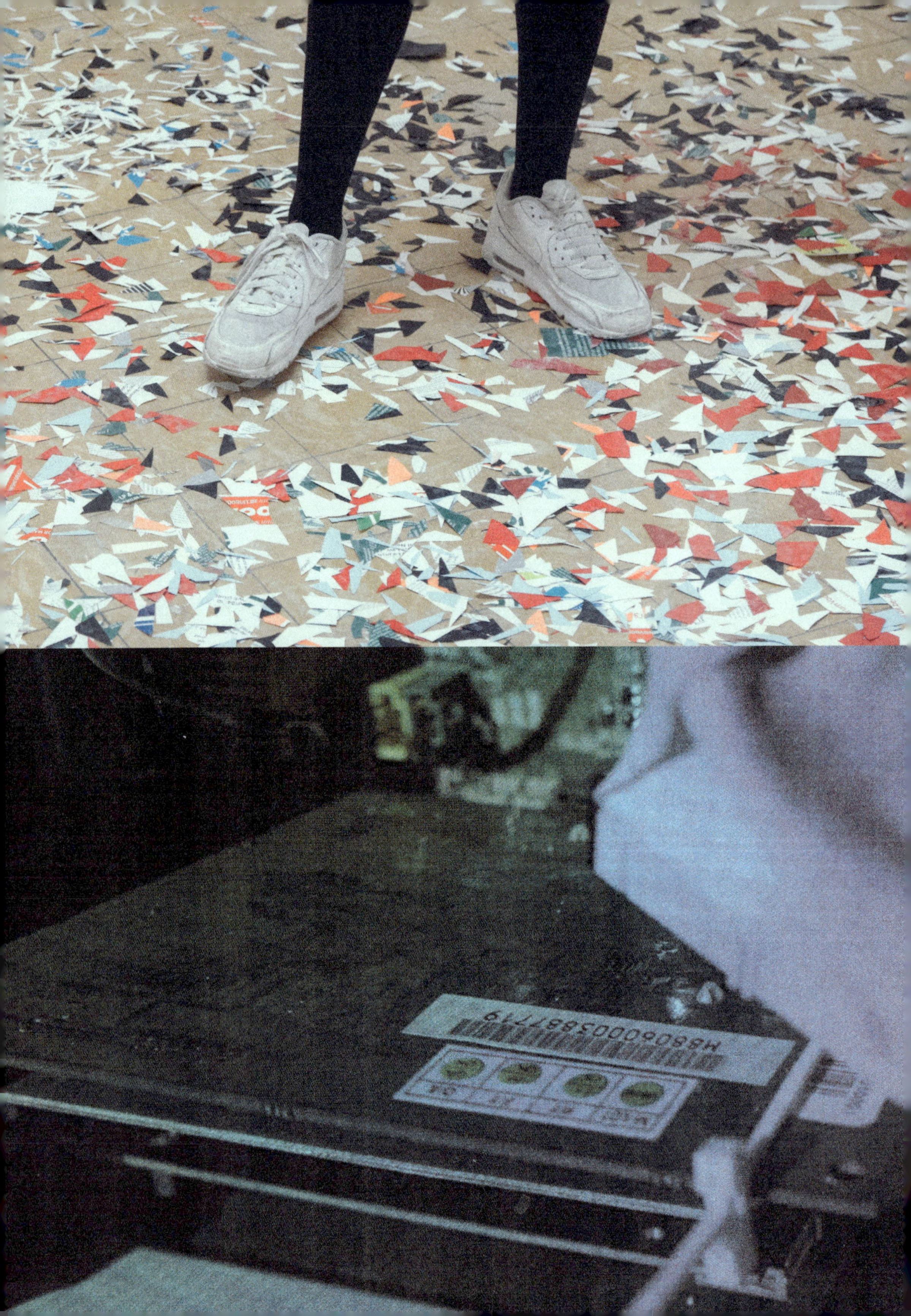

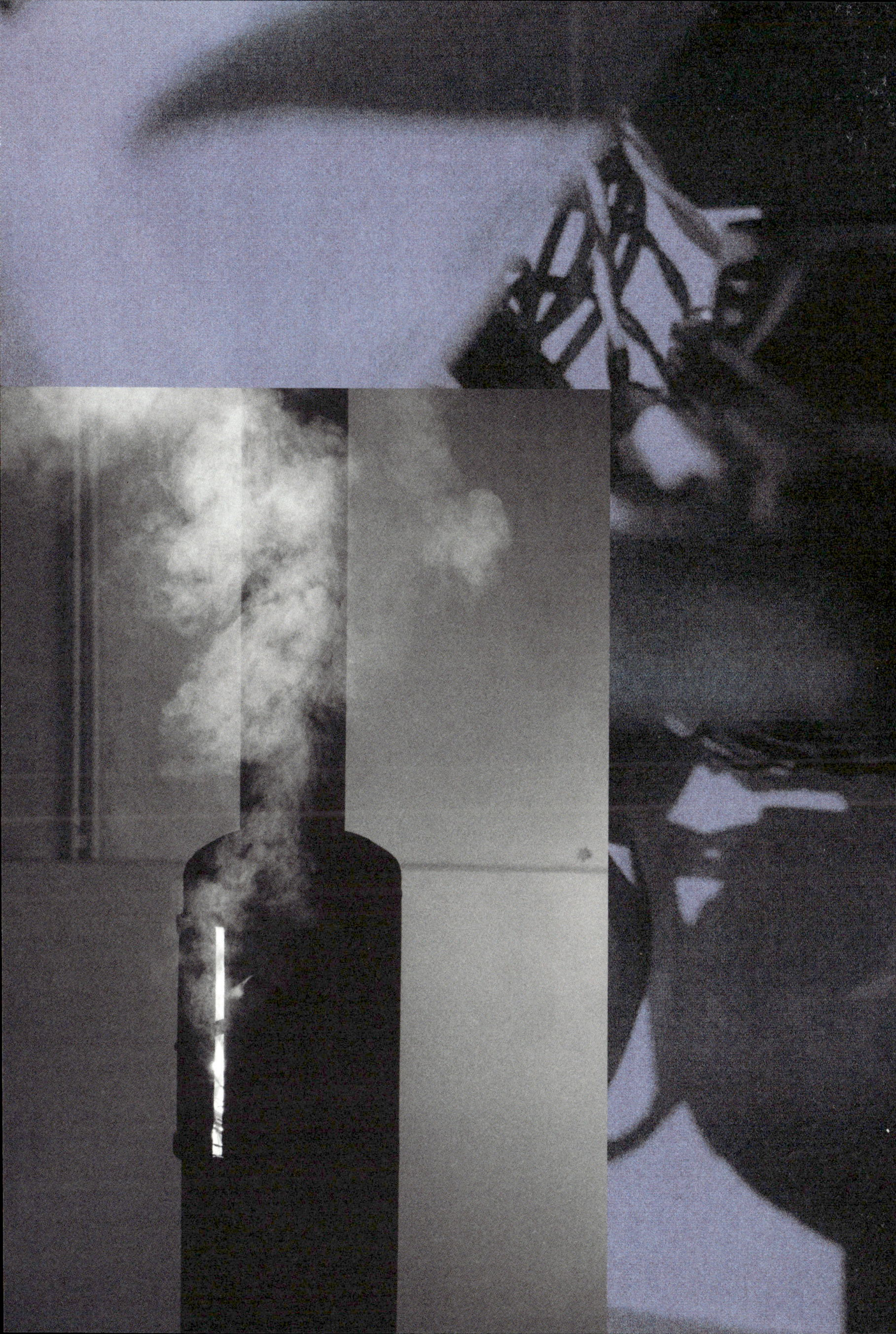

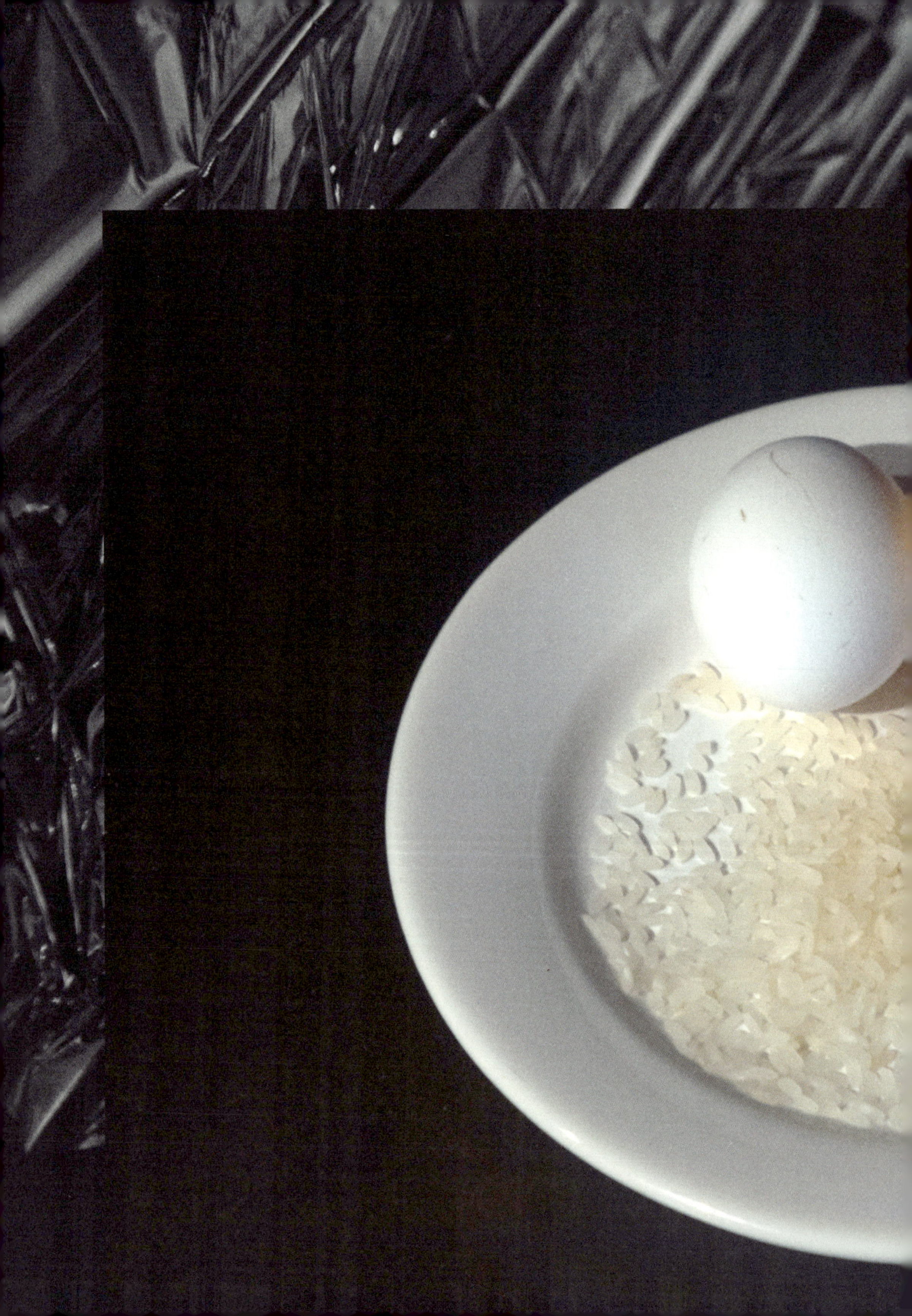

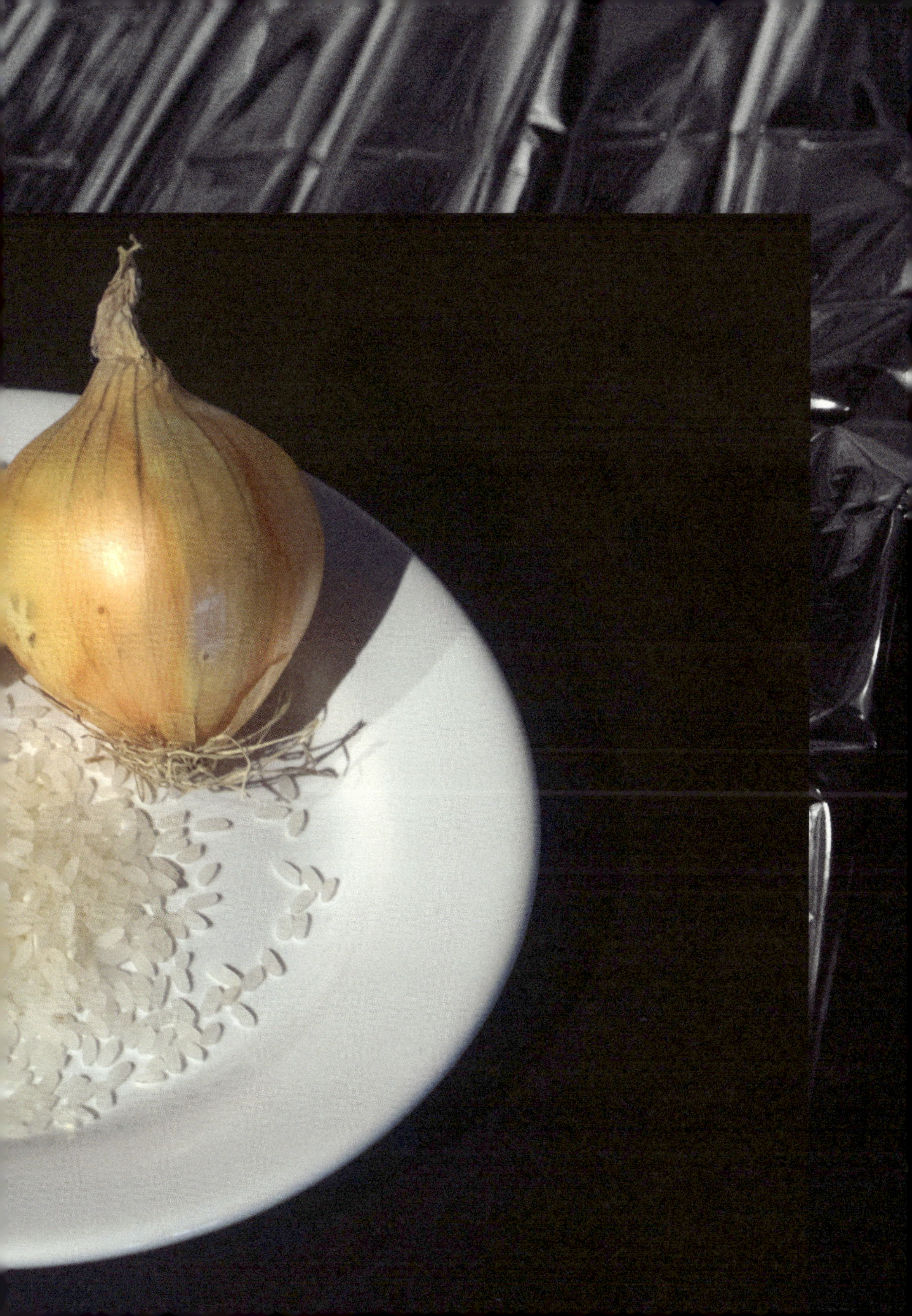

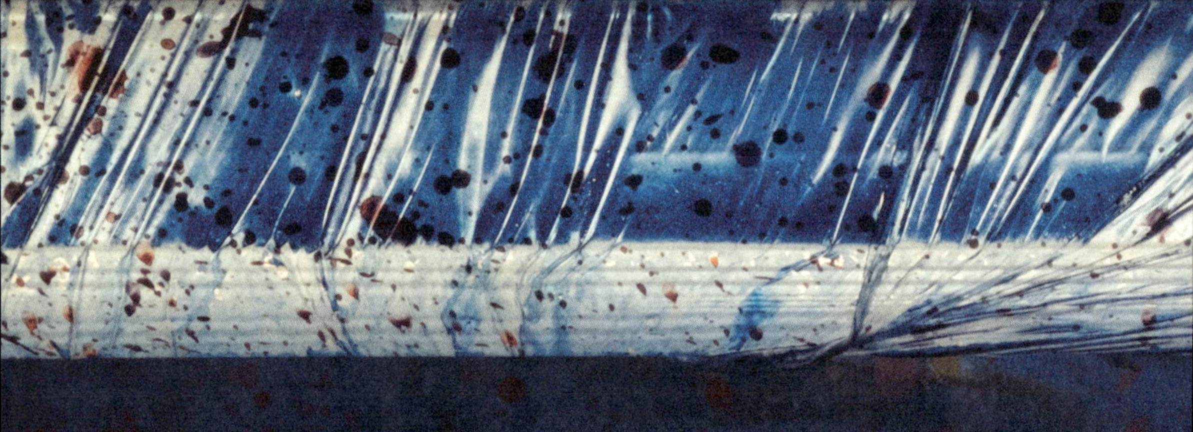

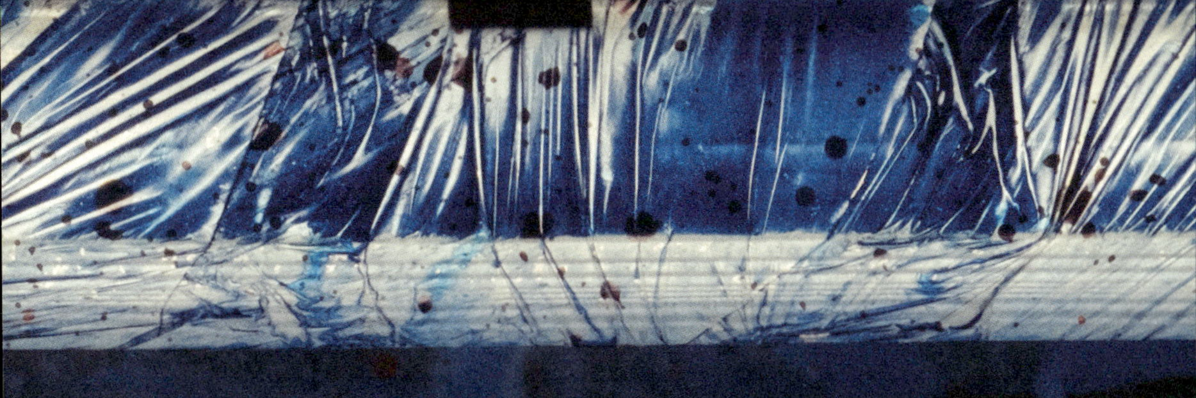

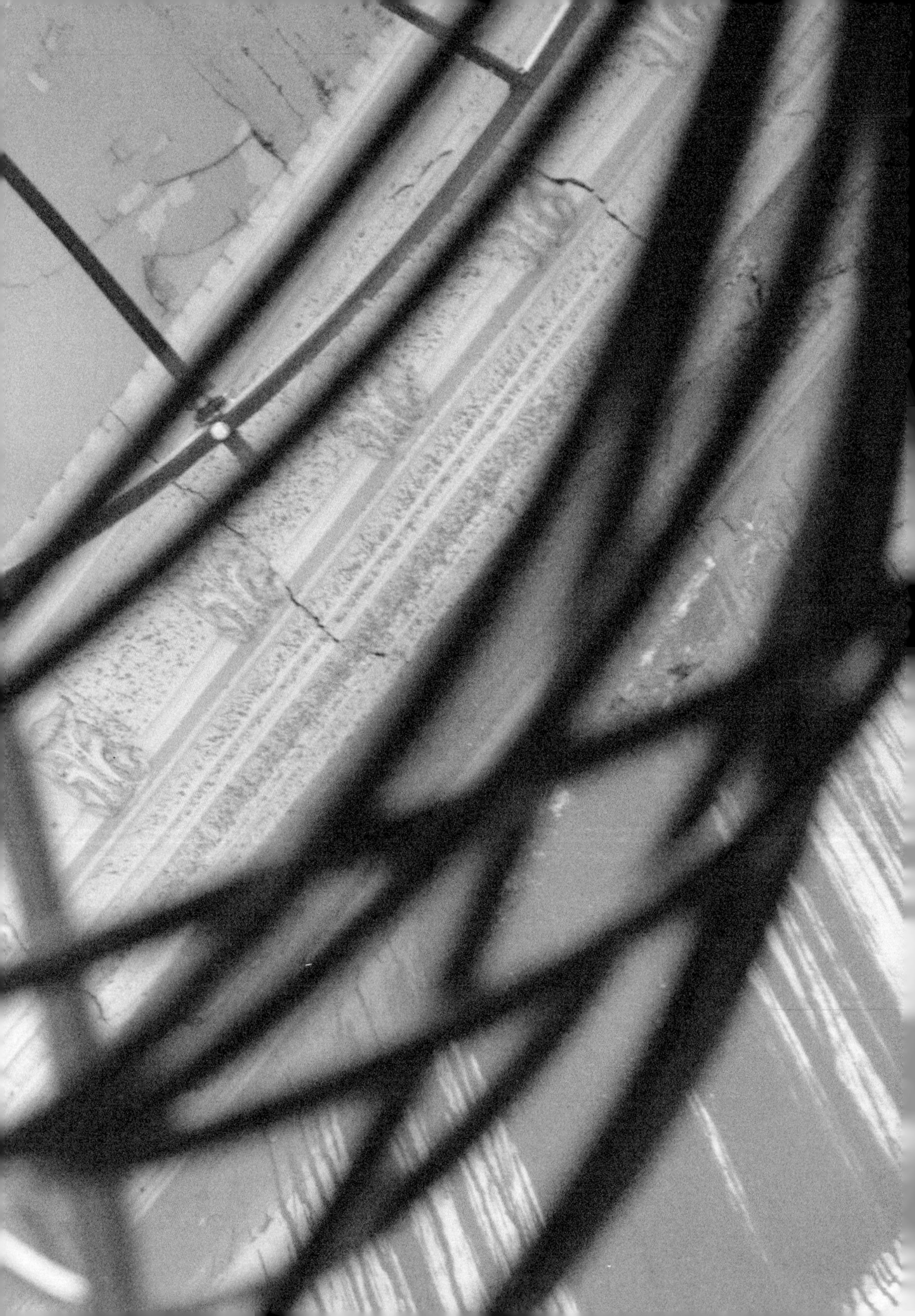

They said they found me in a lifeguard chair
playing accordion for a dying pear tree.

They said they found me under a balcony.
I was dead.

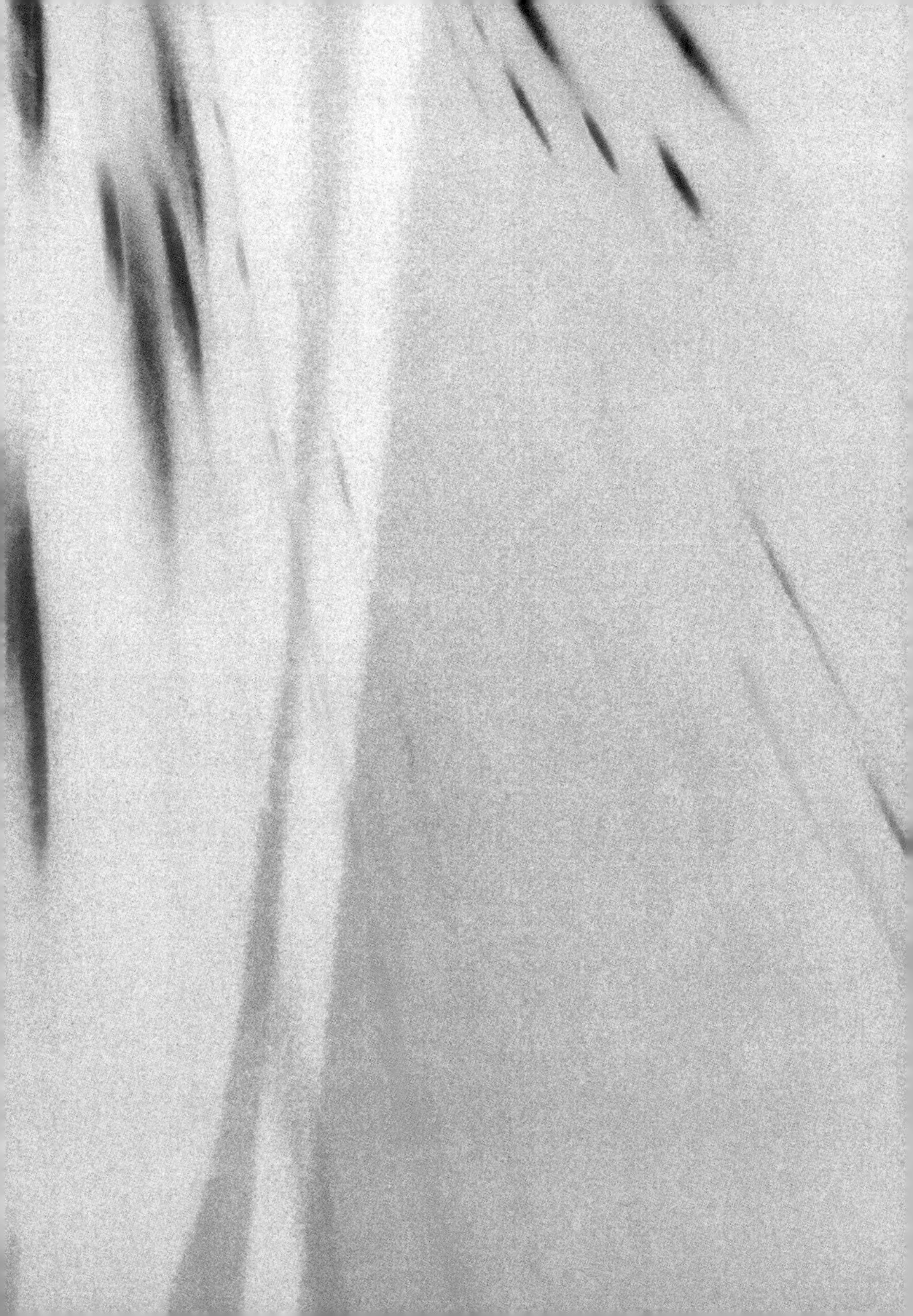